Gangsters Up North

Mobsters, Mafia, and Racketeers in
Michigan's Vacationlands

Robert Knapp

CLIOPHILE PRESS
CLARE, MICHIGAN
2020

ISBN: 978-0-9912557-2-6

Library of Congress Control Number: 2020903685

Cliophile Press
Clare, Michigan
cliolibri@gmail.com
www.cliophilepress.com

To all the fine historians Up North.

Contents

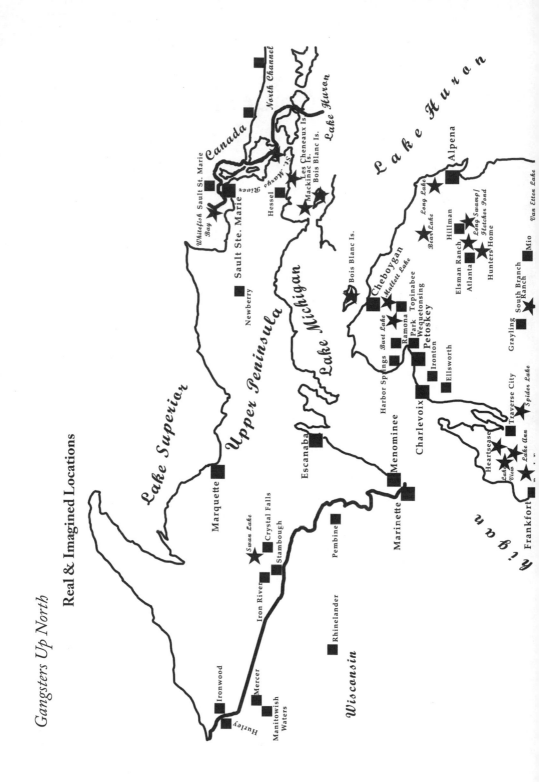

Gangsters Up North

Real & Imagined Locations

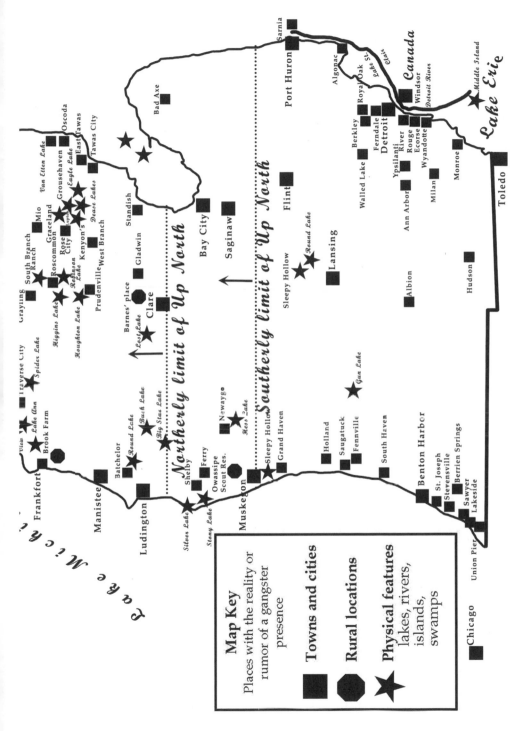

Map Key

Places with the reality or rumor of a gangster presence

Towns and cities

Rural locations

Physical features
lakes, rivers, islands, swamps

Lake Michi...

Lake Erie

Canada

Northerly limit of Up North

Southerly limit of Up North

Chicago
Union Pier
Lakeside
Sawyer
Stevensville
St. Joseph
Benton Harbor
Berrien Springs
South Haven
Fennville
Saugatuck
Holland
Grand Haven
Sleepy Hollow
Muskegon
Owassipe Scout Res.
Ferry
Shelby
Stony Lake
Silver Lake
Ludington
Manistee
Frankfort
Brook Farm
Batchelor
Lake Ann
Vista
Traverse City
Spider Lake
Round Lake
Buck Lake
Big Star Lake
Hess Lake
Newaygo
Gun Lake
Sleepy Hollow
Round Lake
Lansing
Albion
Hudson
Monroe
Milan
Ann Arbor
Ypsilanti
Walled Lake
Berkley
Royal Oak
Ferndale
Detroit
River Rouge
Ecorse
Wyandotte
Windsor
Detroit River
St. Clair
Lake St. Clair
Algonac
Port Huron
Sarnia
Flint
Saginaw
Bay City
Gladwin
Clare
Barnes' place
Lost Lake
Houghton Lake
Higgins Lake
Prudenville
West Branch
Kenyon's
Robinson Lake
Dease Lakes
Rose City
Roscommon
Graceland
South Branch Ranch
Mio
Grayling
Eagle Lake
Grousehaven
Van Etten Lake
Oscoda
Tawas City
East Tawas
Standish
Bad Axe
Middle Island
Toledo

vii

Preface

"Up North" Michigan has a charm all its own. Generations have enjoyed relaxing, fishing, hunting, and a wide range of other delights over the last hundred and forty years. Gangsters just joined the millions of others who came north. Sometimes they, too, simply sought rest and relaxation at a cabin, a gangster-friendly retreat, or a resort hotel. Other times, they saw opportunities for furthering their own interests in gambling, bootlegging, and even kidnapping, bank robbery, and murder. In the normal course of events, hoodlums did not advertise their presence, preferring to maintain a low profile as they recreated or as they invested in enterprises that sprang up in corners of Up North where rich men and their families spent summers. Ferreting out their activities is a challenging and rewarding project. While here and there others have written about what these gangsters were doing, putting together the whole picture gives a clear idea of how extensive their presence was Up North. Along the way, colorful stories abound—some true, some not—about these outlaws.

At each stage of my investigations, I had to assess the rumors and stories told about gangsters. Why are there so many tales to follow up on, to check out? What is fact, what fiction? What creates the crazy-quilt of gangster accounts Up North?

The most obvious origin of such stories lies in a desire to capitalize on the gangster motif. Businesses often seek a link to some famous person or event in order to attract patrons. For example, a resort near Rose City (Ogemaw County) created an intricate web of fictional mob involvement with the place, even including a report that Al Capone visited. Another venue melded half-true advertising copy with completely

uncorroborated details of a gang using the place as a hideout. A golf
course created on land once owned
by gangsters constructed from a
kernel of truth a whole narrative of
unlikely or impossible gangster details.
A hotel built interest around supposed
gangster patrons of yore, including,
once again, Al Capone, and purveyed
stories of long tunnels this way and that
to provide escape routes for the fictional
gangsters in case of a raid. A final example involves the famous Graceland Ballroom, which may well
have seen a gangster or two in its
heyday. Here, a subsequent owner
embellished unabashedly, even to
putting a gangster manikin with a
submachine gun on a balcony.

A similar process—exaggerating for effect—happened when a local
person decided to add to whatever historical basis existed in order to
impress visitors to a place. Harry Bennett's Lost Lake retreat in Clare
County became a Boy Scout camp in its later life. A scout leader at the
camp apparently relished making up stories about gangster-like activities and structures—tunnels, machine gun outposts, spikes in a moat—
all sorts of imaginary things. These stories then made their way into
newspaper articles and became historically true facts for most people.

What to make of the local eye-witnesses who told stories? At a most
basic level, such stories as they were told and retold within families or
communities tended to accrete details. But, how did they start in the
first place? In some cases, gangsters were present, and that presence created an environment for embellishment. Underworld figures certainly
lived or vacationed at places like Tawas City, Clare, the Petoskey/Harbor
Springs area, and Topinabee on Mullet Lake. Locals aware of this
added imaginary details to agree with stereotypical gangster-related

doings and infrastructure. Therefore, almost everywhere supposed eye-witnesses swore to escape tunnels, secret rooms, machine gun nests, se-cluded hideouts, bootlegging adventures, covertly buried dead enemies, bullet-ridden cars at the bottom of lakes, and so on.

Newspaper accounts of gangster doings provided another active in-ducement to the imagination. Newsmen often had nothing more to report than whatever rumor came to their attention. People often re-ported a gangster completely removed from where the gangster was at the time. Published photographs encouraged reports of look-alikes, reports that sometimes actually led to the false arrests of innocent dop-pelgangers. The report of John Dillinger in Sault Ste. Marie and Clare and the multiple reports on Fred "Killer" Burke exemplify this wide-spread phenomenon. A false sighting then led to accompanying stories that were repeated to friends and relatives down to the present day.

In other cases, a stereotypical appearance led to a false identifi-cation of a person or automobile as "gangster." Fancy cars, especially black ones—Cadillacs, Buicks, and so on—were enough to start ru-mors. A group of men from outside the local area inspired identifica-tions as gangsters. In a paradigmatic instance, a small businessman from Ohio decided to build a cabin in the backwoods near Harrison (Clare County). In the late 1940s, he bought supplies to build his getaway and brought them north in trucks driven by some of his Ohio employees. Locals quickly identified him and his crew as Mafia—the business-man's Cadillac and entourage seemed the giveaway. Locals reported an escape tunnel from the house to under a nearby pond. The actual pump house became a prison for enemy gangsters. These tales spread to Har-rison and rumor quickly became fact. To this day, locals tell of an erst-while Mafia hideout near town.

Physical remains also inspired stories. In a recent instance, a person breathlessly identified a mysterious chamber in a hillside as a gangster hiding hole. What is patently an ice cellar dug into a hill, something very common on a farm back in the day, has become a gangster artifact. In another instance a wine cellar in a large home was identified as a gangster jail where enemies could be held before execution. In yet an-other, a water tower and a fenced entrance were enough to breed stories of a machine gun emplacement situated to spray any invaders who tried to enter by the locked gate—all to protect Al Capone, of course.

Faulty memories could also add to the confusion of tales. With no dishonest intention at all, recollections could blur, and rumors heard in by-gone days could turn into absolutely statements of truth. Whole stories welled up from fragmentary recollections or vague rumors of gangsters and their activities. To say that a person's story of a gangster's presence was a fiction is not to say that the person was lying. A person could firmly believe in an event or experience reconstructed from scattered memories. But the reconstruction would still be wrong.

A more nefarious origin comes from using false gangster accusations to attack a resident. In Iron River a man named E. C. Bradley, a road contractor who was active in local politics, engineered the removal of the local superintendent of schools. This angered some of his fellow citizens. In an attempt to intimidate Bradley, a local "person of unbalanced mind" wrote threatening letters and signed them "Harry Fleisher," a particularly notorious Purple Gangster of the time.[1] Such attacks, whether they were successful, would lead to stories about the presence of gangsters.

Finally, I believe it is possible that sometimes people from downstate came north and enjoyed a "gangster" self-presentation. The violent reputation of gangsters was a fundamental part of the whole persona. A fellow—it would almost certainly always be a young male—could put on a swagger, insinuate gangster connections, and excite the locals—especially, perhaps, the local young ladies. I believe that many testimonies to gangsters at the Graceland Ballroom near Lupton may have their origin in this scenario.

Sorting out the facts from the stories is the intriguing, but daunting, challenge. *Gangsters Up North* brings together the real activities of mobsters, racketeers, and mafiosi in Michigan's northlands. At the same time, it lays bare many misunderstandings, exaggerations, and outright fabrications that here, as elsewhere, accompany gangsters' lives. A coherent picture of the real and the imagined brings to life little-known aspects of Michigan's fascinating history.

Gangster Presence Up North

Al Capone hid out in Sault Ste. Marie!
John Dillinger passed through Clare as he fled from the law!
Purple Gangsters danced until dawn at the Graceland Ballroom!

"Up North"

Sandy beaches, sylvan lakes, meandering streams, quiet forests. Year after year, millions come by car, boat, and airplane to enjoy what Michigan's northland has to offer. They have been coming for a hundred and fifty years. The rich settle into their splendid "cottages" all along the Great Lakes. The not-so-rich enjoy more modest getaways that pepper the shores of virtually every lake and river, great, large, or small. Sun-lovers crowd the beaches; hunters roam the woods; hikers and bikers trace the trails; vacationers fill the resorts, bars, and restaurants. Magnificent sunsets, cool, soft mornings, lively nights all offer a siren's call.

At first, it was the steamships. Coming up from Chicago and Detroit, they arrived on boats making stops all along the coasts of Lake Michigan and Lake Huron. By the 1880s, railroads had pushed north along the same shores. Their tentacles reaching out to St. Louis, Indianapolis, even Cincinnati, they brought resorters within a long day's travel of a northern paradise. Churchmen saw the wilderness as ideal for calm retreats and set up extensive, well-appointed camps. Wealthy magnates bought up large swathes of land for their own private hunting preserves. Entrepreneurs built luxurious lodges and hotels and plastered newspapers for hundreds of miles around with advertisements of their amenities. Real estate speculators platted the shores of lakes and offered lots that even common laborers could afford.

Then the true revolution came. The automobile disrupted the fairly staid vacation industry. With tanks full of gasoline, a tire repair kit, and some knowledge of how to apply baling wire to a problem, early motorists forged north. At first, their narrow tires often meant their cars had to be dragged out of the mud or sand by a friendly farmer's horse

team. Roads, restricted by law to those built by individual township planning and labor, proved abysmally inadequate for the newfangled contraptions that multiplied like rabbits, taking over from horse and horse-drawn travel. By the 1920s, state and federal governments began to reckon seriously with the need for good roads. Trunk lines were laid out, numbering became regularized. Most of all, well designed and constructed roadbeds proliferated. Oiled gravel was a great improvement over sand and dirt; hard paving allowed travel at average speeds of forty-five or even fifty miles an hour. As highways U.S. 31 and 131 snaked north on the west side, U.S. 27 headed for the Straits through the middle of the state; U.S. 23 edged along Lake Huron, U.S. 2 cut through the Upper Peninsula east to west, and state highways populated the rural areas with another series of good roads. By the mid-1920s, automobile traffic to Michigan's northern vacationlands supplied by far the most tourists and resorters. The automobile opened virtually the entire area to vacationers of all types and classes.

Michiganders use the term "Up North" very loosely. The general idea is that you must go "north" for a vacation. For someone living in Battle Creek, perhaps Stevenson Lake near Clare is "North"; if they live in Detroit, it may be Lake Huron's shore north of Bay City; if in Muskegon, then Crystal Lake near Benzonia could beckon. Clare long advertised itself as the "Gateway to the North." By that reckoning, the line of counties from Mason County on Lake Michigan to Arenac County on Lake Huron would

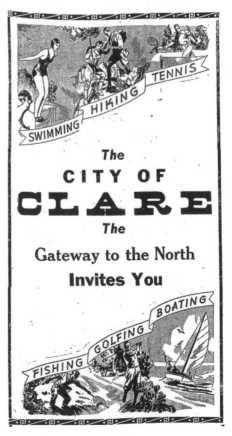

SWIMMING HIKING TENNIS

The
CITY OF
CLARE
The
Gateway to the North
Invites You

FISHING GOLFING BOATING

be the southern edge of "Up North." Residents of Grand Rapids, Flint, and areas south might dispute that line, considering anything to the north of a line from Muskegon to Sanilac to be "Up North." The term usually excludes the Upper Peninsula, normally thought of by natives and others as a distinct "Yooper" land. A resident of Lansing with a cottage on Lake Superior would not say that it is "Up North." Rather she would say it is "in the U.P." And certainly, a Yooper would never say, "I live Up North"; rather, "I live in the U.P.," or "I live in northern Michigan."

I use a modest definition of Up North, the one that holds that Clare is, indeed, "Gateway to the North." Thus, of Michigan's eighty-three counties, twenty-seven of the Lower Peninsula make up the area. I also include the Upper Peninsula simply because it was part of the same vacationing habit as the northern counties of the Lower Peninsula. To simplify the narrative, I broadly and, as I just mentioned, rather incorrectly refer to this entire area, the northern Lower Peninsula and the Upper Peninsula, as "Up North."

What were gangsters doing in this recreation land?

"Gangster"

The definition of gangster is almost as elastic as that of Up North. Linguistically, a gangster is a member of a gang; a gang is a group of people working together in an activity, be it legal or illegal; the suffix "-ster" indicates agency or membership. Quite early on the term came to have the connotation of a group bent on nefarious acts. In the late nineteenth century, it was vigorously applied by both Republicans and Democrats to cabals of their political rivals, inter- as well as intra-party. Only in the 1890s did the word begin to be applied to criminals as well as politicians. Overwhelmingly, it retained its political cabal meaning well into the twentieth century. But by around 1910 it became the familiar term for any group undertaking criminal activity. This could take many forms, from mere thuggery and robbery, to kidnapping, extortion, and murder.

A companion word, "racketeer," appeared for the first time in 1927 to describe criminal influence in a labor union. "Racket" meaning "dishonest activity" goes back a century before. The meaning of the word in America gradually centered on non-violent criminal activity. Examples are gambling, prostitution, bank fraud, drug dealing, intimidation, extortion, counterfeiting, money laundering, and bribery. The distinction, if often a fuzzy one, is between such criminal activities and violent crimes such as murder, torture, armed robbery, and the like. In fact, the United States criminal codes include as "rackets" pretty much any criminal activity. However, I will use racketeer to mean only less violent forms of such activity.

A gangster can be, and often is, also engaged in running rackets. So, alongside those who are pure racketeers, I also use the term to include anyone who is part of a group that engages in thuggish and/or less-violent criminal behavior. I exclude small-time, independent criminals such as pickpockets, occasional thieves, robbers, and the like because they are not gangsters or racketeers. On the other hand, I do include otherwise law-abiding citizens who engage gangsters or racketeers to provide services, for example the employment of gangsters to provide security at a Ford Motor plant in the 1930s or as strikebreakers using violence to thwart pro-union assemblies.

The Mafia is a special class of gangsters. I refer to these criminals by this name because of their peculiar origin and strong self-identification. Although disputed, the term "Mafia" seems to come from a Sicilian-Italian word meaning brave or fearless. Criminal gangs in Sicily have existed forever, but in the seventeenth to nineteenth centuries, especially, bands formed to survive in a land oppressed and ravaged by self-centered, uncaring, and often foreign elites. At the end of the nineteenth century a complete culture of self-preservation, group loyalty, and banditry came to America along with the thousands of Italian immigrants, most of whom came from Sicily and southern Italy. The Black Hand, criminal activity bred first in Naples, brought institutionalized extortion

5

and protection as well as other rackets. Feeding on fellow immigrants, the Black Hand was greatly feared. However, it overplayed its hand and by the mid-1920s reaction by police and the immigrant community had practically finished it off. At that time American-born gangsters were evolving a new type of criminal life based on entrepreneurial gangsterism rather than strictly thuggish behavior. Italian-Americans, especially those from or with roots in Sicily, created a new approach as well. It was dubbed the Mafia after a popular Italian usage for a criminal gang. Mafia members were bound together with strong ties of ethnicity and an even stronger sense of honor. Their early focus, as with the Black Hand, was extortion and protection, but soon activities branched out into all the lucrative areas favored by organized crime at the time, especially prostitution, gambling, and bootlegging. As before in Sicily, no mafioso ever admitted that there was a Mafia. But the term, long familiar to Sicilians, became the standard way Americans referred to Italian organized crime. At some point mafiosi began to call their operation "our thing" (*cosa nostra*), but this term does not appear in print until 1945 and remains rare until 1961. Mobster, much as gangster, is a word applied to all these criminals—gangsters, racketeers, and mafiosi.

Gangsters Up North engaged mostly in racketeering sorts of criminal activity—gambling and bootlegging most of all. Violence was rare. I found only a little evidence of kidnapping or extortion. Indeed, many gangsters were not Up North to further any criminal ends at all. In some cases, they were born and/or raised there but conducted their criminal activity entirely outside of the area. In others they, like the other thousands of resorters and hunters, just wanted recreation, rest, and relaxation among the lovely lakes and streams Up North.

Truth, myths, and legends: The problem of sources

Gangsters accrete stories about gangsters. Gangsters did truly exist. They did truly engage in a wide range of criminal activity. They did live and work in a wide variety of places. But because of the many stories, writing a true history of any gangster or gang presents daunting problems of sources and verification. Some gangsters loved the spotlight. Al Capone welcomed newspaper stories about him, even at times sought

them. John Dillinger enjoyed reading reports of his escapades. Newspapers engaged in fierce, cut-throat competition for circulation that led to a taste for sensationalism fed by real and imagined gangster activity. By 1930 the rampant publicity showered on gangsters led to the golden age of gangster movies: *Public Enemy*, *Scarface*, and *Little Caesar*, classic films from 1931 to 1932, encouraged a trend that continues to the present day. The gangsters themselves became anti-heroes beloved even more than feared by the American public. Popular passions urged crime-fighting police and city mayors to stop the violence and depredations, but the stories of outwitted cops played extremely well with the people. One result of all this publicity, and some might say perverse heroization, was the widespread creation of mythical encounters and hide-outs without number nationwide. Sorting truth from fiction is daunting.

As I researched this book, I read and listened to many accounts about gangsters Up North, almost all second- or third-hand, heard by descendants from uncles, grandparents, or parents. They told of Al Capone being here or there, John Dillinger hiding out, Baby Face Nelson threatening a druggist, or mafiosi in their always-black Cadillacs. While many stories provided valuable leads and information about gangsters, others were simply impossible to work into any narrative dependent on historically known facts about a gangster's deeds and whereabouts. Online posts by ordinary folk interested in sharing their knowledge of this or that gangster are usually filled with errors or fictions. Newspaper stories are a much more reliable source of information because, leaving sensationalism aside, they contain many contemporary details that, pieced together, can form a reliable picture. Occasionally I have found letters or personal written accounts that shed light on an episode.

The secondary literature on gangsters varies widely in quality and coverage. Some of it is virtually impossible to find. There are additional problems. Many books about gangsters are written by the author simply reading other people's books and adopting whatever is found, elaborating the most famous aspects of a gangster without delving deeply into other possibilities. Also, in the gangster literature, few authors cite their sources thoroughly and systematically so that another researcher can discover where information is coming from. I have benefitted greatly from the authors who do cite their sources, go beyond received knowledge, and bring to light new facts and perspectives. Their hard work is an inspiration.

Michiganders look forward to time Up North. So did gangsters. Their stories add richness and texture to the history of Michigan's fabled vacationlands.

CHAPTER 2

Capone (Almost) Never Slept Here

One of the most famous gangsters of all, Al "Scarface" Capone, made his mark throughout the nation. His exploits in Chicago form the core of his nefarious activities, but both rumor and fact place him in many corners of the United States and even Canada. Was "Big Al" also in Michigan? Certainly, he crossed over into the state from time to time. Was he ever Up North? Myth and legend provide a bewildering cacophony of stories and sightings. It is time to sort out the reports and rumors. I will first take up what is known to be true about Capone in Michigan and then turn to tales that place him Up North.

Big Al in Michigan

Alphonse Capone was born on January 17, 1899 in Brooklyn, New York. His father and mother were hard-working immigrants who after coming to American made ends meet through long hours of work, he as a barber, she as a seamstress. Young Al was an unruly child. Although quite smart, he could not control his temper. A burst of anger, a smack to a teacher's face, and Al was out of school and onto the streets at age fourteen.

There was not much positive about roaming the New York City streets in that era. He joined a series of gangs of similarly wayward boys, gangs with colorful monikers such as "Junior Forty Thieves" and "Bowery Boys" and "Brooklyn Rippers." His big break came when he joined the important Five Points Gang out of Lower Manhattan. There he associated with serious criminals such as Frankie Yale and Johnny Torrio. In 1917 he also managed to get the slash across his face that forever made him "Scarface"—although he hated that nickname with a passion. In 1920 he left New York and, after a brief stint

Al Capone

in Baltimore, came to Chicago in 1921 as an aide to Torrio who had decamped to that city to be an enforcer for "Big Jim" Colosimo, the head gangster of the time. Torrio saw Capone as a very good henchman and elevated him quickly from bouncer at whorehouses' manager to a trusted right-hand man. Early in 1925, Torrio, skittish after a near-fatal assault, withdrew from the front-page management of what came to be known as the "Chicago Outfit." He handed day-to-day leadership to young Capone, then only 26 years old.

In the tit-for-tat murderous atmosphere of underworld Chicago, Capone became more and more concerned for his safety. The murder of his brother, Frank, in April 1924 instilled a fear that haunted him the rest of his life. He narrowly escaped murderous assaults in January 1925 and again in September 1926. As I trace Capone's movements outside Chicago during the next six years, 1926-1932, it is important to keep front and center his absolutely justifiable fear of being murdered.

Capone appears in many accounts of gangsters in Michigan and, more specifically, Up North in Michigan. Careful examination of his movements from 1925 until his trip to federal prison in 1932 helps us to decide which accounts are fiction and which fact.

Actual trips outside Chicago

Capone took over the Outfit when Johnny Torrio retired in the spring of 1925.[2] Late that year, he and his wife, Mae, visited Havana, Cuba with Torrio and his wife.[3] Capone would visit Havana several times, but he never hid out there. He always stayed openly in a fancy Havana hotel.

In December 1925 he took his son, Sonny, to New York City for an ear operation. He returned in January 1926 and spent the winter in Chicago.[4] While in New York, he made no attempt to hide his presence.

In April 1926 a major Chicago prosecutor, William McSwiggin, was machine-gunned by Capone's gangsters.[5] In the aftermath, Al high-tailed it by train to Hot Springs, Arkansas, for a bit of rest and relaxation.[6] He could not have been at the Arkansas resort for very long because by May he was back in Chicago.

There, Al tried to keep out of sight by staying with one of his henchmen, Dominic Roberto, at Roberto's home in Chicago Heights, almost 25 miles from Capone's usual stomping grounds. Some days he would drive with Roberto up to Milwaukee and back, just to break the boredom.[7] He remained fearful of an attempt on his life, the same fear that he had had for the two years since Frank Capone's murder by police. He was constantly on the move between Chicago locations (the Hawthorne Inn, the Metropole Hotel in the city itself, or his home on Prairie Avenue on the South Side). Later in life he would resort to the kind of hideout Roberto's home offered, that is, staying with a friend or relative near Chicago when he did not want the police or press to find him. He always felt safer hiding with people he knew—the location was not as important as the certainty that the people could be trusted. This habit increases the need to examine very closely accounts of hideouts in other sorts of places.

Capone in Michigan: 1926-1928

One of those hideouts that withstands scrutiny is in Michigan.[8] The somewhat unlikely venue is the state's capital, Lansing. "Capone became a fixture in Lansing during the summer of 1926 and four subsequent summers."[9] The basic story is that he went to Lansing in late

May 1926, was protected by a detective in the Lansing police department thus avoiding being outed, and then went on to nearby Round Lake where top lieutenants, Jake "Greasy Thumb" Guzik and Frank "The Enforcer" Nitti accompanied him. He remained in the area about two months, returning to Chicago only in July to face charges of involvement in the McSwiggin murder.

Laurence Bergreen is the only person who writes authoritatively about Capone in the Lansing area.[10] He only describes extensively the summer of 1926, although it is possible that the narrative, quite dramatically constructed, mashes Capone's experiences from all those summers into a description that focuses solely on 1926. In opposition to this scenario, Lawrence Cosentino claims that careful research by members of the Lansing Historical Society has failed to turn up any direct evidence such as a photograph that proves Bergreen's claims.[11] Cosentino suspects the whole story to be just yet another mythical "Capone slept here" tale. However, to discredit Bergreen's account it would be necessary to believe either that he made up the whole thing, or that a group of witnesses he found in Lansing constructed a coherent and consistent account of Capone and his stay(s) in the Lansing area, an account that they then conspired to foist on Bergreen.

Bergreen gives his main sources pseudonyms, so there is no way to follow up on what he says they told him. However, when a name appears that can be checked, all seems to be in order. For example, his sources state that a Lansing police captain, and later chief of police, one John O'Brien, helped hide Capone and protected him for a payoff of $150 a week.[12] The source does get O'Brien's end wrong—he says he retired in disgrace and committed suicide. In fact, he was indicted by a grand jury around 1942, tried, and found guilty of protecting the slot machine business in Lansing and then went to jail.[13] The only other person Bergreen mentions by name is a "veteran Lansing journalist," Lloyd Moles. Moles was, indeed, a reporter for the *Lansing State Journal*. The only other historically verifiable item is mention of the Club Roma at Laingsburg on Round Lake. This club did exist during the time Capone could have visited it and it was a jazzy place, where, presumably, illegal liquor was available. The vignettes that Bergreen has his sources recount paint a picture of Capone that is completely familiar from other accounts—his generosity, his suave dress, his general niceness (when he wasn't ordering people murdered). Either these sources had a similar experience, or they were making up a Capone they were familiar with from reading about him. Still, it seems hard to believe either that a clutch of Italian-Americans claiming to have interacted extensively with Capone in the Lansing area could have coordinated their stories to come out with a unified account such as Bergreen details, or that Bergreen would invent the whole affair just to flesh out a report of Capone in that area.

Bergreen's account is straightforward. Capone headed for the Lansing area because a former henchman offered to provide a place to hide out. (As I noted, Capone wanted to get out of Chicago to escape the heat resulting from Billy McSwiggin's murder in April 1926.) This trusted henchman put him up in his family home in Lansing. Later, he helped arrange for Capone to rent cabins on Round Lake, just outside of Lansing. Capone made no attempt to hide. Rather, he walked about without a problem. Bergreen does not mention bodyguards, but it would have been foolhardy for Capone to go around without them, given the attempts on his life and threats of more. The police were complicit in this business and no one bothered the Chicago gangster. The general picture is of a hoodlum taking a pleasant vacation and getting along well with the natives. Although Bergreen states that Capone went to Michigan at some point during each summer from 1926 through 1928, he does not detail events there in any year but 1926.[14]

Another story about Capone in Michigan is probably related to his stay at Round Lake. A photograph of Capone and a henchman, Ralph Sheldon, at "Happy Hollows" photo studio in Hot Springs, Arkansas, has been wrongly linked to "Sleepy Hollow" in Michigan, making this picture of Big Al the only hard evidence of his stay in the area. Michigan's Sleepy Hollow State Park is on Lake Ovid, created by damming the Little Maple River in 1974. So, this Sleepy Hollow is not "Happy Hollows." It has nothing to do with Capone because "Sleepy Hollow" and the lake within the park did not exist in Capone's time.[15]

Capone in Wisconsin: 1927

It might seem odd to talk about Capone Up North in Wisconsin in a discussion of his movements in Michigan. But understanding Big Al's actual and well-known stays in Wisconsin's northern woods not only provides background for why Michiganders would make up stories about him in northern Michigan. His Wisconsin days also provide background for Capone sightings in Escanaba and elsewhere in the Upper Peninsula. Therefore, examining Capone's visits Up North in Wisconsin is crucial to contextualizing Capone Up North in Michigan.

Although a city boy through and through—he was raised in Brooklyn—Capone, like so many others, enjoyed time spent in rural resort areas. In 1927 he went to northern Wisconsin (no specific place is mentioned) with some pals for a week in late November and early December.[16] This was an intrinsically odd time to go there for we know Capone up until then had shown no interest in hunting. For someone who loved the sunshine and warmth of Florida, a decision to freeze in the far north seems odd at best. Although a complete neophyte, he supposedly spent between $3,000 and $5,000 to outfit himself and his cohort in the finest hunting togs.[17] Everyone in Chicago assumed that Capone had headed north to escape the heat generated by a recent gangland slaying and in fear of his life. The party came back with some ducks and a bear, though it is hard to say whether Scarface was the successful hunter. The most likely supposition is that Capone just enjoyed the camaraderie. For anyone unfamiliar with the male habits in a hunting camp, let it just be said that drinking to excess and card playing through the night tended to be just as important as any carcass brought back to put on the family table. However that may be, this time Capone did not go north so much for rest and relaxation as to play the part of an innocent in the ongoing drama of gangster mayhem in the Windy City. In addition, this was no retreat to a hideout. Everyone knew where Capone was going, and he came back in a week. Capone seems to have enjoyed his hunting experience. He returned to hunt deer in northern Wisconsin in December 1928.[18]

Capone probably stayed at his brother Ralph's northern Wisconsin retreat. Ralph had a hunting lodge there by May 1926 so, probably unlike Al, he genuinely enjoyed semi-roughing it and hunting. When

Al disappeared from Chicago in the summer of 1926 and ended up in Lansing, Michigan, one of the places police looked for him was Ralph's place in northern Wisconsin, near Mercer.[19]

Ralph was not the only gangster to build a retreat in Wisconsin's far north. Joe Saltis, once on good terms with Capone in the beer business in Chicago, then on the outs with him, had built a retreat in Winter, Wisconsin, called the Barker Lake Lodge. After the final break with Capone in 1929, he retreated and lived there the rest of his life. Part of the lore of the place, perhaps not to be taken at face value, is that Big Al fished for sturgeon at the lodge.

Did Capone himself have a retreat in the north of Wisconsin? Many accounts relate that he built and occupied a place called "The Hideout" on Cranberry Lake near Couderay.[20] The details we come to expect from folktales about Capone certainly apply here. There is a garage with loopholes for machine guns high in the stone walls as well as a "fieldstone machine gun turret overlooking the entrance road" (the fortress theme); evidence of it being a center for smuggling booze (bootlegger theme); a specific room where Capone slept; a fieldstone jail where Capone kept...who? Eyewitness accounts of Capone abound.[21] Supposedly, he started this hideout in 1926 and completed it in 1928.[22]

Indeed, Capone was building a retreat on Cranberry Lake. In spring 1929 an Associated Press article stated that Capone "intends to spend his summers near Couderay, Wisconsin when he gets out of the Pennsylvania prison [in spring 1930]."[23] But, when Chicago newspapers got wind of Capone's plans, he backed out of the project, which was still unfinished.[24]

Ralph Capone

An Oshkosh newspaper gives the most accurate description of what happened regarding this "hideout":

"Chicago agents for Capone" had been buying up land. "The main lodge was erected last summer (1928) on Cranberry Lake and it was supposed to be owned by Capone, although held in the name of George Bonesch, of Cicero, Illinois, said to have been financed by the gang leader. It is also said that a crew of men was busy this spring [1929] building garages and cabins but that the work was stopped about a week ago [~May 13, 1929] and only a caretaker is at the resort now."[25]

Did Capone ever actually occupy the place? Bryan Bolton, a member of the notorious Barker-Karpis Gang, told the FBI that the plot to carry out what became known as the St. Valentine's Day Massacre (February 1929) took place "at a place on Cranberry Lake, six miles from Couderay, Wisconsin, where one 'George' [Bonesch] operated a resort." If true, this indicates that Capone did occupy the house in the unfinished resort. To coordinate with planning the massacre, that meeting would seem to have been in December 1928.[26] Capone's experience at his brother's place near Mercer and at Joe Saltis' place at Winter gave him the idea of following suit with his own place near Couderay. However, he clearly never finished his resort as his troubles after his release from the Pennsylvania prison in Spring 1930 did not allow him the leisure to enjoy Wisconsin's northwoods at his own retreat.

Finally, there are persistent rumors that Capone made it to Hurley,

Wisconsin, supposedly to supervise the transport of Canadian whiskey to thirsty Chicagoans. Rumors—as though Capone personally supervised such things on the spot—extend so far as to the claim that he went up to Winnipeg and/or Moose Jaw to secure his supplies. Further south, the Four Seasons Resort on Miscuano Island in the middle of the Menominee River just outside Pembine, Wisconsin, and very close to Michigan, also boasts of his presence for fishing and hiding.[27] To the west of Pembine lies Rhinelander. At Bugsy's Sports Grille, the owners thoughtfully built an escape tunnel for Capone to use should the authorities appear unexpectedly at the door of the saloon. Here the current bartender dismissed the rumors, saying, "You can't swing a cat around here without hitting a place where they say Capone has been."[28]

This Wisconsin background showing Capone's presence in a northern area for rest and relaxation among friends and relatives makes it highly unlikely that he sought respite in similar places elsewhere. At the same time, articles about his doings in Wisconsin's north provided inspiration for tales of sightings of Capone in northern Michigan: If Al Capone hid out in Wisconsin, why would he not hide out in Michigan?

Capone's supposed place, "The Hideout"

Michigan again

As I mentioned, Capone's every move, especially after he came to Chicago, is known. Evidence proves his occasional presence in Michigan during 1926-1928. Attention now turns to his movements from 1929 to 1932, when he went to the federal penitentiary in Atlanta, Georgia. Details of those movements must be laid out in order to exclude any significant presence in Michigan during those years.

Capone wintered in Florida in 1929, conveniently out of town for the February St. Valentine's Day massacre. He returned to Chicago in early May. He then traveled to Atlantic City for a gangsters' conclave (May 13-16). This was the first "national commission" meeting toward setting up organized crime in the United States. There, Capone's rivals humiliated him. Returning to Chicago via Philadelphia he arranged for the local authorities to arrest and convict him for carrying a concealed weapon—his goal was to spend some safe time away from murderous rivals. Capone was out of commission as a guest of the State of the Pennsylvania prison system from May 1929 until March 1930. He returned briefly to Chicago, then spent the late spring and early summer at his home near Miami; during that time, he took a one-week trip to Havana, Cuba in late May. Back in Chicago from August through December 1930, in January 1931 he headed once again for Miami, returning to Chicago in late February. He did not leave Chicago before the government charged him with tax evasion on June 5, 1931. For the next year, he still remained in that city. After his conviction in May 1932, he was sent to federal prison in Atlanta. This chronology of Capone's movements shows that he did not visit any hideouts or vacation spots from winter 1929 on except for a week in Havana in 1930. Capone's whereabouts leave no free time for being Up North in Michigan. It serves to restrict hideouts and vacation spots to the period from winter 1925 through winter/spring 1929.

The only exception to this conclusion comes during a time very close to his imprisonment. Although certainly not "Up North" by any stretch of the imagination (as I stretched it to include Lansing in my narrative), Capone did visit Michigan cities around the bottom of Lake Michigan, just across the border from Indiana. This area could be reached from Chicago in a couple of hours. Several Chicago gangsters visited or even lived there. It barely counts as leaving the Chicago area.

Where Capone never slept

Al Capone was one of the most well-known and, in his own way, most celebrated men in America between 1925 and 1932. While the murder and mayhem, the gambling and the bootlegging, the prostitution and bribery managed by gangsters at that time drew a continuous stream of wrath and indignation from the nation's press and, presumably from many of its citizens, the anti-hero outlaw—flashy, daring, ruthless—generated a special and pervasive type of awe, curiosity, and sense of adventure among the general population. Leading big-city newspapers routinely ran stories, and these were picked up by even the smallest-town newspapers via the news agencies such as Associated Press. National magazines added to the publicity—Capone was on the cover of *Time* magazine in 1930. As radio became more and more accessible during the last half of the twenties, more and more people heard broadcasts that routinely followed the latest foul deeds, escapes, and scandals. At the local theater, folks got their first taste of gangster-esque behavior in Josef von Sternberg's 1927 silent classic, *Underworld*. Although this was more of a traditional good-guy-destroyed-by-bad-stuff type movie than subsequent gangster films, it began a trend and is now viewed as the beginning of the gangster film genre. In 1928, *Me, Gangster* (now considered a "lost" film) appeared, but it was really the release of *Public Enemy* that got the ball rolling. Based unabashedly on the gangster facts and mythology current in popular culture, the film, starring James Cagney, premiered in April 1931, just as Big Al was going to trial. Soon thereafter Darryl Zanuck released Edward G. Robinson in the iconic *Little Caesar*, a film based upon a 1929 novel by W. R. Burnett. By the end of 1933, almost 80 gangster films had flickered onto the silver screen.

Much like the craving for association with celebrities of a gentler sort, people were quick to make up stories about experiences with famous gangsters such as Capone, John Dillinger, and Baby Face Nelson.

A good example is what happened when Al Capone came by car from Pennsylvania, where he had been released from prison, to Chicago, in the spring of 1930. He stayed overnight in out-of-the-way places along the route to avoid notice. Rumors of his whereabouts, often sworn to by locals but all fictional, proliferated wildly along the routes his car might have taken.

Not only was Capone famous, people knew exactly what he looked like. He loved, even craved, publicity. His picture appeared often in various media. Reporters dogged his every step both while he was in Chicago and away from there. Sometimes he sought to elude them, for example, during his return from his Pennsylvania prison term or when he spent time in the Lansing area. But his vacation time Up North in Wisconsin is well documented in the press, as are his movements while in Florida. We must approach reports of Capone-sightings Up North in Michigan with a good deal of *a priori* skepticism, given the avidity with which the press attempted to follow his every move and the fact that reporters failed to document any travel Up North.

This is the context that brings us to a summary of places Up North in Michigan where Capone supposedly stayed or was seen. The mythic tracks of Capone in Michigan follow two basic routes. One goes east from Chicago toward Detroit. Sightings abound all along this route as Capone allegedly traveled to and from Detroit in his dealings with illegal liquor from Canada and its major distributor, the Purple Gang. Kalamazoo, Battle Creek, Jackson, you name it, and someone has claimed a Capone sighting. I do not treat these because by no stretch can this area be called Up North, rather the opposite.

The second basic route goes along U.S. highways 131 and 31 north from Benton Harbor to the Straits of Mackinac. Passenger trains also followed this route and there were steamers on Lake Michigan to accomplish the same. That is the route I will trace, starting even below what can be called Up North because the line of sightings makes a coherent, if entirely fictional, whole.

The exception to these two trajectories is Lansing, in the east-west center of the state but not strictly Up North except in the sense that Michiganders tend to think of any lake anywhere north of where they are as someplace "up north." As I have already detailed, Lansing is the only documented Capone presence in Michigan outside of the border area with Indiana along Lake Michigan.

The list that follows is taken from a wide range of Internet and published documents that claim a Capone connection to a given site. None presents any clear evidence of Capone—no contemporary, local published statement by police, g-men, or other dependable source, no picture that shows Capone in a location that can be identified. Every sighting is based only on individual reports, often second- or even third-hand, but allegedly originally by contemporaries. "I was told..." or "I understand..." or "'X' told me..." is the evidence that is reported. I do not believe any represents a true Capone presence.[29]

I begin at the Michigan-Indiana border north to South Haven.[30] I have already mentioned Capone's vacation in Benton Harbor before he was sent to prison.[31] This was a real visit. Indeed, there is plenty of evidence that gangsters from Chicago got at least as far as Benton Harbor/St. Joseph regularly for some rest and relaxation along the lake. Capone's bodyguard, Philip D'Andrea, seems to have actually had a home in St. Joseph. Capone supposedly stayed at the Whitcomb Hotel in that city[32] and ate at restaurants in Benton Harbor. Outside of Benton Harbor, in Keeler Township, a place called Bronte Vineyards alleged that Capone had owned it for years and used it as a hideout; owners showed visitors secret tunnels and places where he stored his smuggled booze.[33]

To this add the fictional stay at the Flynn Mansion on Flynn Road in nearby Sawyer, complete with the usual tunnel, this time to escape to the local river—or maybe to Lake Michigan; accounts differ. Just to the south, in Lakeside, people claimed that Capone stayed at the Lakeside Inn. Berrien Springs claims a Capone house and farm at 1400 Kephart Lane, later owned by Muhammad Ali. Big Al supposedly played golf at the Berrien Hills Country Club.

Stevensville once saw a home owned by a Capone accountant named Irwin at 2135 W. Glenlord Road. It is now demolished. It is true, however, that Fred "Killer" Burke, one of the participants in the St. Valentine's Day Massacre and a Capone goon, had a home in this town.[34]

South Haven lies about 30 miles further north. Getting there, Capone bought gas at Prusa's in Union Pier. The usual "old timers" swear the Sleepy Hollow Resort has a house where Capone stayed. An account of the resort's history includes a statement that "Al Capone was purported to be have invested in Sleepy Hollow."[35] It was said he had a house on the Black River and a tunnel so that he could escape to it and thence onto Lake Michigan.[36] Capone, an avid golfer, played at the South Haven Golf Course according to numerous eye-witnesses. Nearby, in Allegan County, Floria, one of the innumerable Capone girlfriends, is said to lie buried in the McDonnell Cemetery in Casco Township. While this area certainly did experience Al Capone's presence, particularly in Benton Harbor, there is no solid evidence to back up the rumors of any Capone sightings further north.

In fact, from South Haven north the trail gets ever more unlikely. That said, it does appear that gangsters made it as far as Saugatuck in Allegan County. Bryan Bolton, a Chicagoan, member of the Barker-Karpis Gang and a familiar of Al Capone, visited his mother who lived in town. Supposedly Al himself visited, staying at the Twin Gables Hotel; owners point to bullet holes in the walls and ceiling attributed to gangster shootings.[37] The story is that he came over to the beach town in his yacht and cavorted at a place called "The Dock," a dancehall featuring the big bands (who did frequently play in such places).[38] Nearby, residents repeat rumors of Capone's presence at the Yellow Hotel east of Pullman on 110th Street. That hotel, now gone, saw Al as a guest according to a person's great-grandmother who "knew him well." Naturally, there were tunnels in the hotel's stables. At Gun Lake's Chicago Point east of Saugatuck he either owned or rented a cottage called the Eagle Nest.[39] (And of course the cottage had the requisite tunnel to the lake.) Fennville boasts an "old mansion that burned down on 112th Avenue," said to be one of Al's summer homes, just another mythological hangout like the one in Pullman. Finally, Tom Fleming of the Allegan County Historical Society relates that he talked with a supposed third cousin of Al Capone. "The cousin could not recall any family stories about Gun Lake but did talk about Capone spending time in Saugatuck and nearby Lawrence" (in Van Buren County).[40]

Continuing north, the town of Holland gets little press, only the rumor that Al had a hideout "underground over in the boonie part of town."[41] By this account, Al did not just have a tunnel to escape, he actually lived in a cave. Near Muskegon, it is claimed, he had a hideout on the Owasippe Scout Reservation just to the north of town.[42]

Football at Muskegon High School boasts one of the oldest and winningest high school football programs in the U.S. The Muskegon Big Reds have drawn several famous fans over the years, including, it was said, Capone, who supposedly attended at least a couple of the games and always had the team's score read to him on Monday mornings at his offices in Chicago. When he was serving time in Alcatraz, he supposedly had a Big Reds pennant in his cell.[43] Muskegon itself was the scene of the manhunt for Capone thug Fred "Killer" Burke when he was on the run after murdering a police officer in St. Joseph to the south. However, Burke eluded police.[44] He was supposedly heading for Muskegon from Newaygo (Newaygo County). Capone was said to have had a hideout in Muskegon, a "big white house located on the top of the hill where Penoyer Creek and the train tracks cross the Muskegon River." Or maybe it was a big yellow house off Stone Road south of M-20 "where the sandpit is in town by the railroad tracks," to the north of the county—or maybe he was at Bush Lake where Big Al and his gang came for privacy and seclusion or, then again, maybe the Bush Lake place belonged to an unnamed "Russian boxer" who ran it as an "escape home from Chicago authorities." All these stories are told.[45]

On up the coast, Oceana County features several mythical Capone appearances. He stayed at a house on Johnson Road just west of Ferry. And in the "last house on Garfield Road" in Benona Township. That one had a tunnel leading down to Stony Creek where a getaway boat could be launched. But, let's be clear: while there were gangsters who did hang around Stony Lake (one of them being Charlie Jameson, whose story will be told later in this book[46]), and a Barker-Karpis Gang member did spend a month on the county's Silver Lake in July 1935, Big Al never made an appearance.

Mason County has its own Capone myth. This centers around the Optiz Hotel, which was built in 1905 by Mary Opitz on Round Lake in Sheridan Township. (Capone stories seem to have had a fondness for round lakes; besides the one near Lansing where he stayed, supposedly there is another hideout at Round Lake, Wisconsin near Hayward and Couderay.) The Opitz Hotel sat near excellent train transportation from Chicago northward to the Ludington area. Passengers got off at Bachelor where a car met them and took them to the Opitz Hotel. The Opitz itself looks like the standard resort hotel of its day: a long veranda for lounging, public rooms downstairs and private rooms upstairs; the structure still stands. As the story goes, Capone used room number 6, one with two windows that provided a cooling cross-breeze and a view where he could see vehicles coming down the road to the hotel. There is even a photograph that claims to show Big Al standing beside a fancy car in the vicinity of Round Lake: "The man is nattily dressed in a suit with light-colored shoes and hat. He is parked at the side of a rural road that has been said to be Sugar Grove Road. The photo is labeled 'Al Capone' in old ink. The man looks like Al Capone."[47] On the other hand, a local person reports that his grandfather, the local constable, told him, "Al Capone did *not* stay at the Opitz Hotel. Old Lady Opitz would never have stood for it."[48]

In this area, people talk about recollections of selling homemade brew during Prohibition. At Historic White Pine Village near Ludington there is a significant archive dealing with local history. An historian collected all the newspaper articles about local booze in Prohibition times. It is very clear that many farmers made their own hooch for sale to wholesalers who shipped the stuff to Chicago via Manistee (Ludington's port was farther away than Manistee's a bit to the north). Police regularly raided stills and caches of booze. This connection to the illegal liquor trade surely gave rise to many of the mythical stories of a gangster presence in the area and, of course, that Capone was the one to whom the whiskey was sold. In reality, no gangster needed to be there, just producers and intermediaries willing to take the risk of making and getting the booze to the coast of Lake Michigan.

To the east of Mason County lies Lake County where, at Big Star Lake, a hotel supposedly hosted Capone. A native of the area wrote, "A guy named Tim Korhorn told me that his aunt owned the hotel on the

Opitz Hotel, Round Lake, Mason County, ca. 1910 and ca. 2015.
Mrs. Opitz is at the front in the left image.

east side of the lake. His aunt housed Al Capone and his cronies when the heat was on in Chicago. They would have to drive through pastures in the Sippy Flats area to get there. She was asked if she knew who he was...she said, 'Yes, I do, and I don't care.'"[49]

Surprisingly, I have found only one rumor of Capone's presence in Manistee County. Locals claim that he stayed in the Portage Point Inn, a luxury hotel built in 1891 to serve tourists coming up from Chicago by steamer. Just to the north, in Benzie County, the stories once again proliferate. As usual, people say that many local residents remember Big Al.[50] The stories center around his presence in Frankfort. The Harbor House is one location. It is a fine brick structure at the end of Main Street at the corner of Michigan Avenue. Capone supposedly owned this. He had a jail cell constructed and a tunnel that led far away to an inn or the local theater, or maybe also to a bank and an elementary school, all 300 to 500 yards away up Main Street. It is not clear why he would need a tunnel to go to those places.[51]

Elsewhere in Benzie County, Capone supposedly owned a whole row of houses on nearby Chrystal Lake. "There are many stories from people in the Frankfort Beulah area that remember the stories from their relatives that housed Capone and befriended him."[52]

The most well documented rumors in the Benzie area involve Lake Ann, a lovely inland area about 15 miles west of Traverse City. Gangsters from Chicago supposedly did their rest and relaxation and some even ran industrial-level stills to make whiskey to transport down to Chicago. Shields' Resort on Lake View, a tiny lake near the larger Lake

Ann itself, had a hotel and cabins as well as a nine-hole golf course where Capone supposedly played. The resort began in 1924 and is noticed for the last time in newspapers in 1928. Twenty years later, a Lake Ann Baptist Camp bought the property. In an interesting publicity move, the Camp advertises, "The place that once housed Al Capone now invites people into a deeper walk with Christ." Campers are treated to the tale that Al Capone was at that site. A local history states that Big Al also appeared at Lake Ann itself: "One of the locally noteworthy periods during the last seventy-five years was during Prohibition when some prominent Chicago families operated whiskey distilleries in [Almira] township. Some known 'gangster' families had property at Harris Point and at what is now the Lake Ann Camp & Retreat during this period. Al Capone visited this area at that time."[53] A Lake Ann cottage advertises itself as a former hideout for Big Al: "A best kept secret since the early 1900s when a Traverse City Furrier built the original cottage. In the 1920s it was a secret place for Al Capone. Capone's men guarded the ¾-mile drive to insure his privacy."[54] The Lake Ann Corner Cone shop even named a frankfurter after him, the Al Capone Dog: "When 'Scarface' came up here it was like Chicago coming to Lake Ann—and that's why we named OUR version of the Chicago Hotdog after the infamous bootlegger."[55] Of course there is no verification that Capone ever visited the Lake Ann area, much less played golf there on the skimpy, nine-hole course at Shields' Resort in the late 1920s.

All of these rumors were probably the result of the presence of someone with a verifiable connection with Capone. That would be Joseph Winkler, then head of the Chicago musicians' union, who was a friend of Capone's. Winkler (not Capone) owned the brick home in Frankfort that locals attribute to Capone himself. Winkler, like many wealthy Chicagoans, loved to come Up North for some leisure time on the lake. There is nothing inherently unlikely that a friend such as Capone could have visited him and even stayed awhile. However, there is no indication that this ever happened. Probably it was the locals who made the connection from Chicago to Winkler to Capone and so created the myths.

There were gangsters in Benzie County, but I treat them when I discuss real presences, not mythical ones.

As far as myths go, the story of Al Capone in Leelanau County pretty much tops the list. The development of the basic narrative is a case study on how these stories become accepted by the public. There was no published inkling of rumors about Big Al in the county until Larry Wakefield wrote a story for the *Indianapolis Times* in December 1983.[56] The basic narrative is that Capone vacationed in the area at a cottage complex called Heartsease (Heart's Ease). Wakefield was inspired by local rumors: "It is certain that Capone and his men stayed there several summers in the late '20s and early '30s. Several local people remember seeing him." From these rumors Wakefield moved to the architecture of the place (none of which survives). A gate to the property becomes guarded with armed men when Capone is present; a 30-foot wooden tower becomes a place where a machine gun sat, ready to spray invaders, according to "old timers." No tunnels, but perhaps the sandy soil made that difficult. Supposedly, Capone vacationed in Leelanau summers between 1928 and 1932. As I noted above, Big Al's movements are well known and there is no inkling of a trip Up North during those years, much less multiple ones.

The background Wakefield provides as evidence is completely lacking in any proof that Capone was present. Allegedly, one of the owners of Heartsease, a Frank J. Prince, was a pal of Capone in Chicago. But Prince was a well-known investigative reporter for the *Indianapolis Times* during the late 1920s and early 1930s and had nothing to do with gangsters in Chicago or anywhere according to numerous newspapers articles about and by him. Even an exposé of his life, written by a St. Louis Missouri journalist to protest the possible naming after him of a building at Washington University St. Louis, contains no hint of gangster connections.[57]

While it is true that Frank J. Prince had a bad early life, serving several terms in jail or prison, he had clearly turned himself around. However, Wakefield implies that even after he went legit, he hobnobbed with gangsters. As proof, he claims that Prince was really one Morris Czech. Now while F. J. Prince himself did use an alias in his delinquent

Heart's Ease, supposed Capone hideout in Leelanau County

years, his name was not an alias for Morris Czech or anyone else. The alias "Frank Prince" does belong to a man named Morris Czech who was, among other things, involved in early House Un-American Activities Committee investigations as an alleged Communist—but he is certainly not our Frank J. Prince.[58] In sum, a story has been constructed to prove rumors when the rumors in fact are just that, rumors of the sort that are reported in numerous locations without any actual Capone connection. Capone never set foot in Leelanau County's Heartsease, but Wakefield's conjecture, published in the *Indianapolis Times* and repeated subsequently in his book, was picked up by a reporter for the *New York Times* and by others so that it now forms part of the standard lore of the county.[59]

Grand Traverse County left few rumors of Capone's presence. I have found no rumors about Capone in Traverse City itself. The only one I know of relates to the L'Da Ru Lakeside Resort on Spider Lake in East Bay Township. The owner, Michael Anton, claims that it was once a hideaway for Big Al. The large log structure was built in 1923. The story is that Al Capone built this house as "one of many rural getaways he had in northern Michigan and Wisconsin."[60] Capone and his boys allegedly slapped down their poker hands on a green-felt-covered card table still at the resort. Interestingly, there is a Spider Lake in Wisconsin that also claims Capone's presence.[61] Does the name, Spider Lake, like the name, Round Lake, attract rumors about Big Al?

Rumors of Al Capone's presence peter out the further north we go. There are none from Antrim County and only the vaguest in Harbor Springs (Emmet County).[62] In Charlevoix there is only the story that Big Al stopped there for lunch on his way north to supposed hideouts in the Upper Peninsula—a story quite unbelievable since Capone-spottings in the Upper Peninsula concentrate in the Delta County area of Escanaba, a very, very long and tedious journey by any route passing thorough Charlevoix.

Sightings of Capone in the Lower Peninsula have almost run their course. There are a few scattered over the rest of Up North. For example, he supposedly stayed at Kenyon's Resort near Lupton in Ogemaw County. Across the St. Clair River from Port Huron (not really Up North), he stayed at the Grand Union Hotel in Sombra, Ontario as well as in neighboring Courtright. And of course, there are the rumors that Capone made it to Detroit to negotiate with the Purple Gang. The many stories about Capone in and around Detroit and dealings there with the Purples are fictional.[63] Capone never got further east than the Lansing area in southern Michigan.

A final note about Capone Up North involves not the man himself, but a sibling. Big Al had a little sister, Mafalda (1912-1988). She moved from New York to Chicago with her family in 1921. She attended a high-quality Catholic school and at the age of eighteen married John Maritote, the younger brother of one of Al Capone's henchmen, Frank "Diamond" Maritote. Her brother, Al, did not attend the wedding for fear of an attempt on his life, but he did send a spectacular wedding cake in the shape of a cruise ship that cost him $2,100.[64]

She was never directly involved in any of Al's nefarious doings. However, Mafalda was a life-long apologist for her family. She remained in Chicago even after Al was released from prison in 1939. When Al died in 1947, she, along with other family members, was at his side. Mafalda and John had one daughter, Dolores.[65] She married George Irvin, an officer in the United States Air Force. In 1979 the Air Force transferred Irvin to Wurtsmith Air Force Base in Oscoda Township. Mafalda, now frequently called Mae, and John moved there in 1980 to be close to the Irvin family and their granddaughter. The Maritotes bought a nice home next to a golf course. They ran an antique store nearby. The Irvins subsequently moved to California, but the Maritotes stayed put in Oscoda.[66] Mae suffered from the onset of Alzheimer's Disease and by the late eighties was not socializing with neighbors.[67] John Marito-

te finally had to put her into a nursing home in nearby Harrisville, as related here:

Mafalda

> To the end of her life, John took very good care of Mae, first in their home and then in the nursing home. A person with direct knowledge wrote: "I was lucky enough to have met Mafalda and her husband, while she was in a nursing home where I was working. She kept photos of her brother Al, and the rest of her family, in her nightstand, as well as photos of her wedding, the magnificent cruise ship wedding cake that Al had made for her and her husband, as well as other trinkets and photos. She had been diagnosed with Alzheimer's at the time I was taking care of her; however, if you opened the nightstand where she kept those photos, and mentioned her brother, showed her those photos, she lit up like the North Star! The sweetest thing was when her husband would come and visit her every single day! He would brush her hair, help with her makeup, help dress her, feed her, etc., looking every part the classy gentleman; pin stripe suits, overcoat, hat etc. You could just see the love they had for each other!"[68]

No, Al Capone was never in Oscoda, or even within hundreds of miles of the area. But his sister, Mafalda/Mae, left a small footprint there to remind us that his family had connections Up North, even if he did not.

Leaving the Lower Peninsula of Michigan, the Upper Peninsula offers yet more yarns about Al Capone Up North. The eastern portion lacks rumors, much like the area from Traverse City north in the Lower Peninsula.[69] The hearsay business picks up in the western counties of Iron, Dickinson, Delta, and Menominee.

Iron County is the area closest to attested appearances of Big Al in northern Wisconsin. The nearest point where rumors locate Capone in Michigan, the Iron River/Stambaugh area of Iron County, was difficult to reach from Capone's known Wisconsin visiting spots. Leaving aside the unfinished hideout at Cranberry/Pike Lake near Couderay, he certainly visited Joe Saltis' place, Barker Lake Lodge near Winter, and his brother Ralph's place near Mercer. Plotted on a 1930 road map, Mercer is 85 miles west of Iron County. The 90 miles over gravel roads between Mercer and Couderay/Winter farther to the west would have been an adventure. About 150 road miles separated Iron River and the Couderay/Winter area. Only small sections of these roads were paved; the rest was graveled, at best. In those conditions, averaging 25 miles per hour would be good, if not amazing—not counting rest stops, blown tires, and so on. So, an auto trip from Couderay to Mercer would take about four hours, while a trip to Iron River would take at least six hours and probably would have required an overnight stay somewhere. These were not trips to be made on a whim. There was no rail connection in either case.[70] To get to Couderay by train, travelers took the Minneapolis, St. Paul, and Sault Ste. Marie Railroad out of Chicago and transferred to the Chicago, St. Paul, Minneapolis & Omaha line for the final leg from the town of Beverly, in all, a fourteen-hour trip. But no direct, or even mildly indirect, rail route existed from Couderay/Winter to Mercer, much less to Iron County, Michigan. There must be a strong suspicion that gangsters would not have traveled for hours over rough roads if they could help it. Certainly, Capone would not have hopped over either from Couderay or from Mercer to Iron River for a drink.

To return to Iron County and Capone, local lore has it that he came there in his Cadillac. This car was purchased in 1930, just after Big Al's trip to the Pennsylvania prison system.[71] Given his problems after he was released as detailed above, it is very unlikely that he drove it to far northern Michigan. Nevertheless, a son reports that his father tuned up Capone's 16-cylinder Cadillac and filled it up with gasoline at Lindahl's Garage in Iron River.[72] "Back then the locals loved to see Capone come around and would not think of turning him in. He always brought a welcome infusion of cash into an otherwise economically struggling area. Capone had a place near Iron River/Stambaugh and frequently hung out there when things were a little warm in Chicago." To add a detail, another person claims that Capone owned a house that exists two or three miles outside Stambaugh on M-189. It was said to have had tunnels everywhere, of course. Finally,

A road in northern Wisconsin, 1930s

rumors of the usual bullet-ridden walls appear in a supposed Capone home on Swan Lake, just north of Crystal Falls, about 25 miles east of Iron River. [73]

Delta County at the southwestern tip of the Upper Peninsula also reported Capone sightings. As it is easy to reach this area by rail from Chicago, it is not surprising that Capone rumors abound. However, it is completely out of the way for Capone to get to either Mercer or Couderay via this part of Michigan. So, any trips had to be deliberate. To begin, there is never a mention of either place in any biography of Capone that is based on facts. So, on to the tales.

Ray Saari wrote up a detailed account of Big Al in the area.[74] He based his work on an unpublished book by Richard Lampinen, *Bottoms Up*. Saari's report is the only record of its contents.[75] "While doing his research, Lampinen uncovered a treasure trove of anecdotes..." Lampinen asked Saari to verify that Capone had owned a house in Escanaba. The journalist reports that he did, indeed, verify that Capone owned a home "on a quiet tree-lined street" in Escanaba and that "he was seen twice by a local historian who remembers one visit of approximately two weeks and another of about a week."[76] Another person identifies this house as at the end of South 10th street.[77]

Russell Magnaghi, a very solid historian at Northern Michigan University, heard stories about Capone in Escanaba while he was researching his important book, *Prohibition in the Upper Peninsula*.[78] An Escanaba librarian told of her grandfather owning a small grocery store to the north of the city: Al Capone came in, bought some cigarettes, and left $5 to pay for candy to be given to kids who came into the store later in the day. Other locals told of the home mentioned just above as well as of him dining at the House of Ludington hotel, the fancy spot in town to hang out. One source reports that Capone parked his custom-made Model T (!) outside the hotel and went in. Of course, the hotel comes complete with tunnel-lore: supposedly there was a tunnel running underground from the hotel, underneath a nearby house, and emerging a block further on; it was built for "quick escape should the authorities find them." Another version says that the tunnel went to Big Al's home.[79]

Al was also sighted in Marinette, Wisconsin, some 55 miles south of Escanaba. In a somewhat breathless article in the *Marquette Mining Journal* of March 25, 1931, the paper reported that Big Al might be on his way with three henchmen to Marquette to arrange for the transport of Canadian whiskey back to Chicago:[80]

Rumor Has It That Chicago Booze Lord Week-Ended In These Parts

Did Al Capone, Chicago's gang and booze lord, he of the scarred face and broad smile, spend the last week-end in the upper peninsula? Did he visit Menominee, Iron Mountain and Marquette? Is he still in the upper peninsula? Did he or is he looking for a chance to establish a nice, quiet summer "camp" where he and some of his gun-toting henchmen may go into seclusion? Is Mr. Capone seeking to establish connections which will enable him to run liquor into Milwaukee or Chicago from the Canadian border at Sault Ste. Marie? These are some of the questions that have been asked in the cities concerned since Saturday night, when Capone was reported to be in Marinette, Wisconsin, with a body guard of three men. Rumor had it that he left Marinette for the upper peninsula and that he was going to favor Iron Mountain and Marquette with a visit.

Rumors Fly Fast

The reports flew thick and fast by telegraph and telephone, some coming from newspaper sources in Milwaukee, others from Marinette. As far as Marquette is concerned the police have been keeping their weather eyes open for the gang king but declare they have seen no one resembling him. The state police also heard about the purported swing through the peninsula by Scarface Al as well as the rumor about his effort to make arrangements for getting Canadian booze through to Chicago. Captain Demaray's men are investigating. There appears to be some ground for the report that Al was in Marinette. In that city a colored person in a barber shop declares he recognized the gangster when the latter was getting a shave and a shoe-shine in the shop while his armed bodyguard watched on the outside. The porter formerly was employed in a shoe-shining parlor in Chicago which, he said, Capone visited daily to have his "dogs" polished.[81]

The date of this article—March 1931—means that Capone, deep into his legal trouble arising from tax evasion and soon to be convicted and sent to prison, was hardly Up North heading for Marquette.[82]

Upon examination, the rumors from Escanaba and Menominee replicate those of other places. As always, there is no solid evidence (e.g., a photograph of Big Al at the Ludington Hotel) to prove his presence. And, again as usual, the geography and timing of Al's travels hardly allows a stay or stays on Green Bay or the Little Bay de Noc.

When the general question of bootlegging comes up, Capone's name always does as well, just as it did in the article above. Bootlegging in the Upper Peninsula is no exception. Russell Magnaghi has documented how widespread it was right from the start of Prohibition in 1920. The St. Marys River between Ontario and Michigan was a popular spot to smuggle booze, as was the entire waterway of the Great Lakes Superior, Huron, and Michigan as they all bordered or were readily accessible to Canada. The question is, was Capone personally involved in Upper Peninsula bootlegging? There is no evidence and, in fact, relatively few rumors that mention him specifically. His men supposedly stationed his boat, the *Norco*, in Batchawana Bay, a favorite transshipment point for Canadian whiskey and other alcoholic delights. Unfortunately, there is no record that Capone ever owned a boat called the *Norco*. His only known boat is the *Acania*; it is never attested as far from Chicago as Lake Superior.[83] Supposedly he used Mackinac Island as another transshipment point, but his actual presence there is, as elsewhere, unproven. This does not mean, of course, that a source for Capone's Canadian booze was not through the Upper Peninsula one way or another. But here, as in many other cases of assuring appropriate supply, Capone had no interest in being personally present. Claiming to be simply a used furniture salesman, he maintained an aloofness from the daily business of running his whorehouses, gambling establishments, and rum-running. Added to the lack of evidence he was ever in the Upper Peninsula is the fact that he had no reason to be there personally, save for some recreation—and even then, his presence in Escanaba and Iron River is highly unlikely. And so, the story of Al Capone and his sleeping habits comes down to a very few cases of Big Al being present in southern Michigan, and not a single certain instance of him personally being Up North. Improbabilities and impossibilities abound in supposed eyewitness' accounts, rumors, and hearsay. The day someone comes up with a trustworthy police report or picture of Al Capone Up North in Michigan is the day we should believe he was ever there.

Although Capone's name became almost synonymous with "gangster," he was not the only famous mobster to make it Up North in legend. Occasionally, some even made it up there in fact. This is the topic of the next chapters.

⊶CHAPTER 3⊶

Sault Ste. Marie's Public Enemy #1

In the early twentieth century, Sault Ste. Marie was already a bustling place. There was a good deal of commerce and industry related to the ship canal that had been completed in 1855 and another, larger, in 1896. The other major industry was tanning. Large stands of hemlock trees attracted The Northwestern Leather Company that employed many local men. The company presence in Algonquin just to the west of the town center encouraged a housing tract where company workers lived.

John B. Hamilton and Sarah Edmonds married in Isabella County in 1882.[84] John was a blacksmith there. About 1894 the couple picked up and moved to Sault Ste. Marie. Then for a short time the family, now including five children, moved to the lumber town of Byng Inlet, Georgian Bay, Ontario sometime between 1895 and 1900. There in August 1898, Sarah gave birth to John B. Hamilton, Jr. Another move by 1901 brought them back to Sault Ste. Marie to live in a house in the Algonquin district. John worked at the tannery and at the same time, or later, as a carpenter. The couple added two more children.[8]

From the age of two, John Hamilton grew up in the Soo. Although he was not born there, he is definitely a Sault Ste. Marie native.

Hamilton's life before crime followed a fairly normal path for a youth in the backwoods of the Upper Peninsula. His younger sister, Valentine Hamilton Martin, recalled her brother's early life.[86] Her husband, Colin Martin, added details as well.

Sault Ste. Marie about 1910

There were five boys and two girls in the family—Johnnie was the third youngest. He was just a normal boy—nothing startling about his childhood nor in his early manhood. We lived in Sault Ste. Marie, in upper Michigan—a quiet, peaceful little town. Johnnie and I and a younger brother [Foye] were still at home when the older brothers and sister went out into the world. We had good times together, we three. Daddy [John B. Sr.] was a carpenter—a good one but there wasn't much building going on in that little city. It was Prohibition that started him [John B. Jr.]—everything he ever did can be blamed on Prohibition. When his father died [in 1923] he took over the carpenter trade the elder man had started. But work was slow in the Sault then so he just started peddling moonshine. John had no bad habits. Although he was a bootlegger, he never drank himself. He never smoked. ... Finally, he was caught bootlegging. That is, it was found out, and he faced a possible prison term. So, he just disappeared one day. We never heard from him again until he was picked up for stealing automobiles [in 1927] and sentenced to Michigan City [prison]. ... John couldn't be downed—even while he was in prison and everything was gloomy, there was nothing but a laugh in his heart, a joke on his lips. He would often write us letters, and his letters would be witty and full of humor.

The Hamiltons struggled to survive on John Sr.'s meager earnings. Young John was only 10 when the family almost lost their house across from the tannery in the Algonquin district to a fire that ravaged the homes around it. The next year, John barely escaped death as he was playing around close to a passing train when a protruding object struck him on the head. Dazed, he picked himself up but stumbled against the passing cars. His hand fell onto the rail and the car's wheels ran over his right hand. A passerby saw the accident and carried the lad to his home. A doctor was summoned and treated the wound. Hamilton's life was not in danger, but he lost the tips of the first and second fingers on his right hand. Authorities later bestowed on him the sobriquet, "Three-fingered," but his friends all called him "Red," because he was a carrot-topped kid.[87]

John made the local news again the next year.[88] It seems that the father had gone out hunting in the early morning, promising to return by midday. When he did not return by late afternoon, worries set in that he had gotten lost or even shot. Twelve-year-old Hamilton set out with a friend to find him. Hamilton senior soon returned, but now the boys were gone. In the pitch dark of a November night three search parties went out. Carrying their lanterns, through the hours they sought the boys in vain. Meanwhile, the two boys, bedraggled, cold, and

The Northwestern Leather Company in Sault Ste. Marie

thoroughly lost, at last stumbled upon a half-overgrown road that they followed until they came to a house. By then it was well after midnight. Daniel Doran, the farmer, took them in, dried them off, and sent them to bed, at the same time sending word to the worried parents. The next morning, Doran took them to the railroad tracks and pointed them toward town. They trudged the five miles back to Algonquin.

In 1914, John's father, under great stress to provide for the family, broke. He repeatedly threatened to kill members of his family. The family notified the police, who came to the house a number of times; each time, he put his .38 pistol into his pocket and escaped into the woods near his home. Finally, two officers approached the property stealthily; spying Hamilton lurking in some bushes and eyeing his house, they disarmed and arrested him. They then locked him up pending charges.[89] His fate is unknown, but evidently, he was an unstable, even violent father.[90] Soon, he disappeared. Sarah sought and obtained a divorce in 1920 on the grounds of desertion.

In these difficult circumstances, family and friends later recalled young Hamilton as a "model boy" and a "perfect gentleman." He attended Sunday School and one story even had it that he had taught in the church school—that while doing that, he met his future wife, Mary Stephenson. Mothers would point to him as an example of piety and decorum, wishing that their boys could be like him.[91]

Hamilton also did the things young men in the Upper Peninsula did. He hunted in the forests and there earned a bit of fame as a good marksman, proficient with a rifle. Somewhere he learned to shoot a pistol as well. In local marksmanship contests, he regularly came out the winner. He later put this talent to nefarious use during his years as a criminal.

In his tenth-grade year of high school, he had had enough of education and took his first job, as a lumberjack, cutting the hemlock trees needed for the Algonquin tannery. A few years later, in 1919 he briefly tried his hand at urban living by moving to Pontiac to work in the burgeoning auto industry.[92]

He married a local girl, Mary Stephenson, in the Soo in 1921; they soon had two boys, Orville and Howard. While he trapped, hunted, did some carpentry, and worked in the forest, his wife cared for their offspring and for a small garden and some chickens. Prohibition came just about this time. Michigan's Upper Peninsula was not a hotbed of support for the Volstead Act. Hamilton determined to earn a bit of extra money making and selling moonshine to the lumbermen. Erecting a small still in his chicken coop, he made some money until about 1924, when he was busted by the local constabulary. Posting a $500 bond, he promptly forfeited it and disappeared into the criminal world.

He returned to southern Michigan. This time he set up his still in Muskegon. That did not go well, either, and he went on to the Detroit area. His talent with a gun and his brawn as a lumberjack presumably recommended him to the bootlegging trade that was blossoming on the Detroit River. In 1926 the police nabbed him in Ecorse on a liquor transportation charge—bootlegging. By now, Hamilton was deep into criminality. He and a former policeman and fellow Soo native, Raymond Lawrence, who also had become a rum-runner in the transport of illegal liquor from Canada to Chicago, went west to Grand Rapids

"Red" Hamilton and Raymond Lawrence

41

and held up a coal company office. The take was a heady $200, but the pair did better robbing a Grand Rapids bank, netting $22,500 in that heist. Early in 1927 the duo struck again and with confederate Curtis Turner, held up the Fulton Street branch of the Kent State Bank. The trio made off with $25,000.

Inspired by this success, he headed south where he and Raymond Lawrence tried to rob a South Bend bank in broad daylight. They burst into the bank, brandishing pistols. $125,000 in cash and securities was almost in their hands when an assistant cashier broke for the door and once on the street raised the alarm. The robbers then beat a hasty retreat to an apartment house in the city that was owned by Hamilton's brother, William. There, a neighbor saw the two changing license plates on a sedan parked in front of the building. Tipped off, the police caught up with them. The South Bend chief's men surrounded the apartment building. The chief himself climbed the stairs to the second story apartment, pushed open the door, and announced that everyone was under arrest—brother William, William's wife, Ray Lawrence and his wife, and John Hamilton and his at the time. The police also confiscated a small arsenal. Taken to the station, the wives gave as much information as they had. Under some pressure from interlocutors, Lawrence confessed to the attempted robbery. Brought in and confronted with Lawrence's confession, Hamilton "dictated a similar statement laughing and joking as he did so, and he complimented the police department for its quick dispatch in solving the local crime." The women and William Hamilton were released. As part of the deal when the confessions were given, the two robbers were not extradited to Michigan for the Grand Rapids robberies.[93] The next day, a South Bend judge heard the confessions and guilty pleas and sentenced the men to 25 years in the Indiana penitentiary.[94] The next year, Mary divorced John on the grounds of extreme cruelty and non-support.[95]

Enter John Dillinger

The American public avidly followed the adventures of John Dillinger (1903-1934). He was a flamboyant gangster celebrity in the heyday of such celebrities. He robbed banks, frustrated police raids, escaped from jails, and had a series of molls. He might not have killed many people—he was not convicted of the one murder he committed—but he focused the media on his exploits through his daring. His colorful personality and derring-do appealed to the general populace even to the extent that they gave him an unearned reputation as a latter-day "Robin Hood."

John Dillinger

Dillinger's beginnings as a kid raised in Indianapolis were unsettling. He could not seem to control his anger and often got into fights. He bullied younger children. He shoplifted. He quit school to take up employment in a machine shop. His stern father who, Dillinger once said, believed that to spare the rod was to spoil the child, became increasingly worried about John's behavior and determined to move to the rural Mooresville, Indiana, area, away from the evil urban influences of Indianapolis. That did not help. Dillinger's first arrest came at age nineteen—auto theft. Could military service set him straight? He joined the United States Navy—but promptly deserted when his ship docked in Boston. He returned home to an angry, disappointed father.

One night in September 1924, a still young John Dillinger had too much to drink and too little sense. He and a friend mugged a Mooresville, Indiana, grocer. In that area, everyone knew everyone else. The day after the robbery, police arrested John. He pleaded guilty and was sentenced to ten to twenty years in Indiana's Pendleton Reformatory. There he met men who would later be his accomplices in crime. Transferred to the state prison at Michigan City by his own choice, he got to know even more criminals. One of them was "Red" Hamilton, serving time for the South Bend bank job of 1927. Paroled, Dillinger and a fast friend, Homer Van Meter, went to work to spring their pals from the prison they had just shared. They succeeded. Hamilton was free. It was September 1933.

Hamilton became an integral part of the Dillinger gang. Over the next half-year, he participated in the Lima, Ohio, jailbreak that freed a newly imprisoned Dillinger and committed several bank robberies with the gang. In one hold-up, he murdered a police detective, William Shanley, in another, William O'Malley. In January he was badly wounded in an East Chicago heist. After Dillinger's infamous escape in early March 1934 from the Crown Point, Indiana, jail using a wooden gun to intimidate guards, Hamilton rejoined the gang and robbed more banks. Mid-March, he was shot in the shoulder by a bystander during a hold-up in Mason City, Iowa. The gang retreated to St. Paul, Minnesota. He remained there with his girlfriend Pat Cherrington when Dillinger drove to his father's farm near Mooresville. On April 9th Hamilton returned to Chicago. On the 11th John Hamilton and another gang member, Homer Van Meter, met up with him there. On the 13th, Van Meter and Dillinger raided the Warsaw, Indiana, police station and made off with weapons and bullet-proof vests. Back in Chicago, police had just arrested Dillinger's favorite moll, Billie Frechette, for harboring him; I tell her story in the next chapter. He became obsessed with springing his girlfriend. John Hamilton was not in much better mental shape. He had been badly wounded twice since January. He was increasingly depressed, repeatedly saying that he would soon die. In this mood, his thoughts turned to his Sault Ste. Marie roots and, especially,

Indiana State Prison, Michigan City, Indiana

to his sister, Anna, to whom he had been very close in younger, happier times.[96] Dillinger remembered his own recent visit to his family in Mooresville and thought of how he missed Billie. He was sympathetic.

A drive to the Soo in 1934 was no easy matter. From Chicago it is about 500 miles to the Soo whether via Grand Rapids and route U.S. 131 or Lansing and route U.S. 27. Some northern stretches were still graveled. About 25-35 miles an hour was the most a car could average,

"a highway through the north woods"

figuring some stops for food and rest. At the straits, the ferry took some additional time. It was at least a twelve to fourteen-hour drive from Chicago to the Soo. Hamilton insisted. His companion in crime finally agreed. Three people made the trip: John Dillinger, John Hamilton, and Patricia Cherrington.[97]

Patricia Cherrington

Patricia Cherrington was a sort of professional gangster moll.[98] When she first appears on the scene, she is a friend of Billie Frechette, the woman who would become John Dillinger's best moll. They both worked in a fairly seedy Chicago nightclub where Billie was a hatcheck girl and Pat danced in the chorus line. Divorced from a husband she had married at age fifteen, rid of a child sent off to her mother in Toledo, by her early twenties she had come from a hard-scrabble upbringing in Texas to seek her fortune in the big city. Outspoken, given to drama, an attractive red-head intent on making the most of her good looks, she entered the world of low-class dives with low-budget, semi-nude performers such as herself laughing and drinking with gangsters and their ilk. One of them, Arthur Cherrington, married her. The relationship ended when, in June 1932, police burst into the apartment where she and Cherrington lived and arrested both. She went free, but her husband was sent to Leavenworth for robbing a drugstore's postal substation.[99] Cherrington did not act like a married woman after that. She took up with one gangster after another. A gall bladder operation ended her dancing career. She roomed with her sister, Opal Long, and with Billie in flop-houses and dated poor choices. In this promiscuous life she somehow met John Dillinger and the gangsters that he ran with. Her moll-dom began with Harry Copeland. She would go on to be Pete Pierpont's moll, and then, finally, late in 1933, John Hamilton's.

46

Once attached to Hamilton, Cherrington remained fiercely loyal, tending to his wound from the mid-January 1934 East Chicago gunfight while living with him in a Chicago apartment and treating him in St. Paul when he was wounded again in the Mason City, Iowa, bank robbery the gang carried out in mid-March. The two were back in Chicago by April 11.

The Soo

Hamilton and Cherrington set out for Sault Ste. Marie in a Ford coup early in the morning of April 17. Dillinger followed, alone with a small arsenal in a Ford V-8. The long drive brought them to the Soo as night was falling. Cherrington in her later statement to the FBI described the scene. Bryan Burrough recreates it vividly:

1934 Ford V8

> When night fell they drove into town. At 8:30 Hamilton's thirty-nine-old-sister, Anna Steve, answered a knock at the kitchen door of her frame house at the top of a steep hill on 14th Street. It was Pat Cherrington. "Are you Mrs. Steve?" she asked, and Mrs. Steve nodded. "Now don't be afraid, don't say a word," Cherrington said. "I've got a surprise. There's someone here who wants to see you." A moment later Hamilton materialized from the darkness, carrying a machine gun wrapped in a blanket. Dillinger was right behind him, holding a rifle. At the sight of her brother, whom she hadn't seen in seven years, Mrs. Steve began to cry. Hamilton held her and said they couldn't stay long. Wiping away her tears, Mrs. Steve said she wanted to go out and buy steaks to celebrate, but Dillinger shook his head and urged her to cook what she had in the house. Shooing her three children upstairs, Mrs. Steve prepared a dinner of bacon, eggs, and toast, and ate it with the trio at the kitchen table as they reminisced about Hamilton's childhood. Afterward both men shaved.

Mrs. Steve took out a pair of clippers and gave the men quick haircuts. For the first time in weeks Hamilton seemed happy. He was home; it was all he had left. Around ten, the kitchen door swung open, startling both men, who grabbed their guns off the table. But it was only Mrs. Steve's eighteen-year-old son, Charles Campbell. Dillinger lowered his gun. "Charles, this is Johnnie," Hamilton said. He didn't have to say more. Everyone adjourned to a sitting room, where young Campbell watched the two men closely. Hamilton made a clicking sound when he breathed, the result of his earlier wounds. Dillinger, still walking with a limp, remained on edge. He sat by a window saying little, reading a newspaper between peeks outside. After a bit, Hamilton sent his nephew to fetch one of his boyhood friends, a man named Paul Parquette, who came over and was stunned to find himself face-to-face with the country's most-wanted man. It was an awkward moment, a parody of a reunion; no one knew what to say, Hamilton showed his old pal how his machine gun worked. This was far too chummy for Dillinger, who rose around eleven and announced it was time to leave. Hamilton begged for just one night to sleep in his sister's house. But Dillinger said it wasn't safe. The FBI was out there somewhere, he said, watching. As they gathered their guns, Mrs. Steve began to cry. Not knowing what to say, she handed her brother a jar of venison to take. Hamilton held her for a long moment and softly kissed her cheek. "Bye," Hamilton said. "I hope we see you again." They wouldn't. The last time Anna Steve saw her brother, he was walking down the muddy hill away from her house; Hamilton left his car behind for her as a gift. At the bottom he and Pat slid into Dillinger's car and drove to the town of St. Ignace, only to find they had missed the last ferry across the Straits. Dillinger found a hotel where they could stay the night, and Cherrington signed them in.[100]

Hamilton, the nice, Sunday School-going kid gone bad, would never see Anna or Sault Ste. Marie again.

On the 18th, a salesman informed the sheriff of Chippewa County (where Sault Ste. Marie is located) that a friend had boasted that he had been with Dillinger the night of the 17th; the salesman added that the story might, or might not, be true. The sheriff immediately contacted the FBI by telephone with the information. The FBI took it very seriously. Agents dispatched from Chicago flew to St. Ignace. They arrived at the Soo on the 19th. Of course, the Dillinger group had already departed.

The agents hauled in Anna Steve and her son, Charles Campbell, for questioning. They did not reveal what Anna might have told them, but from Charles they got juicy details. He told them that Dillinger had walked with a limp and that Hamilton favored an injured arm. They were, Charles averred, heavily armed with rifles, machine guns, and bullet-proof vests. The local and federal authorities then raided the Steve property where they found and impounded John Hamilton's abandoned automobile they found in the barn. J. Edgar Hoover was determined to get something out of the failure to capture Dillinger. His instruction to his g-men was to prosecute Anna Steve to the fullest for harboring a fugitive from justice. The ensuing drama would go on for well over a year.

Anna Hamilton Steve was not one to take sitting down what life threw at her. She demanded that the car her brother had left be returned to her, noting that it had been searched and seized without a warrant. Judge Fred M. Raymond ruled that, "in the face of current crime conditions precedents of other days cannot be followed." In a ruling contradicting all rules of law, he claimed that because criminals used the law to evade punishment, the law could be broken by authorities to punish such law-evading criminals.[101] Anna did not retrieve the automobile.

Her trial on a charge of harboring a fugitive was scheduled for the fall of 1934 in federal court, Marquette. Judge Raymond, the man who had recently approved of search and seizure without a warrant, was to preside. But the trial was put off to early 1935 and the venue changed to federal court in Grand Rapids. It was then moved back to Marquette and again postponed to the April term while the U. S. district attorney in Grand Rapids denied that the government would drop the charges. In Marquette, a district court returned an indictment against Mrs. Steve on a charge of harboring the criminals John Dillinger and John Hamilton; Steve pleaded not guilty. Charles Campbell also was indicted and also pled not guilty. Then a further continuance was announced, moving the trial to Sault Ste. Marie and the June court term.

When the trial finally got underway on June 5, 1935, more than a year after the gangsters' visit to the Soo, the government made its case for the harboring of the gangsters. Mrs. Steve took the stand in her own defense. She contended that she had taken the gangster in only because she feared for her life—she told how Dillinger had sat by a window with a gun in his hands while the visit went on.

After deliberating for seven hours, on June 7th the jury returned verdicts of not guilty for Charles Campbell, but guilty for Anna Hamilton Campbell Steve. Judge Raymond sentenced her to four months at the federal detention farm for women at Milan, Michigan, and fined her $1,000.[102]

In Sault Ste. Marie, the outcome caused an uproar. Anna Steve was a respected fellow citizen. She was an active church member and had been the president of the local Parent-Teacher Association. Fellow Sooites quickly organized to circulate a petition. Signed by 1,500 citizens, probably at least half of the adult population, its text requested President Franklin Roosevelt's intervention to lift the "curse of John Dillinger" from Mrs. Steve by issuing a pardon. The accompanying letter argued that she had been "the victim of circumstances" and so innocent of evil intent. The Soo's city commission added to the chorus by adopting a resolution asking that Mrs. Steve be pardoned immediately. A few days later, the Justice Department refused to recommend a pardon.

End of the line

Hamilton had returned to Chicago with Dillinger and Cherrington on April 18th, 1934 after his brief and exhausting visit to the Soo.[103] Once there, the Dillinger gang decided that a bit of rest and relaxation was in order. On the morning of April 20th Dillinger, Baby Face Nelson, Homer Van Meter, Hamilton, Tommy Carroll and three women including Pat Cherrington set out north in four cars heading for a remote

Little Bohemia Lodge, 1930s

Wisconsin resort, Little Bohemia Lodge, near Manitowish Waters.[104] Through a local informant, the FBI found them there and launched the infamously unsuccessful raid on April 22nd. Dillinger, Hamilton, and Van Meter escaped the raid, fleeing toward St. Paul. They almost made it, but just south of the city, at Hastings' bridge over the Mississippi, a policeman recognized the license plate number on their stolen vehicle. He and some deputies gave chase. The gangsters noticed that they were being followed and sped away at eighty miles an hour. Catching up, the police opened fire on the fleeing vehicle as Dillinger broke out the rear window and fired in return. Suddenly, Hamilton collapsed in the front seat. A bullet had pierced his back. He was badly wounded. Dillinger realized that police would be all over St. Paul looking for him. The gangsters stole another car, carried Hamilton in terrible pain to it, and headed for Chicago. There, Dillinger hoped to find a sympathetic doctor he knew who would fix up Hamilton. Failing in that, Van Meter and Dillinger fled to Aurora, a little west of Chicago, where they found a hide-out apartment. They carried Hamilton to a bed, but he was clearly in very bad shape. Gangrene had set in. There was not much to do but try to minimize his great suffering. On April 26th, he died.

They had to dispose of the body. There was an abandoned gravel pit nearby, in Oswego. Four gangsters including Van Meter and Dillinger dug a shallow grave and laid Hamilton in it. Dillinger poured lye over

Public Enemy No. 1

John Hamilton, former first lieutenant of John Dillinger's mob of desperadoes and one of the few major criminals still at large, has received the designation of "Public Enemy No. 1" since the death of George "Baby Face" Nelson. (Associated Press Photo)

his face and hands to prevent identification saying, "Red, old pal, I hate to do this, but I know you'd do the same for me."

Authorities had no idea that Hamilton was dead. Two months later, the FBI enlisted Ana Sage to help them end John Dillinger's crime sprees. On Sunday, July 22nd, "The Lady in Red" actually wore an orange dress that evening to identify the gangster as he emerged from the Biograph Theater in Chicago. Apparently, there was no attempt to arrest him. The moment Dillinger seemed to reach for a gun in his pants pocket, the waiting FBI agents shot him down.[105] Homer Van Meter fell in August 1934. Pretty Boy Floyd in October. Baby Face Nelson had a fatal run-in with agents in November. At that point, newspapers promptly elevated John Hamilton to the rank of Public Enemy #1.

For a year and four months, rumors and bad information led nowhere. Where was Hamilton? Late in August 1935, the FBI got a tip: Look in the gravel pit at Oswego.[106] They did. They compared the corpse's teeth to a dental record in Hamilton's police file. It was him.

With almost two months' time already served, Anna was released from

Hamilton exhumed, *Indianapolis News*

custody in mid-August 1935 after the additional two months in jail. She returned to her home in Sault Ste. Marie. There, she learned of her brother's fate. She telephoned the authorities offering to pay for John's burial. That was fortunate, as two of his siblings had already refused to do this and Hamilton was heading for a potter's field. At dawn on August 31st, a damp fog enveloped the graveyard of the Oswego Township Cemetery as the mutilated body of the Sault Ste. Marie gangster was lowered into a grave. Six persons watched, but no mourners wiped tears from their eyes, no flowers were laid on the grave.[107]

More Public Enemies Up North

Although John Hamilton was the only Public Enemy actually from Up North, others came or were reported by rumor. I begin with John Dillinger, as his visit to Sault Ste. Marie was only one part of his story Up North.

Dillinger Tales

Michiganders' interest in Dillinger's whereabouts rose in earnest on March 16th when in Port Huron deputy sheriffs cornered and shot Herbert Youngblood, a fellow prisoner freed from the Lake County "escape proof" jail in Crown Point, Indiana, during Dillinger's great escape on March 3rd 1934. On his deathbed, Youngblood told police that Dillinger was just outside Flint and heading for Canada or, as other accounts had it, was heading for southwestern Michigan. Authorities took the information seriously. Police launched searches into Canada as well as around Niles in the southwestern corner of the state. In fact, though, around March 16th Dillinger was in St. Paul, Minnesota, far from Michigan.

By the end of March, Dillinger sightings were rampant throughout virtually the entire nation. Reports came in from locations as disparate as southern California, Arizona, Oregon, and even Sonora, Mexico—not to mention Iowa, New Jersey, Louisiana, and many places in between. Michigan hosted several of the sightings.

In Detroit, along with numerous reports to police of individual sightings, he supposedly robbed a railroad freight terminal. He was reported

WHERE DILLINGER SEARCH CENTERS

Map shows cities and towns in which John Dillinger has been seen since his escape from the Crown Point, Ind., jail March 3rd. The desperado's latest exploit is the daring raid he and a companion said to be John Hamilton, member of Dillinger's mob, staged on police arsenal at Warsaw, Ind.

seen in Jackson, Flint, Niles, and many other places. The possibility that he could appear almost anywhere at any time was very lively in people's minds. Dillinger's real appearance at Sault Ste. Marie in early April added fuel to the myth-making fire. By an odd coincidence, on April 15th, two days before Dillinger, Hamilton, and Cherrington arrived at Anna Steve's home in Sault Ste. Marie, the sheriff in the Soo had taken Ralph Alsman, age twenty-four, of Brookville, Indiana, into custody.[108]

The sheriff demanded proof that Alsman was not John Dillinger, for he bore a "marked resemblance" to the gangster. Fingerprinted, Alsman protested that he had left Indiana, fearing that someone would mistake him for the gangster and shoot him. Of course, he was not Dillinger and soon went on his way. The arrest of the unfortunate Alsman exemplifies the high alert locals were on everywhere when it came to sighting the infamous gangster.

Bois Blanc Island

This sort of false sighting, added to the very real presence of Dillinger Up North, produced another fictional appearance at nearby Bois Blanc (pronounced locally "Bob-Low") Island, a fair-sized, quiet wilderness just south-east of Mackinac Island and across Lake Huron from Cheboygan. There in the middle of the island, locals point out the ruins of three cabins where, they claim, John Dillinger hid out. One story ties together the Soo sighting to make this hideout a stop for Dillinger on his way to the Soo to visit his (not Hamilton's) sister there. There is even a novel that fancifully fills the story out even more.[109] But Dillinger's movements are well documented and there is no time when he would have been hiding out in such a remote Up North location. The rumor is but another untrue tale of the famous outlaw.

DILLINGER DOUBLE SEEKS SANCTUARY AND GETS JAILED

SAULT STE. MARIE, Mich., April 16—Ralph Alsman 24 years old Brookville, Ind. bears such a close resemblance to John Dillinger the desperado that the sheriff's office here took him into custody and fingerprinted him to check his identity.

He told officers that he left Indianapolis for fear that his resemblance to the outlaw might induce someone to take a shot at him on general principales.

Dillinger visits Clare?

During the Dillinger frenzy, amusing anecdotes emerge about his presence in Clare as well as a rather spectacular false sighting there.

Jack Livingston, a fixture in the local oil businesses, operated out of the Doherty Hotel in Clare during the 1930s, and was a notorious practical joker. One of Livingston's pranks was inspired by Dillinger. While newspapers were full of breathless reporting on Dillinger sightings here, there, and everywhere, Livingston was living at the Doherty. When he overheard the night clerk boast about what he would do if he came "face to face" with the man also known as "Jackrabbit," Livingston went out and found two country boys whom he enlisted for a prank. They came into the Doherty late at night and demanded a room. One of the boys had a red-stained handkerchief pressed to his forehead. The night clerk registered them and, filled with apprehension, led them to their room. Once they were inside, the boys closed the door, blocking the clerk's exit. "Do you know who I am?" "No," replied the clerk. "Well, I'm Dillinger and if you know what's good for you, keep quiet. We want liquor and food. If you mention this to anyone, we'll kill you." They kept this charade going for two days, with the clerk furtively bringing food and drink throughout. Livingston finally revealed the truth to an uproarious response from everyone in the hotel's lobby. He apologized for this prank by paying all the expenses for the room, food, and drink.[110]

In a second incident, Larry Knapp, who repaired slot machines in and around Clare and often was at the Doherty Hotel, told of the time he connived with local oilmen to pull a practical joke on a bellboy at the Doherty. "Some [oilmen] were quite sports as they would spend two or three days hatching up to play a joke. About 1935 or 1936 [actually, 1934], John Dillinger was supposed to be coming through Clare on his way up north and was to stop at the Doherty Hotel overnight. I was chosen to play the part of Dillinger and they poured ketchup all over my shirtsleeve and arm so when the new bellboy opened 'John Dillinger's' room door to hand him what he had ordered, the boy was sure scared and about fainted."[111]

Then it happened: On Saturday evening, April 21, 1934, Dillinger and his pal, John Hamilton, were sighted in town![112] Mrs. Johnson, the wife of the owner of Johnson Radio Service Station, was sitting in the shop reading a newspaper article that described the two men and the car they had supposedly been seen driving. "She had just remarked to herself, 'what if they came to Clare?,' when she happened to glance out the window and saw a car being parked that was exactly as described in the paper, even to a broken window and license plates. As the men alighted and came toward her, she quickly saw that they also tallied with the description." The two men strode into the small shop and asked about a Philco short-wave radio. She showed them one, then turned and unsuccessfully tried to call her husband on the telephone. Meanwhile, the men tuned in to several police bands "and then left the building, appearing extremely nervous and anxious to get away." They were there a scant seven minutes. Immediately, Johnson grabbed a bystander, Sheral Callihan, informed him what had happened, and told him to contact the sheriff. Deputies and State Police

DILLINGER THOUGHT TO HAVE VISITED CLARE LAST SATURDAY EVE.

Traveling Partner of Gangster Answers Description of John Hamilton

Two Men Are Identified at Several Places in Northern Part of State

The *Clare Sentinel* reports Dillinger sighting

swarmed. Johnson told them, "They perfectly answered the description of these nationally known gangsters." Perhaps needless to say, Dillinger had not paid Johnson a visit. The *Sentinel* story explicitly relates this event to the supposed sightings of Dillinger in Escanaba, Newberry, and Sault Ste. Marie, all related to the recent story of Dillinger at the Soo. The editor points out, however, that the Clare story does not match the Soo story because no woman was in the car with the two men.[113] It also does not match the chronology of Dillinger and Hamilton's actual trip to the Soo.

Evelyn "Billie" Frechette

Evelyn Frechette's life began as inauspiciously as it ended, fifty years later. She was born in Neopit, Wisconsin, just outside the Menominee Indian Reservation centered at nearby Shawano, September 15, 1907. Her father was French Quebecois. Her mother, Mary Labell, had one parent who was French, the other who was American Indian.[114] The area was poor, the prospects slim for a "half-breed," as anyone with partial American Indian genealogy was called at the time.

Evelyn "Billie" Frechette

Evelyn had some formal schooling.[115] At age eighteen, about 1925, she went to Chicago. There she worked as a domestic.[116] It is likely that such employment either directly or indirectly led her into prostitution. That led three years later to pregnancy with no father in sight. This was a difficult situation to be in. A social worker directed the desperate young woman to Edward Brooks' hospital on North Clark Avenue in Chicago.

Edward Brooks, who saw himself as a compassionate Christian missioner to the downtrodden, had established a hospital that served such desperate patients as Frechette.

Evelyn Frechette gave birth to William Edward on April 24, 1928.[117] Brooks suggested to her that she travel with the child to his "baby farm," that is, a private institution that took in the children of unwed mothers. Baby farms were well-known establishments. At their best, a farm could be a sort

Edward Brooks

of day care, a place working mothers could safely park their children. But more often, these were commercial adoption and/or baby-selling operations. Edward Brooks' baby farm in Benzie County, Michigan, followed a pattern of ostensible social service turned to exploitation and inhumanity. Unwed mothers had long faced terrible problems. Their families often rejected them; city social services, if they existed, proved woefully inadequate to meet the need. Recourse to help offered by religious organizations involved humiliation at best and at worst (as the recently exposed situation with Catholic-run baby farms in Ireland showed) exploitation or death for the child. In the United States, baby farms existed throughout the nineteenth and early twentieth centuries. Authorities tried to snuff them out when their behavior became too outrageous and too visible with scandals regularly erupting in urban newspapers. The excesses gradually led to their suppression during the 1920s and the licensing of their primary operations.

Brooks coordinated his hospital in Chicago with his baby farm. He claimed his only motivation was the milk of human kindness. The train trip around the southern tip of Lake Michigan and north to Brooks' farm brought Frechette to a ramshackle series of buildings where unwed mothers awaiting delivery, or having just delivered, were hoping to leave their children behind, perhaps for adoption.

Frechette's baby died at three months in Benzie in the summer of 1928. The little child suffered from congenital syphilis (*treponema pallidum*), passed from mother to child during fetal development or at childbirth.[118] Some years later, when Frechette had gained notoriety as John Dillinger's primary moll, Brooks remembered her. He recalled her in his Chicago hospital (which was eventually closed by local authorities) and that she had traveled to Benzie with William, but that was all. She was just one of many desperate customers.[119]

Evelyn Frechette left Benzie, though we do not know whether before or after her William died. In an odd way, she kept the memory of her only child alive by taking the nickname "Billie," a sobriquet that appeared later in the newspapers. Apparently, she went back to her home on the reservation.[120] She appears there in the 1930 Census married to a man named Albert.

Her next two years are obscure. But she continued to get mixed up with a disreputable crowd. Along the way, she met Weldon Walter Sparks and she married him in 1932. After he was almost immediately sent to Leavenworth for bank robbery, she divorced him in January 1934.[121]

Frechette, now commonly known as "Billie," met John Dillinger, by her own account, in November 1933, but it probably happened a couple of months earlier.[122] She had worked in dives, sometimes as a hatcheck girl, sometimes "toe dancing," that is, performing in risqué dance performances in the follies mode. She was his moll until she was arrested on April 7, 1934, tried, and sent to prison for two years for having harbored Dillinger in Minneapolis. So, she was his girl for only about six months. Upon her arrest, Billie had her second experience in Michigan, but this time not Up North. She spent her two years in the federal woman's prison in Milan, near Detroit. After her

"Billie" Frechette and John Dillinger

release, she made a living for five years touring the country with some of Dillinger's family and lecturing on the topic, "Crime Did Not Pay." Then she returned to Shawano, Wisconsin, where she died in 1969.

Other famous gangsters Up North

There are brief mentions of two other well-known gangsters in the northland, Alvin Karpis and Joe Roscoe, both members of the infamous Barker-Karpis Gang.

Alvin Karpis

The FBI pursued Alvin Karpis, a Public Enemy, Up North. Karpis, after a youth filled with crime and incarcerations, joined Fred Barker in Tulsa, Oklahoma to form the Barker-Karpis Gang. This group was notorious for its violence. It committed pretty much any crimes available—kidnappings, bank robberies, murder for hire, and other outlawry. The gang, which may have numbered as many as twenty-five hoodlums at its peak, was seriously harmed after the FBI focused its attention on them and their activities. Ma and Fred Barker were killed early in 1935; Karpis, on the run, rose to the rank of Public Enemy #1, one of very few criminals to reach that height of infamy. (Pretty Boy Floyd, John Dillinger, Baby Face Nelson, and John Hamilton were four others, all killed by government agents.) By early 1936, the FBI had traced Karpis to New Orleans. A raid in May caught Karpis at last. He was convicted of kidnapping and spent the next twenty-six years on Alcatraz Island, a guest of the U.S. government and a companion of Al Capone on The Rock.

The FBI had little to go on in manhunts like this besides tips from citizens. These tips sent agents on many wild goose chases. Apparently one tip pointed to Karpis being seen in the vicinity of Petoskey/Harbor Springs in northern Michigan. Agents were sent. An extensive report followed that started by stating, "no indication of

Karpis or Campbell (an accomplice) have [sic] ever appeared at these resorts although it is not without a possibility."[123]

Harry Campbell, a leading member of the Barker-Karpis Gang, did, indeed, come Up North. On May 29, 1935, Gertrude Billeter married a "Bob Miller," Harry Campbell's alias, in Toledo.[124] In November of that year, Campbell and other members of the Barker-Karpis Gang robbed a train in Garrettsville, near Youngstown, Ohio, making off with almost $50,000. (The year before, the gang had exacted a $200,000 ransom for the return of Edward Bremer, a wealthy St. Paul, Minnesota banker.) Evidently, the Garrettsville job was meant to be Campbell's last. He had settled into married life in Toledo under an alias, at first living in a camping

Harry Campbell

trailer on his in-law's property. The summer of their wedding, the couple took the camper Up North to Silver Lake (Benzie County) for a month's fishing trip. Thoughtful Harry brought back a big mess of fish to Toledo upon his return and gave some to friends.[125] Among those friends was Lucas County's sheriff, James O'Reilly. When the FBI, led by J. Edgar Hoover himself, descended on the Millers' home in Toledo virtually on the couple's anniversary in 1936, Sheriff O'Reilly protested that he had no idea that one of America's most wanted had been his drinking buddy for months. Hoover had ordered his agents not to notify the corrupt Toledo constabulary of the raid. Harry's wife, Gertrude, was found to be completely in the dark about who "Bob Miller" really was. At least she had enjoyed a summer's vacation Up North.

A lesser known Barker-Karpis man, Joe Roscoe (born Rascio or Roscolli and known as "Vedo"), appeared in the northland: the Petoskey postmaster had not seen any mail directed to him, but stated that "it is not without possibility that Joe Roscoe has been [in the resort area] during past seasons."[126]

Joe was originally a Toledo gangster who may also have served some time in New York State. He specialized in gambling and bootlegging. At one point he owned a small island (Middle Island) just north of Sandusky, Ohio, in Lake Erie where he had a mini-hotel offering pros-

Joe Roscoe

titutes and a casino.[127] It seems to have operated throughout Prohibition and for a time afterward as a base of smuggling premium beers and liquors into the United States via Monroe, Michigan, and Toledo to avoid (first) the law and, after Prohibition ended, alcoholic beverage taxes.

When Toledo's Jimmy Hayes was murdered in 1934, Joe took over his gambling places. In 1936 J. Edgar Hoover called him "the reputed gambling king of Toledo."[128]

He was also a ruthless killer. The 1936 FBI report stated that, "Joe Roscoe is known to place men on jobs and to go out on jobs himself."

He became involved in the Barker-Karpis Gang. He participated in the Bremer kidnapping in 1934 and then in the gang's Garrettsville, Ohio, train robbery in 1935 where Roscoe drove a getaway car. He was later convicted of harboring fugitives and helping them escape and served a 7½ year sentence. He then operated the 42nd Street Cafe in Toledo until, at the last stage of his life, he went into the real estate business.

Roscoe's connection with Up North is quite tenuous. He took over Jimmy Hayes' interests in Harbor Springs' Ramona Park Casino after Hayes was murdered in 1934, but he must not have been much on the scene given his connection with two Barker-Karpis crimes in 1934 and 1935. However, that connection to Emmett County gambling and to the Barker-Karpis Gang was of interest to the FBI when they poked around Up North in 1936.

Fred "Killer" Burke

Born Thomas A. Camp, Fred Burke (1893-1940) moved on from a big-family, rural Kansas environment to become a Public Enemy as one of the most feared assassins of the Prohibition era. He fully deserved his sobriquet, "Killer." He started out modestly in mostly non-violent criminal enterprises such as land fraud and forgery schemes. His first stop was Kansas City, but soon he moved on to St. Louis where he joined the top criminal element in that city, Egan's Rats. To escape trial after being indicted for forgery, he enlisted in the U. S. Army and served in France in a tank unit. Military service did nothing to change his ways. Upon his

Fred "Killer" Burke

return, he became involved in a Michigan fraud scheme that imploded. Arrested for obtaining money under false pretenses, he was sentenced to one to five years in Jackson Prison. He served just one year but then also had to deal with the earlier forgery charge in Missouri, which got him another year in the slammer.[129]

Unredeemed by his prison time, Burke rejoined Egan's Rats and, along with some other Great War veterans, undertook more violent criminal activity that included armed robbery. A crack-down on gangs in St. Louis in 1924 led to the dispersion of many of Egan's Rats to Chicago and elsewhere. Via Chicago, Burke and some others headed for Detroit where they became involved with the leading gangsters of the day, the Purple Gang and Pete Licavoli's crew. Burke was one of the gunmen in the Miraflores murders (1927). In 1929 he was implicated as one of the assassins at the St. Valentine's Day Massacre in Chicago.

During 1929, Burke also made appearances Up North. One witness told the FBI that Burke had been seen at the Ramona Park Casino gambling operation in Harbor Springs. This was a place partially financed by Cheboygan's gambling racketeer, Mert Wertheimer. The FBI was also told that Burke and a fellow ex-Egan's Rats man, Raymond "Crane Neck" Nugent, had been behind the kidnapping of Wertheimer from a golf course at nearby Mullet Lake.[130] I tell that story later.

Like many gangsters, Burke moved around quite a bit, robbing banks and generally engaging in mayhem. However, in late September 1929, he decided to settle down. He bought a house near Stevensville, Michigan, just south of Benton Harbor/St. Joseph in 1929 and settled in with his wife, Viola.[131] Burke presented himself as Fred Dane, a gasoline station owner from Indiana. To the locals he seemed a bit peculiar at times and some even guessed that he had got his money from bootlegging, but in general they accepted him and his wife into the community.

Barely two and a half months later, Burke's stab at the quiet life came to a violent end when he was in a minor automobile accident with a local. No one was hurt, but a policeman, Officer Charles Skelly, stepped up on the running board of Burke's Hudson and motioned him to drive on down to the station to make a report. Burke pulled out a pistol, shot Skelly three times, and then sped off. Skelly's murder set off a massive manhunt for Burke.

Burke's home on Lake Shore Drive

At first Burke, fleeing as fast as he could from the Stevensville area, headed north to Newaygo County. At some point he had arranged with William Smith of Grand Rapids to use his rural cottage as a hideout at Hess Lake. In July 1930, police got wind of the hideout. Officers from Chicago, Grand Rapids, and the local county sheriff's office armed themselves heavily expecting a gun battle with "the most dangerous man alive." Alas, someone tipped off Burke. A half hour before the lawmen closed in on the cottage, he and his wife fled at top speed. He had escaped yet again. State Police throughout Michigan were placed on alert.

What happened next is classic for the time. On July 14 newspapers spread the word that "Killer" Burke was on the run; they printed his picture. This brought in an avalanche of sightings. Mason County, Lake County, Kent County, north in Wexford and Mecosta counties, east near Bad Axe in the Thumb, even Marquette in the Upper Peninsula sent word of his imagined presence.[132]

As it turned out, Burke had fled Michigan. He headed for northern Missouri, hoping to elude pursuit in the countryside. He married again, assumed yet another name, and settled near Green City in Sullivan County. He seems to have continued robbing banks. Then one day in March 1931, a citizen in Green City recognized Burke. Police closed in and arrested him without incident.

Returned to Michigan, his trial took place in Berrien County where Burke had murdered Officer Skelly. He was convicted and sentenced on April 27, 1931 to life in Michigan's maximum-security prison in Marquette. The next day a three-car, well-protected caravan set out with the prisoner, bound for the penitentiary. When they stopped for breakfast in Cadillac, locals lined up to get a look at the gangster. "Look at the lions," Burke remarked as he gazed over the crowd. On to Petoskey and then to Mackinaw City the entourage went as fast as they could. While he ate lunch before boarding the ferry to cross the straits, 200 locals gawked. On the ferry, Burke turned a bit green, but back on land he was fine. North through Newberry and then, finally Marquette. Now prisoner number 5293, his last trip Up North had ended in permanent residency.[133] He died in prison in 1940.

Baby Face Nelson

The gangster known as Baby Face Nelson, another Public Enemy, was born with the much more prosaic name of Lester Joseph Gillis in Chicago in 1908. He makes his one and only appearance Up North in August 1933. The scene is Grand Haven, a town south of Muskegon on the shore of Lake Michigan—a location that just barely, by the most liberal definition, counts as Up North. Nelson had been engaged in criminal activity from age twelve. By 1930 he had established himself as an efficient and effective gangster among the many gangsters of 1920s Chicago. His specialty was robbing the homes of

Baby Face Nelson

the wealthy. In 1930 he was in full form, robbing banks and roadhouses as well as engaging in home invasions and murder. Arrested and convicted in 1931, he escaped during a prison transfer and spent the next two years out west engaged in a variety of crimes. There, Alvin Karpis of the Barker-Karpis Gang introduced him to bank robber Eddie Bentz, who became his partner in the adventure Up North.

At that point, Nelson concluded that it was time to rob another bank. After scouting possibilities, Bentz recommended the People's Savings Bank in Grand Haven. Enlisting additional thugs, the gang arrived in town. One man stayed in the getaway car while the others, including Nelson and Bentz, stormed into the bank waving submachine guns and shouting for the six people present to hit the floor. The teller managed to press an alarm that was connected to a store across the street. The owner, Edward Kinkema, a veteran victim of a previous bank robbery in Lansing, rushed into the street brandishing his Remington repeating shotgun. Seeing an armed man, the getaway driver panicked and drove off, stranding the robbers in the bank. With the alarm ringing loudly, grabbing what money they could, Nelson and his cronies used terrified patrons as human shields and escaped out a side door. Armed citizens had quickly assembled in the street. In the ensuing shoot-out, four citizens were wounded. One robber was mobbed and subdued, but the others seized a vehicle and drove off. Michigan police could not cross the state line, but instead of heading straight south to the Indiana border, Nelson and the remaining bandits headed east. In Hudson, Michigan, their car blew a tire. They stole a third car and sped straight south at last. Crossing over into Ohio, they eluded pursuit. That was the last Michigan saw of Baby Face. The bank robbers had netted a grand total of $2,300, but at least they had escaped being caught after committing one of the most inept bank robberies of the time.[134] Late in 1934, Bureau of Investigation (BOI) agents caught up with Baby Face in Barrington, outside of Chicago. A fierce gun battle ensued. The agents riddled Nelson with bullets and shotgun pellets. He fled the scene, but soon died from his wounds.

CHAPTER 5

Purple Crude

The Purple Gang

The Purple Gang were Detroit's most well-known mobsters.[135] Their origins lie, as in so many American cities, in the neighborhoods crammed with recent immigrants from Europe. In what was to become at the time America's fourth largest city, Jews who had fled the pogroms of the Russian Empire settled around Hasting Avenue. This area teemed with life. Young men, whether infants at the time of immigration or born in the United States, struggled with what it meant to be part of the culture of the "old country" and at the same time Americans in an entirely different milieu. Some took up their fathers' businesses. Some studied hard, went to college, and began professional lives. But the streets beckoned a different kind of youth. Poor students at school or simply dismissive of education, these boys were immune to their parents' entreaties to "be good boys." Envious of the seeming freedom that life in the streets offered and enticed by the prospect of taking what they wanted rather than working for it, these boys became what used to be called juvenile delinquents. The camaraderie of other boys lent a sense of belonging in a world that was torn between the old and the new.

In particular, four brothers from one solid family went bad. Harry Burnstein had four sons: Abraham (Abe), the eldest, Isadore (Izzy), Joseph (Joe), and Raymond (Ray), the youngest. They all entered the world of criminal activity. Starting out with petty theft from local stores and stalls, they went on to a low-octane protection racket in the

Purple Gang leaders: Abe, Joe, Izzy, and Ray Bernstein

neighborhood. But gambling soon became the focus of both their interests and activities, for all were gamblers themselves.

That is how the group later known as the Purple Gang got its start. A good deal of misinformation and downright mythology began to circulate by the mid-1920s as the gang came into its own. In fact, there was no "gang" in the early years, just a loose association of miscreants with similar ideas and goals. The very name, Purple Gang, probably did not exist until newspapers invented it in 1927 for the sake of a striking headline. Although criminals, none of the brothers, or the later men associated with the gang, appear in any significant criminal activity before about 1924. There was some illegal gambling, the occasional assault or robbery, and, after Prohibition came into force in 1920, manufacture and bootlegging of illegal booze—not much that would separate them from the normal riff-raff of Detroit's underworld of the time.

The situation changed drastically with the beginnings of the Cleaners and Dyers War around 1924. By then, Abe Burnstein had become Abe Bernstein, the spelling most common in newspaper reporting. He had a brother-in-law, Charles Jacoby, who owned a large laundry and dry-cleaning business in Detroit. Competitors attempted to undercut his prices. Furious, Jacoby was determined to drive those competitors out of business if they did not charge the same prices he did. He pressured them to do so. The competitors retaliated by hiring men to attack Jacoby's delivery trucks and generally harass his operations. So, Jacoby in turn sought strong-arm help by bringing in Abe, his brother-in-law, and Joe Bernstein, who was already employed as a driver for the firm. They arranged for their friends to ride shotgun on Jacoby's delivery trucks. As the conflict escalated into a war, plants and shops on both sides of the dispute were terrorized with stink bombs, dynamite, and arson. The on-going mayhem got the attention of the Detroit police, who tried without much success to stem the violence.

Abe Bernstein now had a gang. He and his three brothers, Izzy, Joe, and Ray, pulled together a motley band of extortionists, bootleggers, kidnappers, gamblers, and pimps into a loose group that branched out and terrorized Detroit while at the same time engaging in the Cleaners and Dyers War of 1925-1928.

The Purple Gang

In Detroit, life had been going well for the now notorious Purple Gang. Then things gradually went south. The police achieved a breakthrough in 1928 by arresting a dozen men they called the Purple Gang as central perpetrators. Their arrest and trial made headlines day after day. In print, the Gang was accused not only of the violence of the Cleaners and Dyers War, but of other criminal activity, most specifically of a number of kidnappings and a couple of murders. But the Purple Gangsters had learned how to manipulate the justice system, and, in the end, none of them was convicted of anything. However, the trial made the gang the focus of anti-gang publicity and also, when the will was there, of anti-gang activity by the police.

That same year, Joe Bernstein, who had fled Detroit, barely escaped being taken for a ride after a botched murder attempt in New Orleans. The next year he married, but that did not save him from another attempt on his life in 1930. That same year, the people recalled the corrupt and gang-friendly mayor of Detroit, Charles Bowles, replacing him with Frank Murphy. Murphy promised to crush the mob with the cooperation of Harry Toy, Detroit's prosecutor.

The gang unknowingly set itself up for destruction. The Purples had successfully done away with rivals in the Miraflores Apartment ambush of 1927, supposedly the first time the Thompson submachine gun was used in a gangland slaying. Police never managed to establish a link between the gang and those murders. But with the next murders, the Purples severely miscalculated. They lured three Chicago gangsters to the Collingwood Manor Apartments and shot them in cold blood. Three of the four Purples managing the plot were caught, quickly tried, and sent for life sentences to the high security penitentiary in far-away Marquette. The guilty included Ray Bernstein, one of the founding brothers of the Purple Gang. The Purples never recovered. Some of the thugs were sent to jail; some were killed by rivals. A few erstwhile members continued to freelance violence, robbery, and gambling into the mid-1930s or even 1940, but the gang as an entity was no more, ended by the disastrous outcome of the Collingwood Manor murders.

A new kind of mobster: entrepreneurial gangsterism

From the mid-1920s, smart money in gangsterdom became more and more invested in legitimate businesses to launder ill-gotten gains. This became especially important as the Bureau of Investigation, as the pre-FBI was called, took to prosecuting gangsters for tax evasion in the late 1920s. Where, the gangsters wondered, could they put their money? Moe Dalitz in Cleveland invested in laundry and dry-cleaning businesses, among other things. Meyer Lansky in New York City invested in gambling operations. Abe, Izzy, and Joe Bernstein went a different direction. They needed someone who could help them deal with their money. They found their man in a fellow Jewish racketeer from Detroit, Sam Garfield.

Sam, a son of immigrants from Eastern Europe, grew up in Detroit's Jewish district. While his contemporaries and some of his friends formed the Purple Gang, Sam was not a thuggish fellow. His expertise was operating gambling establishments in and around Detroit. He had a good head for business. In 1929, Isaiah Leebove came to town and introduced himself. Leebove had been a fixer attorney for the mega-gangster, Arnold Rothstein, in New York City. After Rothstein's murder in late 1928,

Sam Garfield

Leebove had decided that a change of scene was wise and headed for Detroit.

Leebove had come to New York from Tulsa, Oklahoma. There, he had been the lead attorney for the Livingston Oil Company for about ten years. An important player in the Oklahoma oil boom of the 1910s, he knew the oil business.

On August 29th, 1925, a gusher spurted up at the corner of Mershon and Weiss streets in Saginaw, Michigan. Just a little over a year later, Standard Oil hit pay dirt across the state near Muskegon. The next year, it was Greenfield Township's turn, at the Midland/Isabella county line. Clare, in the middle of the petroleum-rich Saginaw basin, joined the oil boom in 1929. The majors—Pure Oil, Sun Oil, Standard Oil, and others—invested in exploration and exploitation. Alongside these big boys, other investors formed companies to drill wells. A nation already in an oil craze had another focus, one that would expand quickly until in just a few years Michigan became the top oil producer east of the Mississippi.

Leebove's arrival in Detroit was no accident. He had his eye on the Michigan oil boom just getting underway. When, through the network of Jewish gangsters, he met Garfield, the two immediately clicked. They soon went together to Harrison, Michigan, to scout the possibilities of taking advantage of the boom. The possibilities looked very intriguing, as they reported to their friends back in Detroit. Dirty money could easily be used to purchase oil leases or to drill for oil—all paid for in cash. If the leases or wells paid off, the resulting money was clean. Gangsters were ready to invest.

Elated, Leebove returned to Clare, formed the Mammoth Petroleum Company, and set up for business in 1929. Of course, the Bernsteins were not listed as investors, nor was Moe Dalitz from Cleveland, nor Pete Licavoli from the Toledo gang. Rather, Leebove assembled a team of front men. Carl Holbrook, the county prosecutor, was treasurer; an important local businessman, Willard Bicknell, was secretary; Leebove named himself president. Listed investors were local businessmen including one-time state senator Ben Carpenter, but more influential Michiganders included soon-to-be governor William Comstock and Clare Retan, a former Michigan attorney general. What Leebove and Garfield were doing was not likely to be scrutinized very much by authorities.

Isaiah Leebove

Two of the Bernstein brothers had little to do with Up North oil. Izzy Bernstein, for one, headed for New York City where he became involved in gambling and murder. Forced to leave, he ended up in California running numbers rackets and bookmaking. Ray, of course, was incarcerated and remained so until 1964. But Abe and brother Joe often came to Clare. Staying at the Doherty Hotel, as all the oil men did, they managed their investments in the surrounding oil fields with the help of Garfield and Leebove, who both lived in town. This symbiotic relationship lasted for years. Halfway through the decade, Joe Bernstein formed his own oil company with Garfield and exploited the new fields in neighboring Gladwin County. Ed Strong from the Cleveland Syndicate came on board as a heavy backer. Sam "Cheeks" Ginsberg from that same city's underground also became an active player.

William Dunlop Clare chief of police, John J. Dunlop
Clare mayor, and Dr L.J. Slattery gaze at the bloody spot
in the Hotel Doherty bar where Leebove fell.

Then Saturday night, May 14, 1938, Isaiah Leebove came into the bar of the Doherty Hotel and sat down with friends. Jack Livingston, a one-time associate and now disgruntled rival in the oil business, approached. Pulling out a .38, Livingston shot him dead. I give details of the murder in this book's final chapter.

In the aftermath, Sam Garfield took over Mammoth Petroleum and Refining and continued to work with Joe Burnstein in his Burnstein Oil Company. But the former Purple Gangsters had lost their taste for investing in oil, preferring to engage in other enterprises such as thoroughbred horses and bookmaking. By 1940 there were no gangsters in Clare except for Sam Garfield himself.

The Purple Gang Up North in Myth and Legend

Like Al Capone and other famous mobsters, alleged sightings of Purple Gang members far outnumber any actual appearances. In northern Michigan, the Purple Gang was the most known gangster band. The many false sightings can be attributed to at least three factors: once in awhile one of the Bernstein brothers actually did appear Up North; hangers-on, would-be thugs, and just visitors who wanted to impress the locals pretended to be Purple Gang members; finally, gossip, hearsay, and rumor fed the idea that someone somewhere had seen a gangster. From there, the stories multiplied. As with the stories about Al Capone and John Dillinger, eyewitnesses are often quoted as having seen a Purple. Virtually all such accounts are reported second or third hand. Eyewitnesses should not be taken as proof and often their testimony simply does not fit with probability or even possibility.

Rather than list the sightings of Purple Gangsters, I have mentioned them in the chapter on holidays and hunting when discussing a wide array of resorts that claim to have had gangster guests.

Meyer Lansky Comes to Town

Excellent businessman that he was, with excellent underworld connections, Sam Garfield kept on working oil fields for his gangster friends. He connected with mega-gangster Meyer Lansky and invested in legal gambling operations in Havana, Cuba, and Las Vegas, Nevada. Lansky had problems with the authorities in the 1950s. His casino empire in Cuba blew up when Castro came to power in January 1959 and soon nationalized and then closed all gambling operations. Claiming that he was broke, Lansky turned to Sam Garfield, who urged him to invest in the reviving oil industry around Clare. Invest he did. When authorities asked his income, Lansky pointed to his around $25,000 yearly income from his Michigan wells, all perfectly legal money, of course.

Meyer Lansky

Meyer Lansky came to Clare frequently. He stayed at the Doherty Hotel, but his connection was with Sam Garfield. Lansky often visited Sam at his home at the end of East Sixth Street, sitting in a pleasant room with a pleasant vista, playing cards and munching on snacks. The FBI was fully aware of his presence in town and often consulted with local police about him. Clarites treated him kindly as a friend of Sam's. He ate at local restaurants, drank at local bars, visited local people in their homes, and exchanged small talk with the mayor, circuit judge, and chief of police. Sometimes his wife was with him, sometimes not. He would stay a week or two, then disappear for a time on business. He was never harassed, and the FBI could never get Clarites to tell them anything negative about him. At some point, Lansky had a falling-out with Sam, perhaps when the oil wells he had invested in went bad in the late 1960s. He then stopped coming. But for a second time, oil had brought gangsters to small-town Clare. The full story of Sam Garfield and Meyer Lansky is told in Knapp's *Small-Town Citizen*.

⇒CHAPTER 6⇒

Toledans at the Beach

Overshadowed by gangsterdom in the larger cities of Chicago, Detroit, and Cleveland, Toledo, Ohio, nevertheless had a home-grown and very active underworld element during the Prohibition years. Some of its leaders came Up North.

Jimmy Hayes and the Ramona Park Casino

The star of the show was an Irish-American named Gerald James "Jimmy" Hayes. Raised in Cleveland, he early-on got into trouble with the law. He left town for Toledo with a close friend, Ed Warnke, around 1900. They made a living driving a horse-drawn hack, ferrying men to local gambling spots—spots that were common well before the explosion of lawlessness brought on by Prohibition. Hayes advanced to an early motor car limousine and formed the first local automobile taxi service. Apparently, it dawned on young Jimmy that driving the gamblers to gambling spots was

Jimmy Hayes

much less lucrative than owning the gambling joints themselves. So, he saved his money and was soon able to buy his first gambling emporium. He had met the gambling community in his work as a hack; now his familiar face and easy manner welcomed those same people into his own parlor.[136]

Hayes had hit upon a career for life. He followed up his business success in Toledo in the early 1920s by branching out to his old stomping grounds, Cleveland. There he opened the Washington Club and ran a local boxing club. Life could be dangerous in Jimmy's profession. And it was. On September 9, 1926, a carload of hit-men drove alongside his car as it was weaving through traffic near Toledo's Jefferson and Sixteenth streets. Twenty slugs from a sawed-off shotgun struck Jimmy's head and upper body; his car crashed into a tree.[137] That same night, enemies bombed his Washington Club in Cleveland.

Hayes recovered. The attack put him off expansion to Cleveland but did not slow him down back in Toledo, the city that remained his home base. There, he continued through the rest of the 1920s unharmed either by competitors or by city officials, men he cultivated assiduously and who systematically looked the other way regarding his gambling empire. Life changed, though, when the River Gang moved down from Detroit to Toledo in 1930. The Licavoli offspring, brothers Damiano, Thomas "Yonnie," and Peter Joseph, ran this Sicilian mob outfit.[138] Peter Joseph and Yonnie were originally from St. Louis. They trained in their dastardly craft as members of that city's notorious gang run by Joseph "Green Onions" Cipolla.[139] When things grew hot there, they moved to Detroit where they established themselves and their fellow gangsters as masters of the bootlegging operations along the Detroit River south of Detroit. When Detroit, too, got hot following the election of crime-busting mayor Frank Murphy in 1930, they moved on to Toledo. The city's underworld then split. Those intimidated by the violence of the Licavolis succumbed to their demands for protection money and worse. Another faction, led by local gangster Jack Kennedy, resisted the newcomers. A gangland war broke out with the usual kidnappings and murders. For three years, 1930-1933, Toledo bled gangster blood in profusion. The Licavolis succeeded in assassinating Kennedy, but a jury found Yonnie guilty of conspiracy to murder.[140] On November 11, 1934, he went to prison for the job. Through it all, Jimmy Hayes ran his operations and survived. That is, until the night of

October 4, 1934 when he was taken for a ride, savagely beaten and shot, his body dumped in a Detroit alley. He had enjoyed a meal at Detroit's Club Maxine earlier in the evening with none other than Peter Joseph Licavoli, Yonnie's brother.

Among the many rumors regarding motivation, the story circulated that he had been killed by Detroit mafiosi who were angry that he had invaded their territory by running a first-class gambling operation Up North in Michigan at Harbor Springs (Emmet County). If true, that would fit nicely with the theme of "Gangsters Up North." In fact, Toledo's Licavoli gang targeted Hayes because he would not cut them in on his Toledo

Hayes murdered in Detroit

gambling profits. It is also possible that Hayes had played a role in gaining Yonnie's conviction just a few weeks before on a capital charge in the Kennedy murder. Although men were arrested and tried for Hayes' murder, they were acquitted. The case remains unsolved to this day.

Jimmy Hayes was never a gambler himself. But he was a good businessman. He realized that the house made money on gambling regardless of what players were winning or losing. While saloons had long been the heart and soul of gambling operations, Hayes realized that times were a-changing. People desired more than a smoke, spittle, and cussing-filled venue for their enjoyment. To meet this need, Hayes began his gambling empire with the Jovial Club.[141] This and similar "sawdust" establishments were far from the fancy "rug joints" to come— they were called "sawdust joints" because saloons usually had sawdust covered-floors to soak up the spills, spit, and vomit of customers. But ordinary people wanted ordinary, but decent, watering holes. For that, they could come to the Jovial Club or its Hayes-owned counterparts such as the Gentleman's Club, also on St. Clair Street, or the Buckeye Cigar Store on Superior Street where the specialty was betting on the horses. It was said that bets at his joints could be made for as little as a nickel (more or less $1 in current purchasing power) on games of craps, roulette, and poker, or on the horses.

Wealthier customers demanded a bit more, and Hayes readily supplied it. His Point Place amusement park drew a federal raid early in Prohibition when over one hundred patrons were present at the faro and craps tables. Earlier, Hayes had established The Villa just over the Michigan border on the Dixie Highway between Detroit and Toledo. This was a blind for a gambling room operated by Charlie Glass that catered to the well-to-do from Toledo and the surrounding area. [142] With Michigan a dry state in 1918 and Ohio still wet, it was ideally located to provide booze to thirsty Michiganders as well as fine food and gambling. When it was raided in 1924, the *Toledo Blade* made much of its profile of Hayes:

> Jimmy Hayes became a name in Toledo, in Cleveland, then in Detroit, he was a regular guy....He's on the square, the boys remarked about him. They heard of his private charities and heard that he booted youths out of his gambling establishments. Jimmy encouraged 'punks' to get an education....Hayes was reputed to be in control of slot machines here as well as all other forms of gambling with other figures in the racket being in his employ. He was reputed to be the big boss in gambling in all its forms here.[143]

Throughout the 1920s, Hayes, his partner, Ed Warnke, and a few other Toledans had the gambling interests in the city sewn up. These men stayed on good terms with the local police and civilian authorities and, basically, everyone went along to get along. As for journalists, Hayes always kept them at arm's length saying such types "were not good for business."[144]

Ramona Park Hotel (l); the hotel's dining room (r)

The gambling operations in Toledo went well for Hayes. However, his probably favorite place was far away Up North at Harbor Springs, the Ramona Park Casino.[145] This was a fine gambling venue for the wealthy summer residents up from Ohio, Michigan, and Illinois.

A resort hotel antedated Hayes' involvement. The Ramona Park Hotel and its well-known mineral spring had been drawing the rich from Chicago and points even more distant since 1910. Hayes located his casino "just a step away," as newspaper advertisements put it, from the famous and popular hotel. The two establishments were not owned by the same persons, but they operated as a unit in offering recreation to wealthy tourists.[146]

The Ramona was definitely a very fine place. The accommodations were first class as was the dining room; the entertainment was made up of well-known bands and performers. For example, Ruby's Orchestra, a popular band that also played at Hayes' Toledo clubs, frequently provided the dancing and background music.[147] The casino itself was downright lavish. The tables, roulette wheels, and slot machines were ready day and night for the wealthy customers. The Studebaker brothers of car manufacturing fame boasted to a local who caddied for them that they had lost $10,000 each in the casino the night before. And the gambling wasn't just for the gentlemen. The resort had the custom of offering an elaborate luncheon to the women and after dessert, giving each $5 in chips to gamble in the casino.[148]

A consortium of well-known Detroit gambling impresarios had built the casino in 1927. Abe Ackerman was a nightclub operator, but in Detroit, not in Toledo.[149] He had been in the gambling business for a very long time—long before Prohibition. In 1909 he had used a barbershop as a front for a gambling establishment.[150] A typically crooked politician, he was an East Side boss involved in the illegal enrollment of voters. Police arrested him and thirty others in 1912 in a gambling den. Abe Bernstein, later a leader of the Purple Gang and a man associated with the nearby Club Manitou, was arrested at the same time.[151] In 1916 police raided Ackerman's own place on Randolph Street in Detroit; Abe Bernstein was again taken in on a charge of running the gaming.[152] Newspapers mentioned Ackerman as a bootlegger working the Toledo-to-Detroit corridor in 1919.[153] He was arrested again in 1922 for running a gambling operation out of the East Side Athletic Club on Monroe Avenue in the Motor City.[154]

After 1922 Ackerman dropped out of the notices in the *Detroit Free Press*. Although it is unclear just why he disappeared, in 1927 Ackerman and investors decided to expand their gambling operations to a place Up North. That year, he built the Ramona Park Casino.[155] He had two co-investors, Bert Moss and Harry Kaufman. The casino was northwest of the Ramona Park Hotel. It was built with the cooperation of the president of the hotel company, Fritz Cremer.[156] On land purchased from the hotel and at a cost of $30,000, it went up as a two-story stucco building in a style that fit with that of the hotel. Cremer clearly saw the casino as part of the Ramona Park Hotel complex. He undertook to engage a local construction company, Fochtman Lumber, and to "make purchases at home [i.e., in the Little Traverse Bay area] for furnishings and decorations, and he also expects to make several improvements to the grounds of the hotel." Per the guarantee the unnamed Detroit investors made, it was completed by June 1, 1927.[157] No interior images of the casino exist, but

Bert Moss

there is an extensive description in the *Petoskey Evening News* upon its opening:

> Tomorrow evening marks the opening of one of the most elaborate and finest casinos in Northern Michigan—Ramona Park Casino. Nothing in any of the surrounding resorts can begin to compare with its splendor and magnificence. The owners of this new outstanding landmark have obtained the services of Edward J. Young, of New York, as manager, who has efficiently managed a large casino in Havana, Cuba.[158] The gorgeous Italian travertine effect which dominates the interior of the building was created by Thomas Lawther, Petoskey, one of the outstanding interior decorators and artists of this region. The large ground floor, which has a California atmosphere, affords one of the finest dancing floors in the north. It is surrounded with scores of tables from which guests are served. At the end of this room is located a massive fireplace, its mantel being beautifully decorated with a miniature schooner on either side of which are rustic lamps. The ceiling is done in a light stipple having a base color of cream with shell green, yellow ochre, green spar and deep green uniquely blending with the basic shade. The five-foot wainscot has one of the many variations of the opaline effect with a rustic finish of chrome green, burnt sienna and black. The two-piece drapes are chrome green with a heavy strip of deep orange velvet on the outside edges. The wall lights are of an unusual type, being copied from the old-time kerosene lamp, and in color they and the ceiling lights harmonize aptly with the rest of the room. The orchestra platform is of the moveable type and decorated in the most splendid Spanish manner. Connecting rooms to the ground floor are a ladies' rest room (with an attendant), also a rest room for men and the kitchen. The kitchen is one of the more modern types with all the available time-saving machinery therein. The hall leading to the club room on the second floor has ceiling and side walls done in Italian swirl with light pink and chrome green the dominating colors. The entire hall having a rustic effect

including the huge chandelier. The drapes are of heavy velvet and of wine color. The club room is of an exclusive design with a huge fireplace—a duplicate of the one on the main floor. The ceiling is paneled effect, small swirl and is tinted a cream shade. The sidewalls resemble the main floor but are finished in a dark color while the wainscot is Italian ochre travertine. The lights, drapes and massive upholstered furniture harmonize with the cleverly imitated stone walls and ceiling. On the same floor is located an office, a guest room and also another ladies' rest room. The entire second floor is surrounded with a large porch on which the guests may look out over the Little Traverse bay on the warm summer nights enjoying the evening's breeze. The orchestra comes from the Addison Hotel, Detroit, and is considered one of the most talented groups in the state.[159] Nothing has been overlooked for the comport and pleasure of the guests and all indications are pointing to a successful season.

The investors in addition to Ackerman are an interesting lot. Bert Moss, a Bay City native, was a fixture of the Detroit gambling and bootlegging scene. His Addison Hotel featured a dance hall that became notorious as a hangout for gangster types.[160] Harry Kaufman was the third of the original investors in the Ramona Park Casino.[161] This man remained in the gambling business and appears in 1940 involved in a significant Detroit horse book scandal along with other stalwarts of the industry, Abe Bernstein and his brother Joey, both erstwhile Purple Gangsters.[162] He owned the Chateau La France gambling place in Toledo, Ohio, in the early 1930s. Besides investing in the Ramona Park Casino, he partnered with Jimmy Hayes in the Hollywood [Florida] Country Club in 1930.[163]

Moss bought out Kaufman in 1928. He and Ackerman shopped the investment around. In 1929 other prominent gangsters signed on, including Mert Wertheimer, a Cheboygan native, and his frequent partner, R. Raymond "Ruby" Mathis. There was also a rumor that Isaac "Forty-grand Ike" Levy got a stake. Ike was a Hamtramck hoodlum who ran liquor and was involved in bookmaking, at least according to various *Detroit Free Press* articles from around 1929 to 1931. Pat and

Joe Morrissey from the St. Louis gangsters were also in on the investment; they had earlier helped run Hayes' Jovial Club in Toledo.[164]

In 1930, Abe Ackerman brought Jimmy Hayes into the mix.[165] Bert Moss, Ruby Mathis, and Mert Wertheimer sold their interests to him. By 1930, Ackerman also brought in Joseph J. "Joe" Murphy, long-time proprietor with Ackerman of the upscale gambling establishment, Ackmur, which was located at Seven Mile Road and Grand River Avenue in Detroit.[166] But, Hayes and Ackerman ran the Ramona until Jimmy's murder in 1934.[167] Hayes was personally present at times at the Ramona. Besides racketeering types who invested, other well-known Detroit gambling figures were seen at the casino from time to time, people such as Bob Rosenblum, Fred Durks, and Danny Sullivan.[168]

In the fall of 1931, a fire damaged "northern Michigan's most extensive and expensive entertainment place." The fire reduced it "to a mass of ruins" with a loss estimated at between $50,000 and $100,000.[169] As it was operating in the summer of 1932, it must have been repaired/rebuilt rapidly. Improvements were made, as well:

> The outside of the building is strikingly different than anything seen in this northern region and is beautiful in its natural wood finish and colored stain. The lobbies are richly furnished with walls draped with luxurious tapestry. The dining and dancing parlor is much larger than the one which was in the older building and much more attractive. The kitchen bespeaks efficiency in every detail. The grounds have been worked with great care, evergreens and lawns making a most attractive appearance. A massive stairway leads from the lawn and drive way to the porch and then into the lobby of the casino. The building is much larger than the old one and the furnishings are much more elaborate and costlier. [170]

It is certain that Hayes was at the Ramona in that year, and certainly he visited often before and after, probably every summer from 1930 and 1934, at least for a period. The Ramona Park may well have been Hayes' favorite among his many holdings, including the Hollywood Country Club, fifteen miles north of Miami Beach.[171]

The original 1927 Ramona Park Casino (l.) and as rebuilt in 1931-1932 (r.)

An FBI report from the mid-1930s offers an overview of gangster presence at the Ramona and other nearby places. R. D. Tripp, the Petoskey postmaster and an active denizen of the area for over fifty years, provided the Bureau with much information. He told the FBI "that there are hundreds of gamblers and racket men who appear at Petoskey and Harbor Point...to practice their trade among the people who appear at the resorts in that vicinity."

Tripp laid out a pattern of local corruption or, at best, complacency regarding the criminal elements in the area. While he held that some fancy places eschewed any association with gangsters, others, including the Ramona, did not.[172] The F.B.I. report included Tripp's information: "Sheriff [Thomas] Bryant of Petoskey has a reputation of protecting the criminal element, particularly powerful gamblers of Petoskey and no doubt is receiving some remuneration in that connection; that the Chief of Police, Patrick Sullivan, has only a small police force and does very little about the criminal situation in Petoskey although [Tripp] does not believe that Chief Sullivan is accepting compensation for protecting various gambling resorts and the like." Tripp went on to claim that "Chief Sullivan has the reputation of not being able to maintain any degree of secrecy in criminal investigation and would probably not be of much assistance" to the FBI. But another local, John Gallister, "a citizen of Petoskey and prominent in State politics, has the reputation of being the fix in the Sheriff's office and is even rumored as having protected the Ramona Park Casino and other gambling establishments from interference by the Michigan State Police."[173]

In October 1934 someone, probably Sicilian hitmen of the Detroit Mafia, snatched, tortured, and murdered Jimmy Hayes. It was Abe Ackerman who identified the victim as Hayes.[174] The Licavoli brothers were suspected to be behind the murder, but no one was ever convicted. The Ramona Park Casino kept going after Jimmy's death. His wife, Eleanor, came north for the next summer season and kept the place open for two years. Bert Moss became again involved. Joe Morrisey, the hoodlum from St. Louis/Toledo, also helped out.[175] In 1935, another Toledo mobster, Joe Roscoe, came on the scene.[176] Roscoe, who had earlier worked with the Barker-Karpi Gang, seems to have taken Hayes' place as a kingpin of Toledo gambling. He appeared at the Ramona Park Casino pretending to be Jimmy Hayes' wife's brother. But after a few summers, Eleanor and Moss seem to have closed the place, perhaps after the State Police raid in 1938.[177] It did not operate in the seasons of 1939-1941. In 1941 someone acquired and refurbished it. Despite the new investment, it closed again after a short 1942 season; the wartime crowd was just not there. No advertisement appears for the casino in 1943-1946. In August 1947 Al Gerhart of the nearby Club Manitou bought it.[178] He sold at auction everything in the building worth the trouble. He then razed the structure itself.[179] An aerial image of 1952 shows only a foundation at the location.[180]

The roulette wheel from the Ramona Park Casino is now in the Harbor Springs Area Historical Society Museum.[181] That is all that is left of Jimmy Hayes' gambling haven on the shore of Little Traverse Bay.

Seagull Cottage gambling and the Ramona Park Hotel

An until now unnoticed bit of gangster-related gambling does take place on the grounds of the Ramona Park Hotel after the closing of the Ramona Park Casino. When the hotel was built in 1909-10 it included a residence called the "Seagull Cottage." It was quite posh as Cremer chose it for his and his family's summer residence after he bought the hotel in 1924. Fast-forwarding a couple of decades, Sam Boston, born Sam Solomon, acquired residence there in the late 1940s. Boston had been a prominent figure in gambling circles since Prohibition days. His main claim to national fame is that he was one of the participants in the 1928 poker game that ultimately cost Arnold Rothstein, the most powerful gangster in New York City, his life.

Sam the gambler continued to use New York City as his headquarters. After his high-stakes brush with death in 1928, he continued his gambling ways, making the headlines on several occasions. His specialty was sports betting. In 1942, for example, one of his partners, Max Fox, murdered two other partners, Robert Greene and Dimples Wolin, and had Boston in his sights as well. Fox claimed that these men had double-crossed him on a $300,000 bet regarding the outcome of the Roosevelt-Willkie 1940 national election. In subsequent developments, Boston was arrested but released on $500 bond and prohibited from betting more than $2.50 at a time. Of course, that didn't happen. The next year, with a new partner, Frank Silinsky, he operated from a luxury New York apartment. Police raided the place. They arrested Boston and charged him with gambling. Convicted on the charge, he fought the conviction on appeal, arguing that since boxing was legal, "betting and wagering thereon" was also legal. Low and behold, four years later, 1947, New York State courts decided that "casual betting" was entirely legal. Boston went scot free.[182]

Sam Boston

In 1946, while fighting that conviction, "Stuttering Sam," as he was known, a "roly-poly kingpin Broadway gambler" became enmeshed in a professional football game-fixing scandal. Police pointed to his close relationship to "a big betting combine in Elizabeth, New Jersey."[183] Around this time, Sam showed up in Harbor Springs. Recall that the Ramona Park Casino, a major gambling place on the grounds of the Ramona Park Hotel, had fallen on hard times and closed down. From the beginning, the placement of the Ramona Park Casino so close to the hotel formed a symbiotic relationship—the hotel could honestly claim that no gambling took place at the hotel, while the wealthy resorters there who wished to gamble could walk a hundred yards to the casino. Seeing an opening now, Boston settled into the Seagull Cottage and started offering the nearby gambling that the hotel lost with the closing of the Ramona Park Casino.

In 1947, the Michigan State Police and investigators from the Michigan Liquor Control Commission "swooped down" on Seagull Cottage. Previously, undercover agents had "played dice, roulette, blackjack, and other games" at the cottage. At an LCC hearing where the evidence from the raid and the investigation was presented, the manager of the Ramona Park Hotel denied any connection between the cottage and the hotel. He had just sublet the cottage to "a mysterious man named Sam Boston" and that person had, unbeknownst to him, run a gambling operation. The manager could not, however, explain how illegal bingo games at the cottage came to be broadcast over the public address system in the hotel![184]

Sam was arrested as part of the raid. We do not know if anything became of that arrest. I have found no further reference to Sam Boston. He died about September 1969.

Charlie Jameson and Stony Lake

Charles C. Jameson is a name connected with bootlegging and gangsterism in Oceana County. His life began in 1877, the first child of his fourteen-year-old mother and eighteen-year-old father.[185] The family lived on a farm in Hancock Township, south of Toledo, when he was born. The story he later offered was that at age thirteen he took off.[186] He headed west and hooked up with a circus in Denver, Colorado. Traveling with that outfit, he journeyed through many towns in the West during the 1890s. Along the way, he said, he learned how to be an expert gambler—a habit he continued to cultivate throughout his life. Slot machines were just coming on the scene—rudimentary compared with later devices, but still a reliable way to relieve gamblers of their money. Jameson learned how to bribe local officials—slot machines were illegal—and ended up owning slots in several western saloons. He made his way back to Toledo.

That tale is all well and good, but according to the 1900 Census, Jameson was actually in the Toledo area and gave his occupation as farm laborer. Anything is possible, but perhaps Charlie made up the story about being with a circus out west and was really living in the rural Toledo area the whole time. That said, the narrative of his life that we have today continues as though his early adventures and his entry into the gambling industry were true.

In 1906 he married Guarda Spellman, a native of Shelby, Michigan, in Oceana County.[187] The marriage record states his occupation as farmer. But in keeping with the colorful story of his early life, Maxine Huggard of Shelby gives an account of how they met and wed:

> When he was in the rackets in Toledo, one day he was riding through town in his big black car, diamond rings and all, and he saw a girl standing and waiting for a streetcar. He said to his driver, 'I want to meet that girl. I'm going to marry her.' So, they went around the block again. Well, he met her, and she wouldn't give him a tumble. She was very refined. Finally, she gave in to the attention and married Charlie.[188]

It was Guarda's connection to the area that eventually brought Charlie to Stony Lake.

The marriage took place in southeastern Michigan, at Monroe. By all accounts, Jameson adored Guarda. The couple lived in Jameson's home area just to the south of Toledo. The 1910 Census lists him as a manufacturer there. The Jamesons were living in Toledo in 1914 when Guarda's father died. Charlie began to branch out. In 1917, his name appeared in the Toledo City Directory; his occupation was in real estate. His address on Hollywood Street in Toledo's Old West End was a prestigious one in those days, so he must have been doing well.[189] He continued to live at this address for at least a decade. But he also visited Shelby where Guarda's family lived. Her father had begun as a farmer in the area and was a blacksmith at the time of his eldest child's marriage.

Jameson got to know the Stony Lake area through Guarda's home connections, for Stony Lake is just 10 miles from Shelby, a mere half mile from the shore of Lake Michigan. At Stony Lake he built cottages for Guarda and the family, one in 1916 and a second in 1923. Shelby resident Levi Reames knew Jameson from the teens. He told an interviewer, "He loved that woman. She was a nice person, and very, very good looking." Those who knew him said that he was a complex man, a "larger than life figure whose joys, plans and exploits forever made him an integral part of the history of Stony Lake."[190]

Jameson's language was often harsh and crude—he seemed to have come from a hard life indeed. People got used to it, but he clearly had a rough edge. He was "brutally honest, but in a crooked sort of way." It looks like besides real estate, Charlie had gotten involved with gambling. Levi Reames continued, "When Charlie came to Stony Lake, he had one of them dice machines in a cage. I was tending bar and he'd come in there and he'd run that machine. It looked like a fair deal. You'd pick a number and bet on it. He'd make us $2 to $300 a night."[191]

Charlie Jameson at Stony Lake later in life

Of course, the stories of Jameson's bootlegging activities became exaggerated and, to make matters complete, he was credited with association with the Purple Gang. That, however, remains undocumented.[192] The popular description of his life as a gangster runs as follows:

> By now a powerful figure in the Toledo political and criminal hierarchy, with connections to Detroit's notorious Purple Gang, Jameson sat on the throat of the liquor funnel [from Canada across the Detroit River] and made it possible to move enormous illegal inventories out of town and directly into the hands of major customers throughout the Midwest. All he needed was a route and a shipping port, and he had it in the back roads of Michigan and the channel at Benona [that led from Stony Lake out to Lake Michigan].[193]

Charlie apparently was resourceful about getting the booze out of Canada and across Michigan. One trick was to drive Dodge touring cars, which were rather large vehicles, across from Detroit with tires filled not with air, but with illegal Canadian whiskey. The cars could then proceed along the 400 miles of often poor roads until they got to Stony Lake. There, the liquor would be transferred to containers, loaded on waiting craft, and shipped away. While the physics of cars driving 400 miles with 1930s tires filled with liquid seems a bit problematic, Charlie is also credited with using fleets of trucks to accomplish the same thing, probably much more efficiently.

While Charlie worked the shores of the Detroit River, his partner in crime, Guarda's brother Leo Spellman, kept the other end of the operation working smoothly at Stony Lake. A garage mechanic by trade, Leo specialized in getting the hooch out to customers who would ship it via the lake to Chicago and other destinations. He had a place right where Stony Creek debouched into Lake Michigan. It was a fine home, high up on a bluff where there was a clear view of the lake. Boats would come in from Chicago and Milwaukee, load up, and sail into the night. Simon Schmiedeknecht recalled that "they used flashlight signals from the Spellman point. They'd flash from the shore, then suddenly there'd be a big boat out there signaling back. Then a speedboat would come in and they'd load the boxes. They had a speedboat on the bigger boat...it just set out there in the water. Then the speedboat would go back and just as suddenly they were gone."

Charlie spent time at Stony Lake, as well. In 1923 he built his second cabin, this time on a grand scale. It was on the northeastern side of the lake. He bought a large piece of land and built Guarda a beautiful cottage. There he entertained customers. It was complete with security and a getaway route, according to locals: "The cottage was continuously guarded by lookouts whenever important guests were on hand making deals or enjoying the atmosphere of Stony Lake. A getaway trail through the woods to the east could secretly empty the cottage in minutes."

When Prohibition ended late in 1933, Jameson's enterprising ways were no longer sought. He stayed at Stony Lake; Guarda died there in

Jameson built Pine Lodge for his wife, Guarda

1935 and is buried at Shelby.[194] Charlie remained a well-known inhabitant of the lake area until his death in 1961.

How much of this is fiction? Careful investigation of newspapers and the Internet failed to find evidence to verify Charlie Jameson as a gangster and rumrunner. Kenneth Dickson, reigning expert on Toledo gangsters, can find nothing about Charlie who, according to the account above, was a leading underworld figure in that city. Among the two dozen and more men associated with the Purple Gang in books and Detroit newspapers, Charlie's name does not appear once. In fact, he is virtually invisible in verifiable sources. When he does appear, there is no hint of any nefarious activity. If we did not have the accounts from Stony Lake people, we would have absolutely no idea that Charlie Jameson was anything but a run-of-the-mill businessman who married a Shelby girl, lived in Toledo, and spent summers in the teens, twenties, and thirties at a cottage on the lake.

CHAPTER 7

Cleveland's Syndicate Comes North

The Cleveland Syndicate was the name for non-Mafia organized crime in the city. Moe Dalitz, Morris Kleinman, Sam Tucker, and Louis Rothkopf formed the core of the Syndicate.[195] They first met and began working together in Akron, Ohio, about 1930.[196] These mobsters had nothing to do with the Purple Gang in Detroit other than that they pursued the same illegal activities. Indeed, by the time the Syndicate got going, the Purple Gang had only a year or two left. Coming on the scene as these men did around 1930, the possibilities and parameters of entrepreneurial gangsterism were already well known in the underworld. They and their fellow gangsters continued with the normal activities of bootlegging, gambling, and prostitution, but also looked out for the best business opportunities.

The Leader

Moe Dalitz had grown up in Detroit and moved with his parents to Ann Arbor. He got into the bootlegging business in Akron, Ohio, and then, with the other three leading figures, moved on to bigger things in Cleveland. Ontario, just across Lake Erie from Cleveland, supplied him with booze to smuggle. Even after Prohibition, he tried to keep making money by setting up an illegal, then a legal, alcohol plant. Both went bust. Dalitz' real expertise was in gambling, and that is what he then

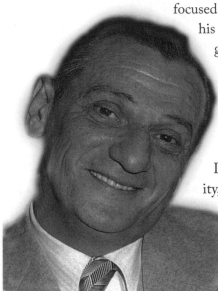

Moe Dalitz

focused on.[197] Throughout the rest of his life, Dalitz choose to emphasize gambling as his special competence. Starting with major casinos in Kentucky and expanding to Florida, he eventually settled on Nevada where gambling was legal. He established himself in Las Vegas. By dint of personality, charitable donations, and Vegas' natural tendency to tolerate or ignore illegal activities, he became a well-known and respected citizen there.

But what to do with the money he took from his enterprises? Investing in oil was an obvious option. There is speculation but no proof that Dalitz was an investor in Ohio oil fields in the northwestern part of the state as early as the late 1920s. He knew Sam Garfield, a gambling figure we have already met and who will figure in this story later on. The two had grown up in the same neighborhood of Detroit and went to the same school there. They remained life-long friends.[198] Sam was purveying oil up in the Clare area and working with Dalitz' acquaintances, the Bernstein brothers. Later in his life, Dalitz worked closely with Sam in various Las Vegas dealings. He often visited Sam at his home in Clare. Although there is little specific evidence, it seems highly likely that Sam worked with Dalitz just as he worked with the Purple Gangsters to invest their money in the oil patches of Clare, Gladwin, and Ogemaw counties during the 1930s. Dalitz then put the clean money that he had laundered through oil exploration and exploitation into his array of gambling operations.

Ed Strong

Edward Strong was another Cleveland underworld figure. Ed Strong's involvement was a significant aspect of Sam Garfield's continuing relationship with the gangsters from Cleveland. Strong was originally from New York City. There, he learned his underworld skills under the tutelage of notorious gangsters Nicky Arnstein and Arnold Rothstein. In Cleveland, although he was involved in prostitution, he specialized in owning race tracks. He was a major figure in horse racing in Ohio and elsewhere, which means he was deep into fixing races and running book making operations. According to the FBI, he was "well known in gambling circles." In 1938 he was an important member of the Cleveland Syndicate and its face in the oil fields: he was vice-president of Isaiah Leebove's Mammoth Petroleum Company in Clare.[199] After Leebove's murder, Sam Garfield became president of Mammoth and moved headquarters to Cleveland, the Syndicate's home.[200] Strong had and retained strong connections with Moe Dalitz. He died in 1948.[201]

Sam "Cheeks" Ginsberg

Short in stature with brown eyes and brown hair, of Russian-Jewish background, born in Pennsylvania, Sam Ginsberg lived in Cleveland from an early age.[202] At sixteen, Sam was already visiting gambling rooms in Cleveland. For this, he was arrested and fined $1 and court costs.[203] Just six years later, Ginsberg had established himself as a gambling impresario in that city.[204] He also segued into managing a boxer through the Perry Athletic Club in the city. By 1912 he had a promising featherweight, Matt Brock, under his care.[205] At that date, Brock had been fighting for four years, so perhaps Sam's managing days go back to 1908 when he was twenty-two. Ginsberg worked hard on Brock's behalf, arranging fights throughout the eastern United States. Boxing then was a very corrupt business. Many people bet on the bouts, and many bouts were fixed. Ginsberg's involvement in boxing mirrors that of other underworld figures of this time. Sam's boxing gig abruptly ended late in 1919 when he and Brock were banned from boxing because Brock (for at least the second time) severely struck an adversary after the fight had officially finished.

Along the way, Sam had made good contacts in New York City with premiere gangster figures. In 1920, Nicky Arnstein, a top-drawer hoodlum, pulled off a five-million-dollar heist of Liberty Bonds. These bonds were negotiable, so could be converted to cash. Arnold Rothstein, another heavy-hitter of the New York underworld, joined in the theft. Rothstein himself brought Ginsberg into the deal. Cleveland underworld contacts assured him that Ginsberg "was a gambler and O.K."[206] According to telephone records, the two stayed in close contact by long-distance.[207] Ed Strong, a man we have already met, was Ginsberg's lawyer in Cleveland. Strong also became involved in fencing the stolen bonds, although, of course, he vigorously denied this.[208] The plot to steal the bonds was hatched in a New York apartment occupied by Sam Ginsberg, "a close associate of Nicky Arnstein and fellow hoodlum Nicky Cohen." Once stolen, the gang dispersed the bonds to fence them. Ginsberg took many of them to Cleveland.

This was not the only securities scheme Ginsberg became involved in at this time. Benjamin Binkowitz stole $178,000 in securities from a Wall Street dealer. After he was murdered and his loot taken from him, many of the stolen securities made their way to Ginsberg in Cleveland and another broker in that same city.[209]

Even as he was busy fencing stolen property, Sam continued to run gambling operations in Cleveland. He and Ed Strong invested heavily in illegal bookmaking as well as actually running racetracks. They got into and out of trouble. In 1920, for example, police raided Ginsberg's cigar store at 715 Superior Avenue N. E. Charged with selling pools on races and baseball games, Ginsberg was found not guilty by the city police judge.[210] When Ginsberg testified in a federal court regarding his possession of the stolen Liberty Bonds noted above, he said that his gambling establishments brought in $40,000 a night—half a million dollars in 2019 purchasing power.[211]

As if this were not enough action for Ginsberg, he also had a big role in bootlegging in Cleveland. Here, again, he worked with Nicky Arnstein of New York. Although there was plenty of liquor to be bootlegged from nearby Canada, New York was always another ready source of hooch smuggled from the Canada, the Bahamas, and Cuba. New

York, in turn, was ready for Canadian whiskey smuggled across Lake Erie. In the early years of Prohibition, "several shipments of whiskey to and from Ginsberg and Arnstein were intercepted by Prohibition agents," although no prosecution followed these seizures.[212] A federal officer described the Cleveland operation as "one of the important whiskey rings of Ohio" and named "Cheeks" Ginsberg, Benny Goldberg, "Yankee" Goldsmith, and Julius Haverman as deeply intertwined with Nicky Arnstein's operations.[213]

Sam met Kitty Kaiser, daughter of Martha Clark, in Cleveland. Martha had married George Kaiser about 1879 and lived in Buckeye Township, Gladwin County, when she had Kitty and a son, Arthur. Through divorce or death, George Kaiser disappeared. In 1892, Martha married Warren Budd and had two more children. They lived in Haynes Township, Alcona County and then at Tawas City in Iosco County.[214]

Warren Budd, Kitty's stepfather, was something of a ne'er-do-well. Raised in the Thumb, he married Martha Clark Kaiser in Mikado, north of Oscoda in Alcona County. They moved south to Tawas City late in the nineteenth century. He and the family found their way to Cleveland by 1900. That year, Warren apparently turned outlaw by attempting to rob a telephone exchange in Windsor, Canada. At his arrest, he gave his residence as Cleveland. For his efforts, he served six weeks in jail.[215] Five years later a northbound train crushed him as he sat drunk, depressed, or extremely careless on the west rail of the Michigan Central tracks outside Lupton in Ogemaw County.[216] The Kaiser Budd family had moved to Bay City by 1913 and to Tawas City by 1924. Kitty's mother owned property in the Tawas area.[217]

During this difficult time in her life, Kitty Kaiser Budd lived in Cleveland, where Sam Ginsberg met and married her in 1921. In that year, Ginsberg was deeply involved in fencing stolen bonds, gambling, and bootlegging. By 1930 the couple was farming in the rural area very near Tawas City.[218] What happened to cause Sam to leave Cleveland?

There is no indication that Ginsberg fell into trouble with the authorities. What changed was the criminal landscape. No single boss controlled the Cleveland underworld at the start of Prohibition. Many small operators worked the criminal offerings of gambling, bootlegging, prostitution, racketeering, and extortion. An area called "Little Hollywood" housed much of the action. Then around 1930, Moe Dalitz came to town. Moe was a player in the underworld games of hoodlum Detroit; he was even thought be allied with the Purple Gang there. In Cleveland, he surrounded himself with competent and ruthless partners to form what became known as the Cleveland Syndicate.[219] The Syndicate maintained good relations with the Mayfield Road mob, the local Mafia. Dalitz put pressure on fellow operators such as Ginsberg. That was enough to make Sam rethink his career. Since his wife had family and land in rural Michigan, he moved there, and passed himself off as a farmer.[220]

Despite his departure from the big cities, Ginsberg maintained his contacts and interests. In the early 1930s, he invested in Mert Wertheimer's Shawnee Club in Cleveland.[221] In the gambling circles he almost certainly got to know Sam Garfield, who was then a gambling impresario and friend of Wertheimer operating in Detroit.[222] Garfield had opted out of the Detroit scene in the uncertainty that abounded as the Purple Gang self-destructed in 1931-1932. He had gone to live in Clare, about 50 miles west of Tawas City. There, he became deeply and successfully involved in laundering gangsters' money into oil exploration and extraction related to the great Michigan oil boom of 1925-1940. Men who had been involved in the Purple Gang were clients as was Ed Strong, the racketeer from Cleveland and Ginsberg's erstwhile lawyer. With that background, it is no surprise that Ginsberg invested some of his take from Cleveland operations into oil exploration. He was deeply involved in the exploitation of the oil fields around Beaverton in Gladwin County. Even as late as 1944 he had five mineral leases in Ogemaw County's oil fields around West Branch to the west of the Tawas area.[223]

Sam apparently was not all that keen on the life of a farmer. He often, even regularly, drove over to Clare and stayed at the Doherty Hotel during the week, joining the whole raft of oil men who either stayed permanently at the Doherty or visited there regularly to check on their investments. In wide-ranging interviews in the 1990s, Forrest

Meek asked about what people at the Doherty Hotel recalled. They remembered Sam Ginsberg as a small, quiet man. (Lucille Doherty added that he always ordered liver in the hotel dining room!) Willard Bicknell recalled, "'Cheeks' came up here and put gangster money into oil. He stayed in the area and married a woman near West Branch. She had a family farm. He used to go there and spend the weekend, but he kept a room at the hotel all that time." Bicknell got some of the details wrong, but what is clear is that the Clare people knew who Ginsberg was and something of his gangster background. Another detail fits what we know about Sam: He was an avid participant in the high-stakes poker games that went on, sometimes for days at a time, in an unused basement room of the Doherty Hotel in Clare, converted by Fred Doherty for their use. It consisted only of a table with two lights hanging over it—that was it, but it was very popular among the local oil and businessmen—and with the local priest.[224]

In 1954, while he was in Clare, Sam was stricken and taken to the local hospital. He died there at the age of seventy. His funeral was held in Clare, not in his hometown; a rabbi came up from Detroit to officiate.[225] He is buried with his wife and sister-in-law in Tawas City.

CHAPTER 8

Mafiosi Up North

U nlike areas Up North that could be accessed easily by boat or rail, the Higgins Lake/Houghton Lake area remained quite isolated even into the early years of the twentieth century. Of course, logging had brought men to the area in the decades before and a few hearty souls had even taken up cabins on the lakes. But with the nearest railroad in Roscommon ten to fifteen miles away and only a rough road going south, no resort boom developed. It was only with the increasing popularity of the automobile and road improvements during the 1910s that the area began to become the popular resort destination it remains today. Leaders of the Mafia in Detroit came to the area by the early 1930s and took up resorting without any attempt to hide their presence. Despite this, the true story of the Detroit Mafia in Roscommon and Crawford counties remains little documented.

Detroit's Mafia

While most of its immigrants were upstanding, law-abiding citizens, the Italian community in Detroit also accommodated a thriving underworld.[226] The Gianolla brothers, Antonio "Tony," Salvatore "Sam," and Gaetano, dominated the usual rackets—protection, illegal beer, prostitution, and gambling. A series of gangland conflicts between 1910 and 1920 provided the proving ground for the men who would soon become the main mafiosi in town, William "Black Bill" Tocco and Joseph "Uno" Zerilli. These men started out as gunmen for the Gianolla gang.

Joseph "Uno" Zerilli and William "Black Bill" Tocco

At the beginning of Prohibition, the Detroit Mafia was split into several rival factions. The Gianolla gang disintegrated with the murder of its leaders. A Young Turk among the Italians, Giuseppe (Joe) Manzello, attempted to take up the reins, but the whole underworld environment had changed radically with the advent of Prohibition. In 1920 alone, one older leader, John Vitale, fell in a hail of bullets as did the leader of another faction, Joe Manzella. From the mayhem, Salvatore "Singing Sam" Catalanotte emerged as the last man standing. He consolidated his control and continued as *capo dei capi* for several years as the Mafia spread its activities throughout the city. Catalanotte proved to be a consummate organizer, assigning various sections of the city to distinct sub-groups to control as much of the lucrative rackets—bootlegging, prostitution, drugs, and gambling—as he could.

Under Catalanotte, two major factions did their work. Angelo Meli, William "Black Bill" Tocco, and Joseph Zerilli led the East-side Gang. Joseph Tocco, Cesare (Chester) "Big Chet" LaMare, and

"Big Chet" LaMare

Angelo Polizzi led the Westside Gang. This worked for a decade of relative peace among the various Mafia factions—until Catalanotte died of pneumonia in early 1930. His successor, Gaspar Milazzo, soon died in the usual hail of bullets. Then "Big Chet" LaMare, leader of the Westside gang, soon followed Milazzo to the grave. This left the Eastside gang to take control of the Mafia. Starting out as young gunmen back in the late 1910s, Angelo Meli, "Black Bill" Tocco, and "Uno" Zerilli were now at the top of the Mafia heap. They, along with some other mafiosi, formed the Detroit Partnership, as the Detroit crime family became known. Tocco and Zerilli strengthened their relations when Zerilli married Tocco's sister, Rosalia. A son, Anthony, later followed his father into gangster life. Another of Zerilli's sisters, Pietra (Petrina), married Pete Corrado. Their oldest son, Dominic Peter, later took up the gangster trade as well. Tocco was sent to prison for tax evasion in 1937. Joe Zerilli took control of the Partnership and retained that position for forty years.[227]

Higgins Lake

" Machine gun" Pete Corrado

This introduction to the Detroit Partnership, sometimes called the Detroit Outfit, brings us back to the Higgins/Houghton Lake area. As early as 1934, Josephine Zerilli, Joseph Zerilli's wife, bought two lots in the Pine Bluffs development on the eastern shore of Higgins Lake near Flag Point. William "Black Bill" Tocco came at about the same time, for he sold Pine Bluff lots to the Zerillis in 1938; he continued to own land there until at least 1946. In 1962, the Zerilli couple bought two more lots on the same side of the lake just south of lots owned by Pete Corrado and his wife.[228] At some point they had also purchased 120 acres at the northern edge of Roscommon County to the east of that town.

Pete Corrado had property on Higgins Lake from at least 1946 when Tocco and his wife sold him a lot on the east side. During the years 1949 to 1950, he bought a good deal more property in the area, some to the east and some to the west of the lake, presumably as hunting land. His son, Anthony, continued to own the property. As late as 2002, this son bought 80 more acres in the area.[229] The Corrados also owned the South Branch Ranch northeast of Roscommon.[230] I treat that property later in this chapter.

Although Joe Zerilli and Pete Corrado always denied involvement in the Detroit Mafia, their resort spots were useful for Mafia business.[231] Joe Zerilli (1897-1977) was very comfortable hosting out-of-state mob luminaries at his cabin on Higgins Lake. One FBI informant reported that he had called Zerilli and asked if he could come up with his family. Zerilli had told him that he was very happy to have him bring his children and wife to the cottage on Higgins at any time.[232]

Joseph Zerilli

Zerilli and Tocco were both very close to Joe Profaci (1898-1962), a New York City *cosa nostra* boss. One of Profaci's daughters, Rosalie, married one of Zerilli's sons, Anthony "Tony Z." Profaci lived in New York City, but his daughter, Rosalie, lived in Detroit. He would come on the train to Detroit and then travel up to Zerilli's place on Higgins Lake. He loved Vernors Ginger Ale, a Michigan original, and on the train back to New York, would take cases of it along with him.

Profaci was notoriously tight-fisted. He also, like many gangsters, habitually carried a large amount of cash. Once, the story goes, he and Tony "The Bull" Corrado were out fishing on Higgins. Their movement

Anthony "Tony Z." Profaci

caused the boat to capsize. Tony could hardly swim and flailed about, but Profaci lunged for his wallet first, more concerned about his money being lost than Tony drowning. In the end, both made it to shore safely.

During one of New York's mob wars, Profaci found himself a prime target of other gangsters. To be safe, he took refuge in the Higgins Lake cottage. Jack Tocco (1927-2014), "Black Bill"'s son, and Joe Zerilli hid him. At the lake, Profaci was often in the company of other dons. Known visitors to the Zerilli place include Joe Bonanno (1905-2002, New York City); Tommy Lucchese (1899-2002, New York City); Stefano Magaddino (1891-1974, Buffalo); John LaRocca (1901-1984, Pittsburgh); and several dons from northeastern Pennsylvania. Carlo Gambino and other New York City dons are not mentioned specifically as visiting but may well have.

Milan "Chip" Shepard, Clare Chief of Police from 1961 to 1966, stated that he more than once witnessed gangsters heading north through Clare. In particular, he once made a traffic stop and saw Mickey Cohen (1913-1976, Los Angeles) in the car. These men were heading for Higgins Lake, he told me, presumably to the Zerilli place.

Zerilli himself behaved like a normal guy while at the Higgins Lake cabin. In 1953 he donated to the Grayling Mercy Hospital building campaign.[233] However, apparently the lake did not appeal to his son, Anthony Zerilli (1927-2015), who told the FBI that he had not visited his father there. "Zerilli said he does not care for Higgins Lake and has not been up for quite some time."

Locals remember the Zerillis and the Corrados among them.[234]

The Corrado and Zerilli families had homes on Higgins Lake, near my hometown of Roscommon, and the Corrados had a horse and cattle ranch (South Branch Ranch) on property a few miles north of town where the up-scale Forest Dunes golf course is now located. During the '50's we frequently saw members of both families and their entourage in town. They maintained a low profile and were friendly with and generous to many locals. I believe that Tony [Zerilli] attended school for at least part of one year. Once when he was an old man Pete "The Enforcer" Corrado, father of Anthony and Dominic, came to town with a Sicilian donkey cart and gave rides to children. Years later I was struck by the similarity between an aging Don Corleone and old man [Dominic] Corrado. Once I was in the barber shop when Corrado came in for a haircut. He was a huge, ominous looking character much like some of the guys in gangster movies. He sat waiting his turn while holding a baby rabbit he found at the ranch. There were rumors that some cattle rustlers had cut the fence and stole cattle by loading them into a truck. Duane the barber asked Dominic if it were true and, if so, what he would do if they caught the cattle thieves. He paused for a moment, then—as he gently stroked the tiny rabbit—he said, "Guess we'll have to have one of the boys talk to 'em." It could have been a scene from The Sopranos or The Godfather.[235]

Margaret Karinen of Roscommon recalls that Pete Corrado had a place on Higgins Lake, and she remembers high school with Pete's descendants, Dominic and Tony Corrado, in 1981. She knew that they owned the South Branch Ranch and lived in Roscommon.

Houghton Lake

Interestingly, there are almost no stories or facts that place these Detroit Mafia families in the Houghton Lake area, despite their documented presence at nearby Higgins Lake. Occasionally, locals would spot one of the Corrados or Zerillis coming to see a movie at the Pines Theater in Prudenville. During the 1920s and 1930s, Johnson's Rustic Dance Palace hosted entertainment and dancing for the nearby resorters.[236] One of the backers, Jack Grablik, had come up from Chicago where he had beaten an extortion rap. The founder, Frank Johnson, also came from Chicago, but I can find no connection with gangsterdom for him. There are no rumors that Mafia or other underworld characters came. This is in stark contrast to the many rumors of gangsters coming to the Graceland Ballroom, a similar establishment, in Lupton.[237] That place features in the chapter, "Gangsters on Vacation."

South Branch Ranch

In the early years of the twentieth century, O.F. Barnes purchased 13,459 acres north of Roscommon for a ranch. He named it the South Branch Ranch, as it sat on the south branch of the Ausable River. Barnes incorporated his property in early 1910 with a value of $100,000.[238] C. P. Downey was the new principal investor within the corporation. He had made his money in Lansing as a manufacturer of a successful cream separator.[239] He also invested in the Reo Motor Works in Lansing and went on to run engineering companies that supplied auto parts for the Chevrolet Motor Car Company and Packard Motor Car Company.[240] He and a few other investors bought more land until they owned 22,800 acres (about thirty-five square miles/sections) along the Ausable river in Crawford County. They kept the name, the South Branch Ranch. The corporation bought sheep and cattle. But as it turned out, the land provided only poor grazing. The company was not a financial success. O.F. Barnes, one of the investors, insisted that the ranch could make money. He purchased from the others all but 1,800 acres along the river itself. Those acres Downey and the partners subdivided into forty-acre plots, each with frontage on the Ausable along a stretch of forty miles. All the original investors also retained hunting and fishing rights on the rest of the ranch. A few years later, in 1919, Downey reversed course, bought up the entire ranch acreage from the remaining investors, and developed his own private hunting reserve along the river. Alas, Downey had little time to enjoy his new haven. Already in ill health, he died in 1921. His family continued to use the place for the next eight years.

In 1929, the Downey estate sold almost the entire ranch to Clifford Durant, the son of the founder of Chevrolet. Durant proceeded to build a grand home on the property. The Michigan Department of Environmental Quality pamphlet for the Mason Tract (which was Durant's land originally) states:

The river is briefly followed [by the current Mason Tract Path] until the trail arrives at the remains of Durant's Castle at Mile 6.3 [just below Chase Bridge]. Only parts of a stone foundation and a fireplace are left, but in 1931 this site held a $500,000 home built by the automaker. The 42-room castle was a retreat for Durant, and included a drawing room, music room, library, barber shop, gymnasium, and seven fireplaces. What amused locals the most, though, was a ticker tape that kept the millionaire in contact with the New York stock market even in this getaway in the woods. The house only lasted a year, for it was destroyed by fire in February 1932.

That setback apparently was enough for Durant. In April 1932, he put the South Branch Ranch up for sale. It then consisted of 17,000 acres, five houses, and other buildings. This was "to close an estate."[241] Whose estate is unstated. Durant himself died five years later, in October 1937. George Mason, another automobile magnate, bought most of the 1,800 acres along the river from Clifford Durant's widow.[242] He donated it to the State of Michigan in 1954.

Enter the gangsters

A different investor purchased the rest of the ranch. Located 15 miles southeast of Grayling and 10 miles northeast of Roscommon, it is in an isolated spot.[243] In 1937 the ranch included 15,760 acres, about 25 square miles. The new owner set it up as a private club for hunting and as a resort. The manager of the club, C. H. Lintz, also continued to run something of a farm there, raising capons and turkeys. In 1940 it was still being run as a private club with "quite a few members."[244] At some point, though, the land was sold to members of the Detroit Partnership, that is, the Detroit Mafia. They called it the South Branch Ranch, retaining its original name dating back to 1910. It became a rest and relaxation retreat for Detroit mobsters—and even, perhaps, as the story goes, for Jimmy Hoffa's remains.[245]

Not surprisingly, verified details about the Mafia's time as owners are hard to come by. The Corrados, one of the Mafia's leading families, were the owners of the property. In 1952 Dominic Corrado, age twenty-two, was arrested in a raid in Detroit. The newspaper stated, "For the last several years, Corrado has operated the South Branch Ranch for cattle breeding at Roscommon."[246] This would indicate that the Corrados bought the property in about 1945. South Branch continued to run as a ranch dedicated mostly to thoroughbred horses and sheep at least into the mid-1960s.[247] The ranch's Appaloosa horses were "some of the most widely known in the Midwest."[248] Horses and cattle continued to be auctioned per newspapers advertisements.

In 1969 the central core of the ranch went to a group that established the Chandra Club, a horse-oriented recreational retreat. This apparently failed. New owners took the property in 1984. By the 1990s the property was in disrepair. A group purchased the land in 1997 and developed it as a golf club resort.[249]

The mob's takeover is embellished with the usual gangster tropes. They supposedly built "one of the largest ranches in Michigan history. The various barns surrounding the primary residence resembled modern day airplane hangars. They included an indoor horse-riding area, dance parlor, interlinking tunnels and hidden rooms." There also was a private runway, hunting reserve, servant quarters, an Olympic-size swimming pool, and even its own junkyard.

Gangsters were there, but the idea that they developed all these accoutrements is a myth. Since the ranch had been built and maintained as a working enterprise, the grounds already had basic structures such as barns for a horse, cattle, and sheep enterprise when it was acquired by the Corrados.[250] A runway and hangars had been built by a previous owner, Cliff Durant. The Chandra Club added the dance pavilion and indoor riding arena in 1969, after the Corrados had left.[251] So the Corrados did not much improve what they bought.

While there is quite a bit of evidence that underworld figures visited the Zerillis at their cabin on Higgins Lake, there is little evidence for mobsters coming to the South Branch Ranch. However, it does seem highly likely that the Corrados hosted their friends for rest, relaxation, and some hunting during the time they owned the ranch, about 1945-1969.

CHAPTER 9

Gangster-friendly Retreats—
Henry Ford and Harry Bennett

Harry Bennett was Henry Ford's enforcer at the Ford Motor Company. Was Harry Bennett a gangster? Absolutely not. Was Harry Bennett friendly with gangsters? Absolutely. Did Harry Bennett on occasion act like a gangster? Absolutely. In a book about gangsters Up North, Harry Bennett deserves a place.

Early life

Harry Herbert Bennett was born in Ann Arbor, Michigan on January 17, 1892. He was the second son of Vernor Bennett and his wife, the former an artist, the latter a schoolteacher. Soon, Vernor died. For a time, Harry was fatherless, but his mother remarried, this time to an engineering professor at the University of Michigan. This union did not last long. At age seven Harry was fatherless, for once again death had intervened. His mother went back to teaching to support the family.

Harry Bennett

When the family moved to Detroit, he quit high school midway through and attended the Detroit School of Fine Arts. He also hung out at Cass Park, near Cass Technical High School and near the then-location of the Detroit School of Fine Arts on Bagg Avenue. He mixed with sailors who told him tales of seafaring adventure and service in the United States Navy.[252] But to Harry's frustration, he was still too young to enlist. And his mother refused to sign for him.

Languishing and longing, young Harry was easy prey for a sailor named Sam Taylor—a man who was both a Navy man and a heavy-weight boxer. Taylor told Harry to come along with him as he went down to Cleveland to re-enlist in the Navy—Taylor would get Harry signed up as well and would eventually teach him to box. Harry lied about his age (sixteen), claiming to be eighteen, and joined up. The day he signed the papers he had a tattoo inscribed on his right arm with the date: January 29, 1909.[253] In the Navy he developed into a fine boxer. He gained a reputation as a tough man with a violent temper. More importantly, he used his quick mind to prepare for a future beyond the Navy.

When his ship had shore leave in New York City, he sought out Joseph Palma, the head of the United States Secret Service in the New York area. Palma liked him and soon Harry was an accredited operative of Navy Intelligence. His experience as a Navy snooper and his connection with Palma became very handy later in his career.

Henry Ford

The Navy stint lasted for two enlistments. Harry liked it so well that he decided to apply to the Annapolis Naval Academy. He signed off and left the Navy in Portsmouth, New Hampshire, in 1913 and headed for New York City, thinking that Palma might help him.[254] When he realized that he would have to wait a long time for any answer to his interest in Annapolis, he decided to take ship on a salvage vessel headed for French West Africa. When he returned to New York City on a freighter, the freighter's captain was suspicious that Harry and a few other American sailors would jump ship, so he ordered them to be detained on board. This did not sit well with Harry; a brawl ensued. The harbor police came to break it up and had to report the ruckus to the U.S. Immigration Office. At this point, Harry used his earlier contact with Joseph Palma to his advantage. Palma got him out of trouble and then a series of coincidences ensued that quickly led to Bennett being introduced to Henry Ford, who happened to be in New York at the time.

Henry Ford had a life-long habit of lending a hand to a worker or anyone in need. When Ford heard that Bennett was from Ann Arbor, just a stone's throw from his beloved Dearborn, Michigan, Ford offered him a job back in Michigan. He also (perhaps not supposing it would ever happen) told Harry to come and see him if he got back to Detroit. Harry remembered, though.[255] And, as it turns out, so did Ford.

Meanwhile back in Detroit, Ford was on the verge of breaking out of the nascent automobile industry's pack. In 1917, he bought land along the Detroit River for a huge manufacturing operation that would become the River Rouge, or simply the Rouge, plant. At first it produced parts for the Model T, a car assembled at Ford's Highland Park plant and elsewhere around the country. Eventually, the Rouge plant would cover 1.5 square miles and, from the late 1920s, produce the iconic Model A.[256]

It was just at this moment of great expansion that Ford again met Harry Bennett. One of many talents Bennett had was as a graphic artist. Tiring of working in New York, he headed west and took a job in Ford's commercial arts department. Ford, who took a preternatural interest in his employees, got wind of his presence. One day he sent W. C. White from the company's secretarial office to find Bennett and summon him: "Mr. Ford wishes to see you," was White's message to Harry. What went on in the interview that followed remains unknown. But for certain Henry expressed an interest in the young man, since information about him spread through the top levels of the organization.[257]

The year was 1918. The United States had joined the Great War, as it was then called, against the Germans. Ford had obtained the contract to supply Eagle-class patrol boats. These "Eagle boats" were specially outfitted, small, fast ships built to hunt and destroy German submarines. As the Rouge plant ramped up to mass produce these warcraft, saboteurs inside the plant struck. Sand was put in parts, bolts were left loose. The plant's manager was desperate to find someone to lead the effort to ferret out the culprits. The head of graphic arts had learned of Bennett's naval intelligence work. "I've got just the man you want in my department," he told the Rouge plant manager

That very afternoon, the manager called Bennett in. They hit it off well. The next morning the two began work on securing the construction sites of the Eagle boats. Harry Bennett used what he had absorbed while in the naval intelligence service. He had learned about gathering information, about personnel control, and about methods of investigation. He found the saboteurs and put them out of business. In the process, Harry ran into Navy Commander Carlos Bean. They had gotten to know each other during Navy service. Bean had been detached from Washington to oversee the construction of the Eagle boats. The commander had a strong recollection of Bennett—his boxing prowess as well as his intelligence and discipline. He favorably mentioned Harry to Ford as they discussed the construction of the Eagle boats and did not fail to note how efficiently Bennett had carried out the anti-saboteur action.

Henry Ford and Harry Bennett, 1940

From then on, Ford would stop by, speak to Harry, and ask him to "take care" of something, sometimes minor, but increasingly major. At times, he would just generally say something like, "I wish something could be done about that," regarding the topic of the conversation. Bennett knew then what he needed to do, and he did it, no matter what.

Bennett became completely enraptured with Ford. A man without a significant father figure, he had run off to join the highly hierarchical Navy and also felt a certain insecurity because of his relatively small size, but he had high intelligence and grit. Bennett relished the satisfaction and power of implementing what the domineering Ford wanted done.

Bennett took up with gusto the job of being Ford's enforcer. He truly believed that Ford was a great man doing great things. He enjoyed being a part of that grand enterprise. He was willing to do whatever needed to be done to carry out Ford's wishes, whether that meant cutting through red tape, intimidating people, or outright violence. He had no office, no title at first, no desk. He moved around as operations needed him, always being careful that Ford knew where to find him. They also communicated regularly, often daily, through early morning telephone calls.

The Enforcer at Ford

Bennett accumulated more and more responsibilities. When he took over security at Ford in 1923, he inherited an already sophisticated intelligence and enforcement operation. He proceeded to hire an even larger apparatus to carry out various jobs for Ford. They performed general security duties. As Bennett described it in 1937, "They watch for thefts of materials. They take charge of the various gates. They show visitors about. They drive trucks. They are, however, in no sense my private army. Such statements make me laugh."[258] They also guarded the one million dollars in cash always on hand at the Rouge plant—money to give the workers their pay. Most of all, though, they spied on workers to see that they were performing well, not stealing things, and not advocating for a union.[259]

Worker unrest was nothing new in the late twenties. The International Workers of the World (the IWW— "Wobblies") had been actively seeking to unionize the plants since the auto industry first boomed in

Detroit. Early on, Ford had thwarted them by offering his $5-a-day sal-
ary scheme and by opening up a "sociological department" aimed at ac-
cumulating information on workers' backgrounds and attitudes as a way
of heading off extremists. When, despite Ford's patronizing measures
and the efforts of his sociological department, labor insisted on organizing and demanding a seat at the table (a table set for one—Ford), he
rebelled. His chosen enforcer was Harry Bennett.

Bennett had accumulated all the personnel-related functions into
his portfolio. It was Ford's assignment to him to fix the labor problem
that led Bennett to resort to his famously violent habits. Bennett was,
first and only, Ford's man. Until a labor agreement was worked out in
1941, Bennett's enforcer mode was at full throttle.

Enter the hoodlums

With labor unrest raising its head, the security force focused more
and more on weeding out unionists real, potential, and imagined and,
when it came to it, providing muscle in confrontational situations. The
underworld was perfectly used to providing thugs for intimidating and
harassing strikers both on the scene of a labor action and at demonstra-
tions. Detroit's Cleaners and Dyers War (1925-1928) featured strong-
armed tactics hired by all sides, the violent men coming from various
elements in the underworld. Thus, it was natural that Bennett allied
himself with a prime source of thug labor in the city. Not that he did
not recruit his own army—often ex-athletes and ex-cons—to be on a
paid force, but he knew he could always count on reinforcements at
critical times if he kept on the good side of criminal elements. At the
same time, good relations helped keep the goons away from service at
the behest of union organizers who themselves were far from above using thuggish men and actions to further their cause.

The most famous (infamous) confrontations that featured Bennett's goons (supported by local police) vs. labor organizers happened
in 1932 and in 1937, both times at the Rouge plant. In 1932, Commu-
nists supposedly instigated a riot at the plant that left four men dead,
nineteen injured by gunshots, and thirty-five more suffering various
injuries resulting from falls and thrown objects. A mob of "about 4000

United Auto Workers leader beaten by Ford thugs, 1937

Communist-led unemployed, armed with stones and brickbats" battled police for almost half a mile along the main entrances to the plant. Police used pistols, tear gas, and water canon to confront the mob. Walter Reuther was prominent as the union leader organizing and directing the unionists. Bennett personally led the defense and was seriously injured when a brick struck him on the head.[260]

Continuing labor unrest let to another riot in 1937. Bennett's Ford men and allied thugs confronted Reuther and his men as they moved along an overpass over Miller Road to access the plant. The bloody "Battle of the Overpass" played out, a seminal moment in the labor movement in Detroit.[261]

Gangsters were useful in another way, as well. Starting in the mid-1920s, the Purple Gang and their ilk began a series of kidnappings.[262] Joseph "Legs" Laman's involvement with kidnappings was especially notable.[263] From about 1925, snatches in Detroit became a favorite method of extortion. The hoodlums responsible began by seizing fellow gamblers and bootleggers; authorities paid scant attention to such acts. But then the gangsters moved on to kidnapping businessmen (with one case leading to murder) and their children. The grandsons of Henry Ford were an obvious, potentially very lucrative, target.

Ford fortified his family residences with guards, escape routes, and so on. Design and construction went to Bennett. The actual existence of back staircases, tunnels, and the like, at Ford's residences are the origin of the later rumors of such things in Bennett's own homes Up North.

Bennett did not rely solely on physical protective measures. His used his close connections with underworld gangster types who could be relied upon to provide an extra layer of security for Ford's family. He cultivated the leaders of the Purple Gang. As I have told, in 1931 a brutal gangland slaying at the Collingwood Manor Apartments in Detroit led to the conviction of three Purple Gang members. Abe Bernstein, once the leader of the Purples, worked tirelessly to get a new trial for the killers, one of whom was his brother, Ray. In 1936 Harry Bennett helped out by writing to Governor Frank Fitzgerald asking for reconsideration of the Collingwood killers' 1931 guilty verdict. Evidently, Abe Bernstein had enlisted Bennett to weigh in on behalf of this entirely fruitless effort and Bennett had helped—surely not just a random act of kindness. Bennett also protected Ford's grandchildren by pre-empting some of the known kidnapping thugs. Sam Caruso and Legs Laman were two such experienced gangsters whom Bennett neutralized by employing them as part of his team at Ford.[264] Besides hiring and working with gangsters, Bennett also had an arrangement that allowed widespread gambling in the Rouge plant, gambling overseen by Mafia bosses Chet LaMare and Joe Tocco.[265] This concession assured Bennett that these mafiosi would not end up causing Ford any trouble.

In 1951, Harry was questioned by Senator Estes Kefauver's Special Committee on Organized Crime in Interstate Commerce. He was asked about gangsters working for him and for Ford. Bennett said that Ford had a soft heart for parolees and wanted to give them a chance, so he hired quite a number. Bennett said that Laman had

Harry Bennett testifies before the
Kefauver Committee, 1951

been paroled to him, but "he left after five days and I haven't seen him since." He further denied that any active criminal was ever employed in Ford's service.[266]

Asked about Chester LaMare, once the head of the Detroit Mafia, Bennett said that he had had nothing to do with him—that Ford's security agents had engaged him to stop assaults on fruit peddlers at the Ford plant. Did LaMare have the fruit concession at Ford? "LaMare didn't know a banana from an orange. He was in with another man who had the contract," was Bennett's reply. He did admit, however, that he was familiar with the West Side faction of hoodlums, Chet LaMare's gang. He also admitted in his memoirs that Ford had given Chet a Ford agency, known as the Crescent Motor Sales Company. LaMare used it for his gang's headquarters.[267]

Bennett denied to the committee that Joe Tocco, another leading Detroit Mafia figure, had ever worked for Ford, "Joe Tocco never had anything to do with the Ford Motor Company." He admitted knowing Tocco— "everyone knew Joe"—but denied knowing other Detroit Mafia figures, Pete Corrado, Joe Massei, and Joe Bommarito.

Asked about Joe Adonis, a Mafia big-wig who was awarded the New Jersey automobile transport contract by Ford, he said, "I never knew Joe Adonis. I didn't have anything to do with the New York office."

Asked about Tony D'Anna, who ended up with several very lucrative Ford dealerships in the Detroit area, he said he never offered him any such dealership; rather, that the Dearborn manager for Ford had done so. Bennett claimed he had no idea D'Anna was a thirty-one-year-old ex-bootlegger who had bribed witnesses. But, he added, "D'Anna was popular in Wyandotte [where the dealership was] and I thought he could sell cars."

In other questioning by the committee, it came out that there were at least accusations that Bennett had feuded with Pete Licavoli, a Toledo kingpin then living in Arizona, and had hired members of Joe Tocco's gang to work for Ford's security operation. The Kefauver people had turned up a good deal of dirt on Harry, all related to his ties to the underworld. Both Bennett and the mentioned underworld figures (those still alive) denied all allegations.

The tales of Bennett's relationships with gangsters are well told in James Buccellato's book, *Early Organized Crime in Detroit*.[268] Bennett never denied entertaining racketeers at his homes—he just insisted it was on his own dime, not with Ford money.[269] There is absolutely no doubt, despite disingenuous and lying statements repeatedly made by Bennett right up to his death in 1979, that his work for Ford was tightly entwined with his positive relationships with Detroit gangsters.

Harry Bennett Up North

Harry Bennett owned two homes Up North.[270] As early as 1935 Bennett had a cottage, a rather grand one, in fact, on Lake Huron. It was a two-story log structure that sat right on the lake north of East Tawas.[271] It is unclear if Henry Ford built the place for Bennett.[272] Probably not, as the deed of sale in September 1934 states that Harry and his then wife Margaret bought the place from a certain Sam L. Anker and his wife.[273] Gossip made this purchase much more interesting: "When I was a child my family owned a cottage built by Henry Ford for Bennett. It was his hideaway and love nest with his private nurse. There was a heart in the cement with their initials outside the back door." This is patently false but does lend an air of mystery and drama to the place.[274]

Harry Bennett's East Tawas cottage in 2018

It is true that Harry Bennett's security work for Ford made him into a very paranoid man determined to be well-prepared against threats; he especially feared that his children might be kidnapped. This situation led to all sorts of stories about the Lake Huron lodge. Supposedly, in the basement there was a tunnel that went out to a waiting boat on the lake;[275] he kept a gun in every room and two exits as well; he was said to have had a leopard chained up by the door, with large cat paw prints in the cement;[276] he had mounted guards;[277] there were lights all the way through the woods.

While many stories are fanciful—there is no tunnel, there are no paw prints—the house is very real. As are inscriptions in the cement walkways pledging the place to Esther, his second wife, "Harry and Esther 1937," and giving the cottage its name, "Ethel B. Lodge."[278] It sits on the shoreline of Lake Huron in an attractive setting and remains occupied in the summer to this day.

Harry Bennett and wife, Esther, 1936

However, Bennett lived there a scant four years before he traded it away. Henry Ford had built a home called the Pagoda House on Grosse Ile for his family, but Clara Ford, Henry's wife, was afraid her children would get sucked away by the strong current in the Detroit River, so Henry swapped the Pagoda for the East Tawas cabin in 1939. Harry has a differ-

"The Ethel B. Lodge 1937" "Esther & Harry" at the lower right

ent account of what happened: "The Grosse Ile property originally was owned by Mr. Ford and had a boat house on it. Mr. Ford had turned it over to a couple of relatives. They got to fighting over the place and Mr. Ford was disgusted. One day in my office he asked me if I had a dollar bill. I said, 'yes.' 'Give it to me,' he said, 'and the [Grosse Ile] place is yours.'"[279]

Once gone from the East Tawas cottage, Harry turned his Up North attention to building a retreat at Lost Lake in western Clare County.[280] There was a small cabin on it when he made the purchase. He built on the estate between 1941 and 1943.[281] Bennett's friends said it had cost him a quarter of a million dollars. It was called the S-Tar Ranch after Bennett's wife, Esther.[282]

In 1945, Henry Ford, in ill health and mentally unstable, yielded control of the Ford Motor Company to his grandson, Henry Ford II. This Henry Ford intensely disliked Bennett and fired him. Shortly thereafter, Bennett went up to his Lost Lake retreat.[283] He subsequently summered there, wintering at his place in the California desert. Between 1945 and 1953, he was at Lost Lake almost every year.

A *Detroit Times* interview at the Lost Lake lodge yielded this description:

> The barbecue pit on the flat roof has a winding outdoor stairway that leads up to it. The pit is there in the hope of finding a

breeze to discourage mosquitoes. Even at close range, the one-story building, 250 feet long, appears to be made of logs. The 'logs' are concrete and cover cement block walls. The 60-foot long living room appears to be paneled with yellow pine. The paneling is plaster. The living room floor is flagstone, principally because that section of the 'cabin' was built during the war when materials were scarce. The room is on two levels. The lower level is a huge semi-circular recess fronting one of the most immense fireplaces in architectural history. This recess is lined by a huge, sectional semi-circular lounge. There is a swimming pool outside, fed by an artesian well with water cold enough to freeze the ears off a raccoon. Out front is a miniature cascade made of flag stone. The water flows into a garden pool and, more importantly, feeds the chubs in the bait boxes. The children (usually there is a house full of them supplied by relatives and friends) charge down the trails in one of the amphibian ducks made by Ford for the Russians when the Soviet was an ally.[284]

In the same interview, Bennett gave this account of the compound:

I own 2,300 acres.... There weren't any secret passages to escape from gangsters, as some newspapers have maintained. The passage at the Grosse Ile house was through a coat closet and led to the boat well below so that we could escape when unwanted visitors were seen crossing the bridge out front. The passage

Harry Bennett's Lost Lake lodge in 2018

in the castle led to a wine cellar and had no other outlet. The passage in the [Lost Lake] ranch house was behind a tier of shelves and led to a play room which had a small bar.[285]

1953 was the last year Bennett used the Lost Lake property.[286] Lost Lake was sold in 1957 for $150,000 to Samuel B. Solomon, president of Detroit's United Steel Sales.[287] In 1965, Solomon sold the property to the Clinton Valley Council of the Boy Scouts of America for $350,000. Scouts operated a summer camp there until 2012. The property is currently (2019) for sale.

Tales

I have already mentioned that Harry Bennett was an important friend and employer of gangsters during his time as head of security for the Ford Motor Company. As Henry Ford's enforcer, he lived a life full of potential threats against him such as an attempt on his life or the kidnapping of one of his children. His dangerous role at Ford created an atmosphere that encouraged contemporaries and later writers to describe all sorts of personal safety measures Bennett allegedly took at his various homes. Some of these measures were real at, for example, his Ypsilanti mansion. Perhaps it was those real measures that spawned ever-wilder rumors about his retreats Up North. His cabin on Lake Huron suffers only a bit from such exaggerations. With his construction of a retreat on Lost Lake, the rumors proliferated. There were tales of armed guards, secret passageways, and raucous behavior.[288] Machine gun emplacements appeared on the roof: "Local rumor had it that the roof was designed to ward off an invasion and at one time there were machine gun mounts on it."[289] A moat would protect from invasion as well: "Bennett's original idea was to dredge the entire area around the house creating an island using the lake's tributary system." Rumors of Lost Lake detail it as a retreat used by a man very worried about his personal safety: the moat with iron spikes, the bridge ready to be dynamited to cut off access, the secret escape tunnel behind the bookcase, the machine gun emplacement on the roof, the fortified cement structure of the cabin itself, the car and airplane constantly at ready to whisk Bennett to safety—all these rumors relate to a Bennett living in constant fear. The Lost Lake estate actually reflects none of this. As the stories were repeated, they created the current view that Lost Lake was a bastion built for a violent gangster. Saner heads knew better all along. Harry Cornell, "a longtime Farwell resident who acted as Bennett's caretaker for many years," "pooh-poohs the legends." "Mr. Bennett just liked the out-of-doors. There weren't any armed guards or anything else."[290] Robert Rowley, overseer of the property from 1965-1986, said, "Most people just thought he [Bennett] was mean. The people up here thought [Bennett and his men] were running around in the woods with machine guns, but that's an exaggeration. They came up here to get away from the city."[291] Rowley told the *Detroit Free Press* that rumors of gun turrets and the like were simply false. He lived in the house after the Scouts took possession in 1965, so he knew the truth.

A stairway hidden behind a bookcase was the only curious thing Rowley or anyone else found on the site. This led down to the swimming pool and bar, as Bennett claimed, and was not an escape route. Rowley's daughter, Rebecca, reminisced, "I was raised at Lost Lake, moving there in 1965 and lived in the Lodge until 1972. It was an awesome place to grow up. There was a moat…but no pointed posts and no secret room that you could hear conversations around the house, otherwise we would have used that as kids. The secret passageway behind the bookshelf was always fun during birthday parties."[292]

The truth about Lost Lake is much less exciting than the many stories it has generated. Harry Bennett was fond of get-away places where he could relax with his family and entertain his friends, among whom were an assortment of disreputable men. His first choice was the East Tawas cottage on Lake Huron. When Henry Ford took this for his own family in 1939, he was left without a retreat. Intense labor troubles at Ford kept him fully occupied. He did manage to purchase the Lost Lake property, but renovations and new construction only began in 1941. During the next two years, Bennett expanded the existing cottage and built outbuildings. By 1943 the retreat stood complete.

During those two years, 1941 to 1943, Bennett's personal situation changed dramatically. In June 1941, Ford Motor Company signed a labor agreement with the United Auto Workers. Labor unrest ended, as did the tension between union thugs and Ford thugs. Harry Bennett no longer had to fear any but the most unlikely threats to his life and family. His Lost Lake compound reflected his newly secure life. There was no machine gun on the roof, no escape tunnel, no spike-riddled moat, and no ready speedboat to take him across the lake to his airstrip for a fast getaway. Perhaps there were some bodyguards still—caution might have dictated that. Bennett did try, unsuccessfully, to have the property fenced. Rather than a measure to thwart assassins, this fence was intended to make it clear to outsiders that his land was private property. However, the Department of Conservation nixed even the fence because it would inhibit deer migration. There were probably some loud parties attended by disreputable people of Bennett's acquaintance from Detroit. That was about the extent of it, especially since, from 1945 until he abandoned the property in 1953, Bennett used the place as a summer residence for his extended family. The truth, as is often the case when the lives of gangsters Up North are investigated carefully, is much less dramatic than the tall tales that their presence—real or, most often, imagined—produced.

CHAPTER 10

Gamblers and Gambling

Club Manitou near Harbor Springs/Petoskey

The Harbor Springs/Petoskey area on Little Traverse Bay was not originally a tourist destination.[293] The first whites to see the area came to save souls, a rather more spiritual purpose. The first permanent settlers arrived in Petoskey in 1852 when Andrew Porter established a Presbyterian mission among the native Odawa Indians. A mission soon followed in 1855. The St. Francis Solanus mission still exists today, the oldest building left in the city. The first gold found in the region was the green of trees, not of dollars. Using the lake as an export route, the great forests of the hinterland were cut and shipped throughout the Midwest as lumber to build a young American nation.

The area was a draw for tourists and summer cottagers from around 1880. Both rail lines and steamship lines advertised their modes of transportation. Tourism and summer residency have played a major role in small towns of the area since that time. Bay View, a planned development at Harbor Springs northeast of Petoskey, came into being as a Methodist summer retreat in 1875. It morphed into an upscale residential area for wealthy resorters and has remained such to this day. Both Harbor Springs and Petoskey had reasonable accommodations available from about the same date. By the early 1900s, there was a steady stream of summer tourists and vacationers. With the advent of the automobile, many drove to the area from around

133

1920 even though it was a two-day trip from Chicago or Detroit due to the condition of the roads.

Alongside the sun and sand of Little Traverse, gambling was wide-open. Some attempt to control it first appeared in 1899.[294] Another campaign came in 1915 after the county had gone dry.[295] The sheriff tried again to get rid of gambling in Petoskey in 1917.[296] But gambling could not be suppressed.

Small-time opportunities to gamble abounded in the resort areas. Almost every drug store and hotel had punch cards and other low-level forms of lotteries that paid out money on the spot. As the take on these was high—20%-40% of the wager—it was very tempting for enterprises to make a little extra money this way. Slot machines were a bit more expensive, but they also paid a good dividend to the owner and so hotels regularly had them available. In Harbor Springs a local man who distributed most of the slots in Emmet County later told a reporter that the resorts were "lousy" with them—he said there were around 200 in Emmet County during the summer seasons of the early 1930s. The supplier would bring slots to the resorts at the beginning of the summer and then remove and store them until the next season.

Juilleret's establishment in Harbor Springs was a good example of a local place taking advantage of the availability of slot machines. Joe Juilleret recalled that in the 1920s and early 1930s there were up to ten slot machines working in his ice cream parlor-cum-cabaret at one time: five nickel, three dime, and two quarter machines. As was customary, the owner, in this case Joe, split the take with the distributor. Besides the slots, Juilleret's offered a full plate of entertainment. There was a band—Ange Lorenzo and his Tunesters were a favorite—and the dance floor accommodated the furious flapping of young and old, cooled by overhead fans circulating the summer air. The cover charge was $1.50 per couple, which the house and the band split 60-40. As for food, the restaurant had a soda fountain that served sandwiches and there was a dining area as well. BYOB was the motto: bring your own booze. Once there with your bottle, you could purchase set-ups. For example, a twelve-ounce ginger ale could be had for 50¢ and a bowl of ice for an additional 25¢—probably about a 1000% markup from cost. The place was so popular that on a good night three hundred people crowded in. Enforcement was spotty at best, but in 1924 there was some effort to clean up the area: in Emmet County, Sheriff Pokriefke ordered all slots and punch cards confiscated in a 1924 ruling.[297] This was definitely pushing water up hill, however.

The hit-and-mostly-miss local enforcement did not, therefore, slow down the illegal gambling activity. The local man who provided the slot machines said that he did not need to bribe anyone—in fact, that he knew of very little bribery in general at that time. Card game opportunities abounded. In Harbor Springs alone there were two or three pool halls running during the 1920s and 1930s. These, according to Joe Juilleret, always had poker games going in the back room. There were larger, more sophisticated gambling opportunities, but these coexisted with the mom and pop gambling that drugstores, hotels, and pool halls offered. It seems that local officials and law enforcement viewed gambling as a way to bring some money into the community since the participants were very often the out-of-town resorters. And the State Police never did anything.[298] This permissive era lasted through Prohibition and into the later 1930s, in fact at least until the anti-gambling administration of Governor Frank Murphy (1935-1937)—and the subsequent governor, Frank Fitzgerald, was once again much more lenient about enforcement.

Many resorters were also eager to drink during Prohibition. A case of high-quality gin could be had for $85 to $90. Al Gerhart, owner of Club Manitou, stated, "I think I sold to 99% of the resort people. I might have missed one or two, but I'll go with 99. If they had their $85."[299] Gerhart sold the real stuff—Canadian export that he purchased from *entrepôts* on the Canadian side of the Detroit River and had smuggled into Michigan and transported by truck on up to the Little Traverse Bay area. He had other options—liquor transported by boat up Lake Huron and through the Straits, or bootlegged booze from the Sault Ste. Marie area, but trucking was the most economically viable method.

At $85 a case (around $1,500 in current purchasing power), locals would have been priced out, but luckily there were sources to supply liquor at much lower prices. Joe Juilleret said he sold booze in his establishment (he did not say how/where he got it), but that ordinary people bought "bunk" gin—juniper flavored grain alcohol—for around $25 a case: "The resort people would be in our place getting drunk on labeled booze while their maids and chauffeurs would be across the tracks at Booth's drinking brown bottle (low quality) whiskey." Booth's was on the waterfront—the dance hall balanced on pilings along the lake side of the building. There were slot machines and the Bob Greenwell Orchestra for the dancers. Booth's was open 24 hours a day, so the availability was basically unrestricted. Juilleret claimed that neither he nor Booth bootlegged; they did not consider buying bootlegged booze (there wasn't any other kind) for distribution to be bootlegging.

Casino gambling—a term used both for highly organized gambling opportunities in hotels and for stand-alone clubs—came to the Emmet County area in the mid-1920s. To the south, John Koch's Colonial Club in Charlevoix had already opened in about 1914. There were multiple gambling opportunities in the Little Traverse Bay area. The first resort spot was Club Manitou located between Petoskey and Harbor Springs. The name, Club Manitou, might come from the Anishinaabe word for a spirit or force of nature, but more probably it derives from the name of the famous lake steamer *Manitou* that brought resorters and cottagers to the Little Traverse Bay area during the late nineteenth and early twentieth centuries. The Manitou made its run from Chicago for the last time during the 1931 season. But in 1929, when Club Manitou was founded, the famous steamer was the jewel of the steamer fleet.

Club Manitou

The main concern of the local authorities in Emmet County was to keep the gangster syndicates out of the gambling. This was a reasonable concern since gangsters in Chicago, Detroit, Toledo, and Cleveland were heavily involved in setting up gambling establishments, supplying slot machines, and so on, not only in their own cities but in outlying parts, especially resort areas. However, local efforts were not successful. Al Gerhart, the owner/manager of the Club Manitou, had direct connections with Detroit gangster money. It was even said that Abe Bernstein, leader of the Purple Gang and resident in Detroit at this time, was the money behind the club. Gerhart preferred, however, to think of himself as a local and, indeed, he did live mostly in Petoskey from the late 1920s until his death in 1987.

The Manitou quickly established itself as a premier club in northwestern Michigan. Patrons rather lovingly called it the "Stork Club of the North," likening it to the famous Stork Club in New York City—or maybe they were just remembering their experience at the Stork Club on Rowena Avenue in Detroit. In the late 1920s, gambling was widespread in the Motor City. Clubs like the Chesterfield drew hundreds of patrons for entertainment and illegal booze. The profit margin was reasonable. Although never as profitable as bootlegging, illegal gambling operations earned big bucks for the gangsters behind the scenes. They almost never ran the joints themselves. They were rather the venture capitalists, investing in operations, some of which were successful while others were failures. It is not surprising that Detroit capital would end up in Petoskey.

Enter Al Gerhart. Born Allah Joseph Schwendner in Reading, Pennsylvania, his father, an immigrant from Germany, was a successful small-time merchant and entrepreneur in that city. He came from Germany with a degree in design and worked as a designer all his life. In Reading he worked for the Reading Hardware Company and obtained several patents for new designs of plumbing items. Along the

Al "Slim" Gerhart

way he was the president and one of the founders of the Temple Malleable Iron and Steel Company. At his death he was also running a small garage out of the back of his home. So, Allah came from a steady, responsible family background. He stayed in Reading into his teenage years. But one by one, all his siblings but one moved west to Detroit. By 1924 he had moved there, too. He was 18.[300]

The next year he was north of Detroit in Algonac, St. Clair County. Police arrested him on a charge of disorderly conduct. He paid a $15 fine and promised to mend his ways.[301] Apparently, those ways involved a girl because the next month police charged him with bastardy. Schwendner, "who was on vacation at Algonac for several months, and who is said to be a bootlegger," promised the judge that he "was willing to make whatever amends he could."[302] The judge ordered him jailed until he could produce a $700 bond (about $15,000 in today's purchasing power) to support his child.[303]

138

His response to his responsibilities was to forfeit the bond and change his name from Allah Schwendner to Al Gerhart. He took his last name from his neighbors back in Reading. Doing this, he could disappear into Detroit and get out of child support. A new name would also protect his siblings living in Detroit from being associated with a bootlegger.

Then things really got serious when, in 1929, Gerhart was an accessory in a bootlegging hijack gone wrong that may have led to murder. His story was that he, Harold Wood, and a prosperous barber-turned-bootlegger, Medis Hull, were driving along Telegraph Road when shots fired from a vehicle in front of them struck Hull in the head; he expired immediately. Hull had a reputation as a hijacker in Wyandotte, south of Detroit. When the police got to the scene, they found Gerhart and his companion as well as Hull's body. An eyewitness indicated the racing car had been pursuing another when Hull was shot. Police at first seemed to believe that Gerhart's car was chasing a rumrunner's vehicle with the intent to hijack it. While Gerhart and Schmidt admitted to having been "down river" to pick up a load of illegal liquor, they denied that they were in the process of hijacking someone else's load when Hull was shot dead.[304] Then, the police had second thoughts. They came to believe that Hull could not have been shot in the head from a car speeding ahead of his vehicle at sixty-five mph. Police also speculated Gerhart and Wood had murdered Hull in a dispute over a load of illegal booze.[305]

This episode indicates Gerhart's involvement in bootlegging over a number of years. As early as 1925, at his court hearing on bastardy charges, the judge knew of his reputation as a bootlegger. Was he a freelancer, or did he work with gangsters? Gerhart himself claimed that he was never more than a chauffeur for the gangsters of Detroit. It is an interesting choice of words, since a gangster's chauffeur often doubled as a bodyguard and confidant.

The next event in Gerhart's life is a puzzle. In 1928, while he was still based in Detroit, he went up to Petoskey and bought enough land in Harbor Springs to provide a place for a gambling and gaiety center. He proceeded to oversee the construction of a significant structure, built in the log cabin style that so appealed to resorters. I describe this building below. His Club Manitou opened on the Fourth of July 1929. The questions arise, where did the money for this venture come from? Why Gerhart?

The common account was that Abe Bernstein, the Purple Gang leader out of Detroit, bankrolled the operation to be created on the model of such clubs around the country that gangsters heavily invested in. Gerhart himself, however, claimed that he alone was behind the club. He said that it was his idea and that he ran it without outside help or interference. He denied any link with gangsters other than his role as a chauffeur for the Purple Gang. What is the truth?

Abe Bernstein

Abe Bernstein was, indeed, in Petoskey from time to time. An FBI report from 1936 places him in the area. But as so often, the trail runs out there. If he did invest in the Manitou, he left no trace of it. That said, Detroit gambling impresarios with whom he was undoubtedly acquainted—men like Al Ackerman and Bert Moss—had recently invested Up North. There was always room for one more. In addition, Abe had gotten to know Clare, Michigan, on the southern edge of Up North, from his investments in oil exploitation there beginning in about 1929. In short, bankrolling a casino in a resort area would not be an outrageous or particularly original idea for a Detroit gangster with cash to invest. It is perfectly logical, therefore, that Abe would have thought about setting up a henchman, Gerhart, at a gambling club Up North.

Another possible gangster connection involves a man whom the press claimed to be Abe's cousin, Sam "Fatty" Bernstein. A long list of newspaper stories from the 1920s to the 1940s associate Sam with various criminal activities of the Purple Gang. He is most often mentioned

Sam "Fatty" Bernstein wanted poster (above)
and working with Al Gerhart at the Club Manitou (below)

regarding murders, robbery, and running a gambling operation.[306] His experience as a speakeasy operator would fit perfectly with Al Gerhart's employment requirements. His heft might also have been useful in case of any disturbance at the club. The only caveat must be that Gerhart denied deep Purple Gang involvement. He enjoyed the thrill he gave to people when he told them he had been involved with the Purple Gang, but insisted he had had only an insignificant, non-violent role. But apparently, he also provided employment for one of his fellow gangsters.

It is clear that Gerhart himself was involved with bootlegging. His rap sheet and unsubstantiated accusation of murder indicate that he was an active gangster. Whether he was with the Purple Gang is another question—for there is no evidence except Gerhart's own words, and the word "chauffeur" seems to have been intended to distance him from the gang's illegal activities. What is also missing from his life story is direct evidence of knowledge either of constructing a gambling establishment or of running one. His father worked as a designer in a hardware store in Reading, Pennsylvania, and so there is some chance that as a young man he was exposed to building operations. It is also likely that he, like so many other gangsters, combined a mania for gambling with their outlawry. There were plenty of gambling houses, some very substantial, in Detroit and surrounding areas to provide evidence on how these places were run. But that is about as far as facts and conjecture can take us. If it is true that Abe Bernstein was the investor behind Club Manitou, then he saw in Gerhart both a trustworthy front man and one who could get things organized and done at a casino. If untrue, then either there were unknown backers, or Gerhart had accumulated a fair amount of cash as a gangster. In either case, it is uncertain where Gerhart got the expertise to build and operate a quite sophisticated gambling speakeasy.

Up North, Al was known as "Slim" because of his lanky stature. The club he created was always referred to by locals not as Club Manitou, but as "Slim's".[307] He got to know and was known by many people in the Petoskey-Harbor Springs area during his long residence there. But according to those who knew him, even well, he did not talk much about his origins or where he got the money to build his club. While running the Club Manitou, Gerhart continued his gangster ways. As one story goes, he wanted some landscaping for his club. The result was armed shrubbery theft gone bad. In late summer 1934, he raided the

Charlevoix County nursery in Ironton. Surprised in the act, he shot at James Wilson, the nursery's caretaker, but missed.[308] Tried and convicted on a charge of felonious assault that September, he was sentenced to eighteen months to ten years in prison and a $2,000 fine.[309] Out on a $1,000 bond, Gerhart appealed. His sentence was finally reduced a year later to nine months to four years in state prison.[310]

But shrubbery? The Charlevoix County nursery at Ironton is just a dozen miles across Lake Charlevoix by ferry from Petoskey. As the *Lansing State Journal* reported, it is much more likely that Gerhart got involved in a bootlegging scheme gone bad and tried to shoot his way out of it.[311]

Or was his outing to the shrubbery somehow part of a counterfeiting scheme? Over the previous four years, $25,000 in bogus $5 bills went into circulation around the state. The cash was counterfeited in Toledo and distributed in Michigan and elsewhere.[312] In mid-January 1935, the Treasury Department's Secret Service arrested Gerhart, Fred Herrick, Ethel Warning, and two other people in a coordinated raid in Detroit. Trapped in their hotel room by agents, Herrick tried to bar the door while Gerhart threw $2,000 in counterfeit bills in packages out the window.[313] Ethel Warning was a well-known jazz singer at the time; she had performed at the Club Manitou. Allegedly, she was the brains of the operation, working with a major counterfeiting ring in New York City.[314] Fred Herrick was a small-time bootlegger from Muskegon who was then living in Harbor Springs.[315] Gerhart and the others pled not guilty to the charges. Apparently, they were not convicted, for there is no indication that Gerhart served time in prison for any but the felonious assault charge in the shrubbery caper.

Gerhart did serve time on that charge. Convicted in October 1935, an FBI report from 1936 stated that the Club Manitou was operated by Gerhart "until the close of the 1935 season" but goes on to state that, "Gerhart is now serving time in the Jackson, Michigan, Penitentiary, yet still owns this place [the Manitou] and intends to open for the 1936 summer season when he is due to be released."[316] So, it seems that Gerhart served his nine months, the minimum possible according to his sentencing.

When Gerhart came back on the scene, he did, indeed, continue to operate the Manitou. Its rival, the Ramona Park Casino, discussed above, fell on hard times during these last years of the 1930s. It probably closed around 1939, and although it reopened under new management in 1942, it did not survive. Meanwhile, Al was branching out from the Manitou. In the mid-1940s he purchased Booth's Bar on the shore of Lake Michigan. The bar was a ratty place at the time. Al rechristened it "Al's at The Pier" and staged a grand re-opening early in 1947.[317] That same year he purchased the now closed Ramona Park Casino. Dismantling that site, he used some materials in his expansion of Al's at the Pier and sold everything else at auction in August 1947. That same month, the Michigan State Police, operating in tandem with the Michigan State Liquor Control Commission, attempted to raid the Manitou. Gerhart blocked entry on the grounds that the authorities could produce no search warrant. Nonetheless, Gerhart was cited for operating a gambling establishment and, for good measure, for failure to cooperate with the State Police.[318] In the end, it all came to nothing. Liquor Control Commission undercover investigators subsequently visited the club once again. One agent even fruitlessly asked Gerhart to allow him to gamble. Gerhart told him, "Nobody gets in here unless I know him."[319] Investigators had to report to the Commission that, "they were unable to find evidence of gambling at the Club Manitou." All charges were dropped.

Gerhart stayed out of trouble with the law until 1965 when we find him on trial in West Virginia. The prosecutor accused him of "interstate travelling and use of mails to carry on unlawful gambling at the Colonial Club, White Sulphur Springs," West Virginia.[30] He beat that rap, too.

Friends' recollections of Al Gerhart are uniformly positive. Neighbors and good friends Emery and Helen Chase knew him for about ten years before his death. According to the Chases, he was a good neighbor to them in their cabin on Crooked Lake. "We were on the phone every day. We'd go out for lunch or dinner together and help each other out," Mrs. Chase recalled.[321] Another neighbor late in Gerhart's life was Jack Feldmann. Feldmann averred that, "With Al, a handshake was

Al and Jean Gerhart and lawyer Al's attorney, Tom Washburne

as important as a signed contract. His word was as good as his bond. I thought he was a neat guy, a good friend." Mr. and Mrs. Tom Washburne of Petoskey had a story about Gerhart's generosity. They told of how "when they were married in 1950, Gerhart summoned them out to the club to give them their wedding gift: $100 in travelers checks (about $1,000 today). "One hundred dollars!" Tom's wife, Betty, remembered. "That was an unheard-of amount in those days." Then Gerhart asked them where they were going on their honeymoon. When they mentioned southern Indiana, Gerhart gave them the name of a friend of his who operated a similar club in French Lick. "When we got there, the friend wouldn't let us pay for a thing the whole time we were there," Betty recalled.

Gerhart was a great storyteller and loved to regale anyone who was listening with stories about how he hosted the rich and famous at his joints in Petoskey and White Sulphur Springs, West Virginia. He bandied about the names of Bob Hope, Monaco's Prince Rainier, Sonja Henie, and Ed Sullivan, although it is unclear if any of these really had come to his club in Petoskey. Another story has it that when he caught a bartender skimming cash, he rewarded him not with dismissal, but with a pocketless suit. A third has to do with a different bartender. When Gerhart hired a man from Saginaw and put him to work, "What do you do on Sundays here?" the bartender asked.

"The same as you do on Saturday," Gerhart replied.

"But you can't serve on Sunday," the bartender protested.

Gerhart paused: "Well, don't sell to anyone with a badge."

Yet another story told of switched Cadillacs. One night in the parking lot of the club the attendants got confused and gave one of two identical Cadillacs to the wrong owner. As the club closed the denizens started to leave. One owner drove off with the other's Cadillac. Chagrined and concerned, Al set everything aside to look for the mistakenly taken vehicle. All night he searched and finally, with the help of the local telephone operators, located the errant Cadillac at a local hotel on Walloon Lake. The hotel's owner, Lawrence Thomas, stole into the driver's room. He quietly retrieved the car keys on the bureau and replaced them with the driver's own Cadillac keys. He then gave the keys to Al, and Al in turn got the Cadillac to its rightful owner. A final tale revolves around young adults frequenting the club. Parents (who probably also paid visits at times) were concerned that their children might come to no good while visiting the club. So as the kids went out, a parent would call Al and ask him to expect their offspring and keep them out of trouble. Al obliged. He let the youths gamble a bit, watched them lose, but not too much, and then he intervened. He told that once one youth came up to him and said, "I'm going to win a vicuna coat for my girl." Al retorted, "I'm buying my wife a vicuna coat and there can't be two vicuna coats in town."[322]

The Club Manitou was located at the corner of Michigan Highway 119 and Pleasantville Road about halfway between Harbor Springs and

Club Manitou interior, l.-r., bandstand, dance floor, dining area

Petoskey. The speakeasy was in the lower level, entered from the outside through a locked and guarded entrance way. One account said that this entrance was outfitted with one steel bar door, two three-quarter-inch steel plate doors, at least four five-inch steel reinforced concrete doors and one four-inch steel reinforced concrete door that was six feet high and nine feet wide.[323] The walls were four feet thick. Inside, it had all the trappings of a night club. There was a dance floor, a lounge, a full bar, and a stage for bands and entertainment. The basement had no windows. To provide a semblance of sun-bright gayety, light bulbs burned behind false windows along the walls. Above the windows, spear-supported awnings and, below, flower boxes added to the desired airy aspect of the room. "Also, the South side to the club had a wall that they could move back and forth to make the club look full, even when there were not many people there. On nights when the crowd was small, they would move the wall forward, so instead of people sitting at twenty tables, while sixty tables were empty, they would move the wall forward so that twenty people were sitting at tables and only four tables were empty. If, as the night went on, they needed more tables, they would simply move the wall back a little which would give more room for additional tables."[324] These moving walls allowed the area to accommodate up to two hundred and fifty people on a Saturday night. The bandstand had a fancy curtain. Bruce Snoap, a keyboard player for the Kingtones, a group that later played the location reincarnated as the Ponytail Club, recalled, "[Club Manitou] also had red, expensive curtains across the stage. I think I might still have one. They were in the back room of the Club Ponytail. I needed some kind of cloth to cover the back of my organ. The owner of the Club Ponytail at that time told me I could have one to cover the back of my organ."[325] There

The kitchen of the Club Manitou

were mirrors lining the rear of the stage, to make it seem bigger and brighter. Two fireplaces in the center of the area provided warmth if needed. A local citizen, Floyd Hoover, each day brought five large bouquets of fresh flowers to decorate the bar and adjoining area. Off to one side, the kitchen provided food for both the speakeasy/casino and the dining room.

The dining room was on the main floor. It occupied the entire space. There were two large fireplaces beside a central chimney that kept the chill out of the room as needed. The second story had four good-sized bedrooms; these were available for rental by the club's employees. The original layout could accommodate two hundred fifty to three hundred fifty persons in the basement and dining rooms combined. As the club was out in the country, habitués came by car, either their own or a cab. Three men worked the car parking area; one washed the owner's car while he was enjoying himself at the club.

The Manitou had no central heating or cooling. The fireplaces provided some warmth, but the place was closed during the coldest times of the year. There were windows and large ventilation shafts located throughout the building. These allowed air to circulate, especially in the lower level, the speakeasy. The shafts were large enough in diameter to allow a person to crawl through. This led to myths about them being tunnel escape routes. Such legends now abound. One rapid-escape tunnel supposedly led from the club to the parking lot, another went under a highway to the local airstrip. The most unlikely tunnel is the one that rumors say led downhill from the Club Manitou to another gambling house, the Ramona Park Casino. Neither this, nor any other tunnel, was constructed to provide an escape route during a raid. Gerhart himself denied there were ever any tunnels in the original building—just a later one to connect the original structure and a newly built addition. He said that the tunnels often mentioned were really related to the functioning of the kitchen and dining areas. That jibes with the mythologizing of ventilation tubing into escape tunneling.

Gerhart's goal was to have the club ready for the 1929 tourist season. Sure enough, the Fourth of July that year had more than patriotic meaning for resorters of the Petoskey/Harbor Springs area as the club opened on that day.

Club Manitou did not advertise. Everything was by word of mouth. While it was easy to access the upper, main level where the dining room was, Gerhart was careful about the speakeasy basement. No one was admitted through the locked door unless approved by Paul Pepper, the trusted manager, or by Gerhart himself.[326] Once approved, however, repeat visiting was easy. Gerhart said, "We weren't interested in anyone unless they were introduced by a friend...Our customers came from Harbor Springs, Wequetonsing, Roaring Brook, Menonaqua, Charlevoix, and the Chicago Club [in Charlevoix]."[327] The clientele was not

Three Manitou patrons. Paul Pepper is on the right. Note the monumental fireplace and the slot machine in the background.

Manitou waitstaff

exclusively the high rollers that the nearby Ramona Park Casino catered to, although of course they were welcome. The 1936 FBI report stated that, "this club caters to the more lower type of gamblers although the club itself is very elaborate..." Gerhart noted, "Our customers were strictly 'pleasure players,' not hard gamblers. For them, gambling was simply a part of the frivolity of the evening.[328]

The dining room on the first level provided excellent service. There was a chef and a sous-chef, both from the Vatel Club in New York City. Patrons were expected to be well dressed—men in coats and ties. The servers were all males. The menu tended toward Midwest heavy with lobster and steak, sometimes together as one dish. Every Thursday the Consolidated Lobster Company of Gloucester, Massachusetts sent four or five barrels of live lobsters for Friday's menu. The French chefs created vichyssoise with fresh cream from the local Bud Parker's creamery.

Dancing was accommodated on the lower level in the speakeasy area. High quality liquor was available both in the speakeasy downstairs and in the dining room. One account has it that in the dining room, liquor was served in teapots and tea cups during Prohibition. By another account, it was served in one-and-a-half ounce cruets along with a bowl of ice (the club had its own ice house) and a small bottle of mix; perhaps this was after Prohibition ended. The bar featured Dewar's Scotch, eight-year-old White Label; there was in addition a selection of four twelve-year-old Scotches, each bottle color coded to a corresponding cruet. Wine was also on hand.

A variety of games was on offer at Club Manitou. Besides the ubiquitous slot machines, there was a table for shooting craps, one chuck-a-luck birdcage, two blackjack tables, and three roulette wheels. Bingo nights happened irregularly to help drum up business.

Larry Knapp visited in 1933 and left a firsthand account of his visit. He was invited along with Bert Kane, a purveyor of slot machines in mid-Michigan, and Clare oilman and money-launderer-for-the-Purple-Gang Charlie Strange on their road trip to Mackinac Island. They stopped at the Club Manitou on the way.

> Along with Mr. Kane was an oilman from Clare by the name of Charlie Strange who had a lot of holdings in the Porter [oil] fields east of Shepherd, Michigan. Later turned out to be a good friend, too. And when we got to Clare it was decided that as long as they were going to Mackinac Island the next day, I would go along with them. On the way north, we stopped at Al & Jean Gearhart's Manitou Club Lodge at Harbor Springs, Michigan, which was underground, and had my first side-car cocktail. The steps down the cellar were wired so they could tell how close you were, and the whole door was a one-way looking glass, so they could see from inside who was knocking.[32]

Gerhart enforced various efforts to guard against disastrous raids. As noted, persons without established credentials with Gerhart and Pepper had to be personally approved by one of them before admittance. Larry Knapp recalled that the entrance to the speakeasy was wired so the doorman could tell when someone was coming; the club door itself was a one-way mirror.[330] Indeed, there were numerous raids. For example, the State Police raided the place in 1938.[331] When that

Paul Pepper

happened, the gambling equipment and setups were quickly burned (there was an incinerator on site). Gerhart told a reporter, "You would burn the layouts. Aw hell, you could dispose of almost anything."[332]

Measures to protect valuable property as well as owners and patrons from raids were quite ineffective, in fact. If the police wanted to raid, they could easily figure out the hiding places of the slots, roulette wheels, and other gambling paraphernalia in back rooms or behind false walls. Similarly, the liquor could not all be destroyed before the law seized possession of the raided building. The surest safeguard was the one all such places preferred: bribing local officials to lay off enforcement of the liquor and gambling laws. Of the raids we know about now, all were conducted by the State Police, not by the local sheriff. Petoskey mayors Norman M. Risk (1929-1932), D. Charles Levinson (1932-1935), and Buell H. Van Leuven (1935-1940) presumably all knew of the illegal liquor (until late 1933) and gambling going on, but Club Manitou was in the county, not in Petoskey or Harbor Springs. Thomas Bryant, sheriff (1931-1941) of Emmet County, who would have jurisdiction, must have had an incentive from Gerhart not to interfere with the club—certainly, he never did interfere, although it must have been obvious what was going on. An FBI file from 1936 certainly suggests as much. In that report Special Agent W. J. Wyn states that local protection explained

Gerhart as philanthropist—Alanson, Michigan, park

the survival of clubs like the Manitou "because Sheriff Bryant has the reputation of protecting the criminal element, particularly the powerful gamblers of the Petoskey area, and is no doubt receiving some remuneration in that connection."[333]

After the demise of the Ramona Park Casino, Manitou's competitor in the gambling trade of the area, the Manitou was the only game in town. It remained prosperous into the late 1940s, surviving raids and the economic downturn of the World War II years. However, the State of Michigan got serious about gambling toward the end of that decade.[334] Increasing pressure from state law enforcement culminated in the revocation of the club's liquor license in 1952. That spelled the end. The club closed and Gerhart in 1961 sold the property to Stan and Jean Douglas who the next year reopened the place as a rock and roll venue called The Ponytail, or just "Tail," as it was known locally.[335] The club remained a hot spot for national and local acts until closing in 1969. Gerhart moved on to purchase and run the Colonial Club in White Sulphur Springs, West Virginia. There he prospered until an FBI raid in 1963 shut that operation as well. Gerhart packed his bags once again and returned to Michigan. He took up the role of a fine citizen, even donating land to a local community for a park. He lived in a cottage on Crooked Lake until his death in 1987.

Ramona Park Casino near Harbor Springs

Jimmy Hayes' Ramona Park Casino between Harbor Springs and Petoskey receives full attention in the chapter, "Toledans at the Beach."

Colonial Club of Charlevoix

Charlevoix lay about 20 miles to the southwest of Petoskey/Harbor Springs. Like the towns around Little Traverse Bay, the Charlevoix area had been a magnet for wealthy resorters since the later nineteenth century. Rail and lake travel made it easy to come for the season from Chicago and as far away as St. Louis and Cincinnati. Since gambling was always a pleasant pastime for these visitors, venues sprang up that were of a higher class than the rough saloons. John Koch, the founder of the Colonial Club, saw an opportunity and grasped it.

Koch, born in 1864, had started his career as a parlor car gambler. He rode the long-distance trains and kept the passengers amused by dealing poker, casino pinochle, or whatever was their pleasure. He himself later claimed that he had been the self-appointed social director of the Santa Fe, New York Central, Pennsylvania, and Florida East Coast railroads.[336] Eventually, he married and settled in Toledo. By 1910 the U.S. Census reported that he was "living on his own income"—income evidently from running gambling operations since in a 1914 newspaper article, John Koch is described as "a Toledo product" who several years before had operated his elaborate gambling establishment in that city. Even then, he was living part of the year Up North on Little Traverse Bay where, a few years before 1914, he had operated "a club house with roulette wheel attachments at Petoskey, Michigan." He also wintered in Florida. From there he executed a business plan to run a resort in the Miami area for winter guests and in northern Michigan for

John Koch

Colonial Club, Charlevoix

Colonial Club original entrance

summer guests. In 1916 he set up shop in Charlevoix. "He has catered to the wealth and fashion of the upper lake regions in the summer time, having become regarded as one of the alluring fixtures of that pastiming section."[337]

The Colonial Club as it existed during Prohibition was a fancy place. By that time, there was already a decades-long history of constructing fine buildings Up North in resort areas. Koch purchased property in 1920 and proceeded to create a Colonial Club in that tradition since he catered to the wealthy resorter crowd.[338] The place burned to the ground in 1923 but Koch rebuilt it to be even more elegant.[339] A grand bouquet of red roses greeted guests in a large entrance hall just inside the front doors. A coatroom and attendant were on the right, then a card room with gold brocade wallpaper where card games such as bridge were played at leisure. To the left was the dining and dancing room. Straight ahead was the serious gambling room.[340]

Like the Club Manitou, the Colonial had two distinct areas. There was the dining room where meals and (illegal) drink were served. This was Orestes Gatti's realm—a first-class restaurateur. With his wife, Margareta, at the cash register and his son, Joe, helping to service, he was an imperious maître d'. His long experience made him a true professional in handling customers, chefs, and the help. He used to say, "I don't mind when my customers complain about the prices—but I do mind when they complain about the food!"

Then there was the "green room" next to the dining room—a carpeted place where John Koch oversaw the gambling operation. While Koch owned the place, the only gambling in the green room was at the roulette tables. Women were allowed to gamble, but at the roulette wheel they were limited to 10¢ chips. Later, when a former associate, Marsh Meek, ran the place, a craps table was added. Gambling went on six days a week; none on Sundays. That day, families would come and have dinner at the club. One oddity was that the Colonial had no bar. Alcohol was served in the dining room as desired. You could bring your own, or you could buy it from the house. In the green room, where the gambling took place, no drinks were served, not even a Coke.

Again, as at the Club Manitou, guests were screened. Frank Poole was the doorman. He only allowed in people he knew. Those admitted were almost all summer resorters. They were dressed to the hilt—coats and ties, evening gowns. Local townies did not need to appear—they would be rejected out of hand. There were exceptions—maybe the local doctors and a banker—but the house rules allowed them only to dine—not to gamble.

The wealthy clientele—men and women from St. Louis, Cincinnati, Cleveland, Toledo, Chicago, and Detroit—expected first-class treatment, and they got it. Fancy cars, often driven by chauffeurs, came up to the club's entrance. A doorman ushered guests from the car into the club while a young man drove the car off and kept track, so it could be returned to its owners later in the evening—all without charge or check. Watching over as many as one hundred fifty cars in an evening was a challenge regularly met—and well rewarded, as a valet parking attendant could earn upwards of $200 in a week in tips alone.[341]

Ernest Hemingway gambled at least once at the Colonial. In a 1920 letter to Petoskey friend Edith Quinlan, he wrote that he had been ejected from his family cottage on Walloon Lake and was considering working at a cement factory in Petoskey. Then one night he went down to Charlevoix and put six dollars to work at the roulette table there. He had won $59 when the wheel stopped spinning at 2 a.m. He wrote that the winnings saved him from the cement plant.[342]

Since the club operated only during the summer, notionally from July 4th until Labor Day, there was no permanent staff. The place closed up after the season and made preparations to reopen when the following June rolled around. John Koch and Orestes Gatti returned to Miami Beach where they owned and ran the Palm Island Club, a sister club, during the winter months.[343]

Edith Gilbert states that the club was never raided in the years when John Koch ran it. This man knew the importance of paying off the right people in order to stay out of harm's way. Every season he went down to Detroit and paid off those who might cause him trouble. However, the State Police finally did raid the place in 1947. An eyewitness reported that the troopers just quietly walked in the front door and carried out all the gambling equipment they could find, loading it onto a waiting truck. The people in the dining room just kept on eating— "What else could we have done?" This happened after Koch had handed management over to Marsh Meek. In response to the raid, Koch said, "Meek didn't put out enough or didn't put it in the right place!"[344]

Meek and Gatti were arrested and the state liquor commission revoked the club's liquor license. Without that, profitability proved impossible. The Colonial Club closed and sat abandoned and increasingly dilapidated until finally torn down in the summer of 1974.

Was John Koch involved with gangsters? He always denied this, as would be expected. Unlike Al Gerhart's clear connections with the

Charlevoix Beach Club and Hotel

Detroit underworld, there is scant evidence that Koch played with that crowd. It is true that he sold his Palm Island Club near Miami Beach to a consortium that eventually included Al Capone. The 1936 FBI report on gangsters in the Charlevoix-Petoskey area did allude to gangsters frequenting the Colonial Club. Certainly, Koch dealt with bootleggers of some sort in order to keep his club supplied. But no direct connection to gangsters seems possible.

Elsewhere in Charlevoix there were other opportunities to gamble. The Charlevoix Beach Club and Hotel in town drew the attention of the FBI.[345] They concluded that it was operated by one Arthur Von Dolke (Von Dalke) "and several Jewish gamblers from Detroit and Toledo." This would be a reference to erstwhile Purple Gang members such as Abe Bernstein and probably a mistake of Toledo for the Cleveland Syndicate. Both the Detroit and Cleveland mobs were Jewish operations, and both heavily invested in gambling. According to the FBI, the Beach Club was known as a "rather tough joint." My research on Von Dolke found very little information and failed to identify any involvement with gangsters, however.[346]

Townies also found other places to gamble and drink illegal booze. As in every town, there were nooks and crannies where a knowledgeable person could find both, whether it was a basement of a hotel or store, the back room of a cigar manufacturer, a welcoming private home, or the second-floor club room of some downtown establishment. All these places, as well as even more public ones such as drugstores and hotel lobbies, often had a slot machine or two. They were fairly regularly raided and just as regularly reappeared.

In Charlevoix, there were rumors of stiff competition between purveyors of slot machines—a regular and lucrative operation of gangsters in big cities who extended their franchises, or tried to, into more rural areas. Supposedly, Al Capone's Chicago Outfit sought to supply Charlevoix with slots and Detroit's Purple Gang fought back. In one specific tale, according to a local named Edward Heise, a barber brought some slot machines up from Detroit to install around town. When the Chicago Outfit got word of this, he was informed that he was going to replace those machines with ones from Chicago. The barber saw the light and the Detroit

Grand Hotel, Mackinac Island

slots were seen no more.[347] Illegal booze was supposedly supplied by ship from Chicago or Detroit sources, but local moonshine and local beer, perhaps supplemented with Canadian imports via Lake Michigan, would have been much more likely found at local hangouts.

A grand time at the Grand Hotel

Located on picturesque Mackinac Island nestled snugly in Lake Huron just east of the Straits of Mackinac, the Grand Hotel began and always remained a tourist-driven enterprise. Opened in 1887, its sole purpose was to create a high-class destination to encourage the use of the Michigan Central and Grand Rapids and Indiana railroads, and the Cleveland Steamship Navigation Company to travel to northern Michigan.[348] In this it succeeded admirably at times, abysmally at others. The central strategy was always to offer amenities that wealthy people desired. One of these was gambling.

Gambling before Prohibition

At the Grand Hotel gambling was available but, as at other high-class resort destinations, it was not the main attraction. Wealthy men and, to a lesser extent, women enjoyed roulette, table games, and the newfangled slot machines that began popping up everywhere in the early twentieth century. When the financially troubled hotel went up for sale in 1911, new management was brought in. This failed spectacularly, and the hotel was ready to go under for good. To the rescue came J. Logan Ballard, an entrepreneur from French Lick, Indiana.

The Ballards take over

But first, Logan's brother, Edward. This Ballard rose from very modest beginnings to being one of the major gambling entrepreneurs of the early twentieth century. From running small-time gambling in the back of a tavern in Paoli, Indiana, he moved to French Lick and there steadily advanced his investments. The big hotel owner in town was a man named Lee Sinclair. Sinclair spotted Ballard as a promising gambling impresario. He hired him to run the gambling at one of his new casinos in town. Even a 1906 yellow-journalism hit piece by William Randolph Hearst's newspapers failed to slow down the action.[349] By 1915 Ballard had parlayed his enterprises into controlling the major part of gambling in French Lick resorts. In 1923 he completed his take-over by gaining possession of the jewel in the crown, the West Baden Springs Hotel. His only competition was Tom Taggart's French Lick Springs Hotel that ran an equally illegal series of gambling operations. Taggart was a well-connected Democrat politician while Ballard bought the Republicans. Between the two of them, authorities never bothered to move against the completely illegal gambling that was thriving in the Springs Valley area.

Edward Ballard brought a younger brother, J. Logan, into the business. There already was some connection with Mackinac Island as the third brother, Joseph, listed his occupation on his World War I draft card as boatman at Mackinac Island.[350] In 1918 J. Logan bought the Grand Hotel. This was a perfect fit for the grand hotels of French Lick: the clientele was the same class of the rich; the outfitting of the hotel was sumptuous, if a bit down-at-the-heels after several financially unsuccessful years. The season meshed well with French Lick, where high season was September into late fall; on Mackinac Island the eight-week season ran July through August.

Although there had always been gambling at the Grand Hotel, Ballard took it to a new level. But he lacked the most important element in the success at French Lick: suborned public officials. While the local officials, such as they were, on Mackinac Island easily tolerated the gambling because it was just part of being a tourist destination, state officialdom was not as bribable as Indiana officials were.

In 1919, on orders of Michigan Attorney General Alex J. Groesbeck, the Michigan State Police raided the "beautiful Monte Carlo of the north" on August 27th, late in the tourist season.[351]

When the police burst in through wide-open doors,

A chuck-a-luck "bird cage" in action

between three hundred and four hundred patrons, "the best dressed and richest assembly of people in the central north," were gambling at roulette wheels and chuck-a-luck. Large sums, as high as $5,000 a turn, were being placed on the five wheels operating. Ivory chips passed from hand to green felt, some in denominations of $1,000. Authorities seized about $8,000 in play at the time of the raid as well as $30,000 worth of gambling equipment. That was a huge haul amounting to about half a million dollars in today's purchasing power.[352] Those arrested included Logan Ballard.

The raid clearly revealed the gambling connection between the Grand Hotel and French Lick. Police arrested W.W. Dale of West Baden, a near neighbor to French Lick, E. C. Wood of Detroit about whom nothing further is known, and J.W. Goodmore of Denver. These were presumably the pit men and dealers. All three worked for Fred "Red" Tully "of French Lick," who was also arrested. Police alleged that Tully owned the gambling equipment and oversaw the Grand's gambling rooms. The men working the gambling at the Grand had come up from French Lick for the season. Tully was a fixture at French Lick and had been involved as an accused in Indiana's investigation of gambling in 1910.[353]

What of the patrons? The State Police apprehended none. Sheriff Robert Benjamin of Mackinac County made no further arrests. He understood that everyone on the island favored the continuance of gambling since it was a central aspect of tourist appeal, and tourism was the life-blood of the island. As for the local mayor, W. D. Chambers, he was put out not because of the gambling on his watch, but because he had been exposed as a non-enforcer of anti-gambling laws.[354] As a final act, the State Police announced a ban on gambling on Mackinac Island.[355]

Prohibition Days

One might think that losing $30,000 in equipment would slow the gambling down a bit, but it was simply too important to be allowed to lie dormant. Too much of the hotel's appeal to the wealthy depended on the availability of gaming for those who chose to gamble. Employees kept an eye and ear out for indications that a patron might enjoy a bit of action. Once identified, they were let in on the "secret." But, the presence of gambling did not escape the authorities' notice. During a 1920 state-wide action to prosecute gamblers, the State Police first cased the joint, then sent in a squad of five men, dressed in plain clothes as regular customers, to enter the ballroom that was the casino. As dancers made their way toward the casino, the officers followed them. Then, in a loud voice, Captain A. A. Downing announced to the startled crowd that he was closing the place. Some women screamed, others wept—but they needn't have, for in the end, no patron was charged. The police arrested Logan Ballard, C. J. Holden, the hotel manager, and two employees, Harry Howard and Albert Jackson. Each was fined $100 by a justice of the peace and let go. Once again, the valuable gambling equipment worth thousands of dollars was seized—certainly that was the harsher punishment.[356]

In 1921 there was yet another spectacular assault on the Grand Hotel's flagrant breeching of gambling laws. Once again, the authorities swooped down at the very end of the season. On August 28, 1921 a raid conducted by State Police Captain Ira H. Marmon netted $15,000 in illegal equipment. This time a bit of subterfuge was necessary: Marmon first spent time at the hotel as a guest. Acquiring a meal ticket, he used this as a pass to access the gambling room. The room was on the second floor of the hotel, reached by first passing through an ordinary hotel room then into a passageway that led to a sumptuously furnished room about twenty feet by sixty feet. There he came upon men and women, finely dressed, playing at roulette wheels, dice, and card games. The chips were $1,000 each. Retreating to the main lobby of the hotel, Marmon called in state troopers from the Marquette/Negaunee post. The jig was up, but even so Murray S. Clark, the hotel manager, did his best to give his men time to destroy evidence by blocking the entrance door. Pushing him aside, the police rushed in, only to find that the gambling equipment had disappeared! Interrogation of an elevator boy led the police to the basement of the hotel where the equipment was found under a pile of mattresses. As Marmon commented, "The equipment we confiscated is about as elaborate as can be purchased. The wheels are of beautiful inlaid work and are mounted with ball-bearings. They are valued at about $900 each. The large tables are handsomely built and covered with heavy green cloth like that used on billiard tables. Even the ivory chips have inlaid designs and little balls of solid ivory were used on the roulette wheels."

The loss of equipment was important— it was taken to Lansing to be burned—but what of the patrons and the people running the operation? No gamblers were charged. Manager Clark was fined $250 plus $5 court costs— that was it. The take from the gambling must have been very significant just to cover the cost of confiscated equipment in the three successive raids.[357]

W. Stewart Woodfill

All these raids occurred while Logan Ballard was managing the Grand Hotel. Before the 1923 season could begin, Ballard was suddenly stricken with a severe illness and died in Bay City even before his wife could reach his side from Chicago. What would happen to the Grand?

Before his death, Logan Ballard had hired William Stewart Woodfill (1896-1984) to manage the hotel. Woodfill had come to the hotel in 1919 as a lowly desk clerk but caught Ballard's eye because of his efficiency and intense dedication to the hotel. In a move that caught everyone by surprise, including Woodfill, Ballard appointed him manager.

Woodfill would be the main person at the Grand for many years to come. But first, he had to gain control of the hotel. Determined to do this, he tracked down Edward Ballard, Logan's older brother, who controlled Logan's estate as a trustee. We have met Edward Ballard before as he rose to prominence in French Lick and West Baden, Indiana. Subsequently, he had expanded his gambling holdings appreciably. Himself a gambling addict, he had a good sense of how to attract fellow gamblers to his establishments in a wide array of locations—New Orleans, Hot Springs, Santa Barbara, and Miami Beach. He had opened the Palm Island Club in 1922 to cater to wealthy individuals who were wintering over in Miami Beach.[358] This is the same club that John Koch invested in as well. For Koch it represented the winter appeal while his Colonial Club in Charlevoix represented the summer appeal. The recent series of raids on the Grand probably put Ballard off, as he was accustomed to operating his gambling locales where he could bribe local authorities into quiescence. Nonetheless, when Woodfill made an offer to manage the hotel, Ballard accepted it. For good measure, Woodfill also brought in Edward's brother, Joseph, who was both an inveterate gambler like his brother and familiar with Mackinac Island and the Grand. Supposedly Woodfill promised Joseph a gambling club at the Grand.

The drama continued to unfold after Joseph died in 1930 and the hotel stumbled along during the early years of the Great Depression. Finally, in 1933, the hotel had to be put up at auction. Woodfill fulfilled his decade-long dream: he bought the hotel outright.

Throughout this period, gambling continued apace at the hotel. Professional operators could buy a gambling concession at the Grand Hotel for a reputed $15,000 fee.[359] In 1926, probably at the inspiration of Joseph Ballard, the hotel company had remodeled its casino by creating the Egyptian Room as an elegant place for gambling. Inspired by the discovery of King Tutankhamen's spectacular grave in 1922, the Egyptian Room aped the decor of similar rooms in other fancy hotels around the country.

Gambling and imbibing alcohol have had a long, probably perpetual friendship. Saloons in those days always had a card game and slot machines going. It certainly was not lost on fancy resort hotels that serving liquor enhanced the patron's experience and the house's take.[360] At the Grand, alcohol was ridiculously easy to obtain during Prohibition (1920-1933). The island lies thirty or so miles from Canada by various routes across the St. Marys River or via Lake Huron. It was perfectly legal to export liquor from Canada even during the years up to 1927 when Ontario had its own prohibition law in force. Swarms of bootleggers took up the business as Willis John McQuarrie colorfully documents in his little book, *Whisky Smugglers of the North Channel*.[361] Besides the favorite rum-running route across Lake Huron from Cock burn and Manitoulin Island, the St. Marys River border between Canada and Michigan provided virtually limitless possibilities for smuggling. The Coast Guard tried valiantly to thwart all this action, but it was hopeless—there were just too many easy (and not so easy) ways to get the booze across the border to the United States' side of the Sault, down to Cheboygan, directly through the Straits destined for the resorts of Harbor Springs and Charlevoix, or even on to Detroit (via Lake Huron) and Chicago (via Lake Michigan). The profits of smuggling could be huge. A tug bound for Detroit seized by the Coast Guard off Mackinac Island in May 1928 held four thousand cases of liquor worth $240,000—three and a half million dollars today.[362]

Few on Mackinac Island cared a whit about the Volstead Act. Or if they did, they kept quiet about it. Even with its small resident population, there were speakeasies. There was also a distillery in Harrisonville that supplied cheap hooch for tourists and locals alike. Some shops on the island openly sold the local stuff.[363] Visitors took full advantage, even, apparently, Michigan governor Fred W. Green (1927-1931). In 1927 he hosted the National Governors' Conference at the Grand. Later in the year E. A. Nowak, editor of the *Michigan State Digest* journal, sued to force the Michigan attorney general to release the expense sheets for the conference. The case went all the way to the Michigan Supreme Court, which ruled in Nowak's favor. The expenses revealed that a significant portion of the $25,000 appropriated by the legislature to pay for the national conference had gone to buy liquor. One story had O. G. Olander, the head of the Michigan State Police, unwrapping the bottles personally. Some state officials turned in bar bills for reimbursement by the State.[364] Clearer evidence of the futility of the Volstead Act would be hard to find.

At the Grand, discretion reigned. Of course, any patron could bring in his or her own stash and drink it in a suite or even, discretely, on the front six-hundred-plus foot verandah. House-supplied drink could be provided in the restaurant, but this, too, was done discretely. Not so discretely in the gambling rooms, however. Alcohol was a necessity. There the liquor flowed openly.

Were gangsters involved in the bootlegging and gambling?

The question must be asked, "Did big-city gangsters play a role?" There is no doubt that alcohol in some quantity moved from Ontario into northern Michigan. But southern Michigan was where the real action was. In the Detroit area, gangsters, most notably the Purple Gang, fed the nation's thirst for quality liquor from across the Detroit River. As for Chicago, direct access to Canadian goods through Detroit rum-runners and thence by rail or truck to Chicago proved a much more efficient and faster source than directly down from northern Ontario. Certainly, the Grand got its quality hooch directly from nearby Canada, supplemented by local moonshine and beer brewed on the spot. But in this case not big-time gangsters, but rather local entrepreneurial men with fast boats and a little daring provided the Grand's supply of liquor.

The end of Prohibition late in 1933 eliminated the need for bootlegging but did not have much effect on gambling at the Grand Hotel. The wide-open illegal gambling at northern Michigan resorts now also had to deal with problems with the Michigan Liquor Control Commission, the entity set up by the state to oversee the sale of alcohol after Prohibition through state liquor stores and the licensing of outlets. The dual issues of gambling and bootlegging led to the Michigan House of Representatives establishing a special sub-committee to investigate both.

In 1937 the House committee investigated state and county officers "involved in the protection of gambling." This broad brush touched the State Police and the state's attorney general, as well as local officials. State Representatives John Hamilton, Chester B. Fitzgerald, and Carl F. Delano formed an investigating team that had subpoena power. One of its actions was to shut down gambling on Mackinac Island—on August 26, late in the tourist season, as usual.[365] But, as had occurred every other time, the gambling reopened right on schedule for the 1938 season.

Former Michigan governor Chase Osborn (1911-1913) responded to Delano's charges of lax law enforcement. He said that he had been well aware of gambling on the island while he was governor but decided that he did not have the police resources to stop it, so it went unhindered. Much later, in 1938, Osborn despaired of ever controlling gambling on the island. In a letter he wrote, "Nothing can stop gambling at the Mackinac Island and other such places except absolute prohibition carried into effect by an armed guard of either State Police or military. Even then one would have to be watchful, that the men were not bribed."[366] The year before, Oscar G. Olander, State Police Commissioner, admitted that he was helpless to stop the gambling.[367]

As we come to the chronological limits of this account, gambling was a bedrock activity at the Grand. And it remained so, despite the disingenuous protests to the contrary by Woodfill. The hotel needed the income and the guests wanted the service. Gambling continued, sold as a concession to the highest bidder. It was not until many years later that Woodfill begrudgingly admitted as much when he said that there was gambling "at one time" for "gentlemen who could afford to lose."[368]

How, exactly, did the gambling work? The same query could be put to the operation of the Colonial Club at Charlevoix or the Ramona

Park Casino in Harbor Springs. The Grand openly sold the concession to professional operators. John Koch at the Colonial Club moved his equipment from Charlevoix to Miami Beach and back again each year; the concessionaires at the Grand did the same thing, alternating with French Lick casinos. As I have pointed out, the equipment was very expensive, especially the high-quality roulette wheels. The return on the gambling was substantial. Was gangster money involved?

Gangsters such as Abe Bernstein (Purple Gang), Al Capone (Chicago Outfit), Moe Dalitz (Cleveland Syndicate), Abner "Longy" Zwillman of the New Jersey mob, and others all invested heavily in gambling operations. These investments can be documented across the country in New York State, Arkansas, Florida, California, and Nevada as well as abroad in the Bahamas and Cuba. Almost always the gangsters were silent partners. It took investigations by authorities to reveal the money behind many operations. Out front were the gambling impresarios, the men who ran the gambling locales. In Michigan, men like the Wertheimer brothers, Ruby Mathis, Sam Garfield, and many others, mostly based in Detroit, ran the businesses. They seemed to run on their own money, but probably many if not all had investors from the hoodlum world. While Logan and Edward Ballard were running their numerous operations at French Lick and elsewhere, and while John Koch had luxury establishments in Florida and Michigan, they all denied any gangster connection. In theory, that could be true; once established, a gambling empire could generate a lot of cash, legal and otherwise. But next to prostitution and bootlegging, gambling was the most profitable enterprise for the underworld. Not for nothing did Al Capone buy a 25% stake in the Palm Island Club in Miami Beach, a club started by Edward Ballard and later managed by John Koch. After Prohibition ended, gambling became the most profitable underworld enterprise. In Michigan, Abe Bernstein helped, at the very least, to finance the Club Manitou in Harbor Springs, while Detroit and Toledo gangster money was behind the Ramona Park Casino. Was the Grand Hotel immune? No gangster name is ever mentioned in its history. That does not mean that gangster money did not lurk behind the long-lasting and lucrative gambling that went on at the Grand for decades.[369]

Wertheimer brothers, l.-r., Mert, Lou, Al, and Lionel

The Wertheimers of Cheboygan

One family of racketeers actually hales from Up North, the Wertheimers of Cheboygan.[370] Originally from Hungary, the patriarch, Isaac Wertheimer (1815-1890), immigrated to America. He and his wife, Laura, lived in Detroit by 1856. This Jewish family always considered Detroit as their home base since the parents and later many descendants lived there. Isaac was a merchant who had retired by the 1870s.[371] His descendants, both male and female, followed in his footsteps, engaging in merchandise manufacture and sales, mostly of clothing. Isaac's sons had stores in Detroit, Bay City, Fort Wayne, Cincinnati, Lawrenceburgh (Indiana), and Danville (Illinois). Two, Joseph (1847-1914) and John (1853-1897), came north to Cheboygan.

After opening the Wertheimer & Company corset factory in Detroit in 1879 Joseph sold it and moved to Cheboygan around 1882. He built the Wertheimer Block and opened a "clothing and gents' furnishing store" called the Star Clothing Company.[372] At the same time his wife, Minnie, continued to manage a store in Detroit that sold knit goods, clothing, corsets, and bustles.[373] Joseph's brother, John, joined him Up North. He had married Yetta (Henrietta) Epstein whose family was also in the retail clothing business. The two men seem to have run a second clothing store in town, the Wertheimer Brothers "one price clothes" store.[374]

John and Yetta had four sons, Myrton (Merton), Alfred, Louis, and Lionel. At John's death in 1897, the oldest, Mert, took over his father's clothing business in Cheboygan in partnership with his mother, Yetta. He was still in Cheboygan in 1914, but Mert and his mother sold all

Downtown Cheboygan about 1910. Wertheimer stores are on the corner.

their Cheboygan assets in 1915. Mert then moved to Detroit with his wife. There, he remained in the clothing business operating two different establishments on Woodward Avenue with one of his brothers, Al. Then they branched out. In 1919 they purchased the Grand River Athletic Club on Grand River. Athletic Clubs were well known as places where betting and gambling took place.

Before coming to Detroit, Al Wertheimer worked in the family clothing stores and, on the side, was running the Model Billiard place in Cheboygan. Pool was a popular male pastime. Pool tables could be in restaurants, saloons, tobacco stores, or in stand-alone halls. In Cheboygan in 1907 there were at least five such; in 1910 ten establishments advertised the availability of pool on the premises.[375] In and of itself, pool was not illegal in Michigan. However, wagering on pool was illegal, as were other forms of gambling. Thus, at least on the books, Al's Model Pool Room was completely legal. However, the gambling that certainly transpired was decidedly not legal. It is highly likely that Al got his start in the gambling industry by acquiring the New Cheboygan Billiard and Pool Hall in 1907, renovating it, and opening the Model Billiard and Bowling Parlor in 1908; later it was called simply the Model Pool

Room. It was a state-of-the-art place with automatic pin setters for bowlers and, in the pool hall, undoubtedly gambling for many patrons. A suspicious fire destroyed the building and a good deal of downtown Cheboygan in 1911.

Al went down to Detroit where, the next year, he was working as a clerk in a clothing store. After a stint in Wichita, Kansas, managing a New York City-based store, he came back to Detroit by the spring of 1917. During 1919, he ran two tailor shops with his brother, Mert.[376]

The third brother, Lionel, like his brothers, at first worked in the family clothing business in Cheboygan. Unlike his brothers, however, he did not settle in Detroit. His specialty became criminal activity involving ownership of retail stores. It seems that he defrauded creditors and acquired and sold stolen goods. About 1925 he left the Midwest for good and settled in West Palm Beach, Florida.

Lou, the fourth brother, had illegal business dealings that remain unclear. He worked in Detroit, served as a sergeant overseas during World War I, then returned to Detroit to work in the clothing business with two of his brothers. His main profession became real estate. He got into the Florida land boom in the 1920s and made a fortune. He then moved to California where he invested in motion pictures and took up the role of gentleman gambler.[377] He died in 1958 in Hollywood, Florida, after a long illness. While Mert never had any major run-ins with the law and was never convicted of anything serious, Lou had an arrest record and seemed to be a much tougher, rougher character than his brother.

Wertheimers in Detroit

Mert and Al Wertheimer had set themselves up in illegal activities in Detroit by around 1919. These went very well. And the brothers flaunted their success in the old hometown Up North. In 1924 this article appeared in the *Cheboygan Democrat*:

> Cheboygan people familiar with the operations of the Wertheimer boys in Detroit since they left here have wondered how they do it. Everybody familiar with their operations in the big city have felt that behind them there must be some sort of

protection that enabled them to get by with the things Cheboygan people know they do. It was along about the close of the war [in 1918] that it first became commonly talked in the old home town that Al Wertheimer was known as the 'King of Detroit's Underworld' and every time the chap came back to the old home stamping ground he left nothing undone to further that opinion. He always came up sporting an automobile of the very finest make and also some attractive female scenery which he took delight in displaying to the edification (?) and envy of the old home folks.[378]

Al and Mert both operated gambling places in Detroit. "These boys are able to pay great fines that may be assessed against them because they are making money in great gobs, and are no doubt spending it just as generously. Mert has some Cheboygan assistance, and we dare say that some Cheboygan fellows have long had Mert's assistance." [379]

In the nature of such things, documentation of how the Wertheimers managed local judicial, prosecutorial, and police interference remains hard to find. However, in 1924 the *Cheboygan Democrat* reported that Lester Moll, Assistant Prosecuting Attorney, Wayne County, was socializing with the Wertheimers Up North in Cheboygan.[380] Another prosecutor also became linked to Al. Paul O. Buckley had been a Detroit assistant prosecutor since 1924. Buckley apparently had done all right for himself—he asserted at one point that he could take up a $75,000 membership on the Chicago Stock Exchange. Unfortunately for Buckley, the police raided Al's Aniwa Club in March 1929. Unfortunately, because Buckley happened to be dining at the club at the time. When he saw the police, he looked up in surprise from his table where he had been dining with friends. Three men were taken off to McClellan police station. Buckley followed them there and interceded on behalf of two of them, entertainers at the club who also were the club's president and vice-president. The Detroit prosecuting attorney, James E. Chenot, took Buckley into his office for a confidential half-hour chat. Buckley's resignation resulted. The raid ended the Aniwa Club— it was dismantled, and its expensive fixtures and equipment removed. It also ended Buckley's career in the prosecuting attorney's office.[38T]

The Wertheimer brothers' reputable (or front) business was in tailoring. Mert and Lou and Al all were partners in a tailor and men's clothing shop on Woodward Avenue. More remuneratively, they ran the Pullman Pool Room on Griswold Street, the same street where their hotel was located. Police raided the place early in 1920. They confiscated 33 quarts of whiskey; they not only arrested the brothers, they picked up Mert's father-in-law, Sigmond "Dad" Wilhartz. Back home, the Cheboygan paper reported it.[382]

Throughout the 1920s, there were a number of articles in Detroit newspapers that spoke of Wertheimer gambling establishments, pool halls, and saloons in the city. In 1921 Mert signed a ten-year lease for 113 State Street.[383] Here he ran the Colonial Billiard Parlor with his father-in-law. In this enterprise, Mert had also connected with Ruby Mathis, a man who would remain a friend and business partner the rest of his life.[384] Renamed the Detroit Athletic Club, then the Grand River Athletic Club (although it was on State Street), it operated for a number of years despite raids, for example the one in 1925.[385]

Al hoped to develop as a prize fighter. He had begun training in the 1910s. By 1919 he had fought in a number of bouts. This helps explain why he and his brother, Mert, went in together to buy the Detroit Athletic Club. In 1922, newspapers refer to Al as a boxing promoter.[386] An athletic club was notoriously susceptible to playing a double role as a gambling house. Men congregated to watch bouts, but they also wanted to drink and bet on the fights, as well as bet on horses and play cards. During the twenties, athletic clubs in Detroit and elsewhere regularly drew police raids. The Wertheimers could indulge two passions in the same locale, boxing and gambling.

"A hodge-podge company of mugs and celebrities" enjoyed booze and gambling at the Wertheimers' place. Mert and Al had used the old athletic club ploy: there were two rooms separated by a flimsy partition. In one room, "a couple of wheatcake fighters padded drearily around" while in the other room dice and cards entertained "a hot assortment of humanity—plungers, gunmen, theatrical people, fistic ones and tatterdemalions..." Here and elsewhere, Mert handled "sportdom" gambling—horse bookmaking, bets on fights, bets on sporting events. Raids were completely ineffective in stopping the action. Mert was invariably absent when the place was raided.[387] In the case of a major 1927 raid, the club was only closed for two months although a judge had ordered it padlocked for a year.[388] Mert's gambling activity here was, again, reported in his hometown Cheboygan paper Up North.[389]

Two years earlier, police had raided the Colonial Billiard Parlor in the Colonial Building, corner of Shelby and State Avenues. It had twenty of the finest mahogany tables and featured all kinds of pool. There was also a restaurant and a "soda fountain."[390] Ruby Mathis as well as Sigmund Wilhartz partnered with Mert in this operation.[391]

In 1923 as well, police "conducted a sensational raid on the near-beer saloon of Al Wertheimer."[392] In the course of the raid, a wagon pulled up behind the saloon. Met by a Prohibition agent, the driver asked for Mr. Wertheimer. Leading the agent to his wagon, he threw open the curtain to reveal "45 cartons of bottled beer, fresh in from Ecorse." The agents raided, blew the safe, and found more booze, obscene motion pictures, and a loaded handgun.[393] The front bar of this "near-beer" saloon was stocked with all sorts of beer and hard liquor.

But Al's major operation was on the eleventh floor of the Charlevoix Hotel in downtown Detroit. The January 27, 1924 *Detroit Times* reported a major police raid on the Charlevoix Club.[394] Shortly before four in the afternoon on Saturday, eight police accompanied by a newspaperman tried to enter the club. Al went to the door of the club to meet them. He had already used a system of lights to warn everyone in the club that a raid was in progress. He stalled at the door, giving his patrons as much time as possible. When the police finally burst into the club, they found only a few men playing cards.

The police called it "the most luxurious gambling den in the middle west." The club was divided into two parts, an athletic club and the gambling club. A thick carpet spread over the floor of the club; luxurious draperies covered the windows and walls. There was a grand piano and Victrolas for music. Bronze statues stood in the corners while shaded lamps cast a soft glow over all. In the library, volumes of Kipling, Wells, Shakespeare, Mark Twain, and Hoyle graced the shelves along with complete sets of poetry and classics of old-world literature. A brand-new copy of Webster's Dictionary lay open on a writing table. "You couldn't find a better library in town," Al said. "Of course, no one reads the stuff, but it looks nice."

Al, comfortably seated in one of his luxurious sofas as he played the genial host to the very end, talked to the newspaperman. He pointed to his system of lights meant to warn when a raid impended. "They didn't get in until after those lights had done their work," he said. He also pointed out the system of doors that fit into the wall panels. At the push of a button, the panel swung open and yielded a passageway to an elevator. "Didn't have any time to use the," Al said ruefully.

Al and thirty-five other men were arrested; police charged four with operating a gambling establishment. Al seemed more concerned about the fate of his pet canary and his police dog than about the raid itself. "I don't suppose we'll open tonight," he said. "But this is what you have to expect in this business." Indeed, in the end, Al was released, and no charge was filed. The judge in the case ruled that the officers had no right to raid the place as they did and that they found no gambling paraphernalia there when they did raid it. One has to wonder about justice in Detroit in those days.

After his other places were closed by police, Al apparently took a break from major gambling operations in Detroit.[395] Then in 1929 he opened the Aniwa Club at the corner of Van Dyke and Jefferson.[396] A remodeled mansion, it was set up as a luxurious furnished establishment with an excellent restaurant. Several prominent Detroit businessmen had invested in the club, putting up $50,000 for renovating and outfitting the place that cost $1,500 a week in rent and another $1,500 a week in overhead expenses. Patrons often wore evening attire. Al's name did not appear on the club's charter while two entertainers were listed as front men: Oscar Herman (President) and Charles Adler (Vice-President).

The club was raided mid-March 1929. It was a high-profile raid, led by Police Commissioner William P. Rutledge, Superintendent James Sprott, and Inspector William Fisher. The intent, Rutledge later said, was to seize Wertheimer and question him about the St. Valentine's

Al Wertheimer's Aniwa Club, "Detroit's leading gambling resort"

Day Massacre, and to see if any gambling paraphernalia could be found in the place. But police found no gambling apparatus, not even in two hidden rooms that seemed designed to hide such things in the event of a raid. As I noted, they did find James Buckley, a Detroit assistant prosecuting attorney, eating dinner—something of a surprise to both him and to the police.

Al was arrested on disorderly conduct charges. He was questioned about three men the Chicago police were looking for in connection with the St. Valentine's Day massacre that occurred in mid-February of the same year. Al admitted to knowing two of the men but denied knowing their whereabouts. Police had had the club under surveillance for some time. When confronted by Detroit police commissioner William P. Rutledge, Al admitted that he had planned to install a few roulette wheels "when the police had eased up a bit," but now simply told him that he would re-open the establishment "after the police surveillance was relaxed." Commissioner Rutledge declared that that was "beyond hope of realization!" [397]

However, Al was right—the club did reopen; the license to run the place was not revoked; all Wertheimer had to do was promise that no gambling would take place on the premises. Detroit's chief prosecuting attorney declared that surveillance of the club since its opening had so far only revealed a legitimate club, catering to wealthy people—people on a list of members. No charges were pressed as a result of the raid and everyone went home. All Rutledge could do was grumble, "These people apparently do not fully appreciate Wertheimer's unsavory reputation."[398]

An upshot of this raid was that the Chesterfield Syndicate—Al & Mert Wertheimer, Charles "Doc" Brady, George "St. Louis Dutch" Weinbrenner, and Danny Sullivan—were put on notice by Commissioner Rutledge that, "I shall never give you another opportunity to run a gambling joint of any kind in Detroit. You...have reached the end of your rope here. If you want to run a clean and respectable club, we will give you a chance to make it a success, but we won't have any more gambling and no liquor."[399] Rutledge would continue to be proven very wrong.

Other activities in Michigan

Lionel Wertheimer does not seem to have engaged in the gambling operations run by his brothers Mert and Al, at least not as an owner. In Albion, Michigan, and other towns he bought and ran merchandise stores. Sometimes these burned down; sometimes they were burgled. He also was caught fencing stolen goods in one of his stores. None of this activity took place Up North, but Lionel, like the other brothers, did maintain his connections with Cheboygan. An interesting detail in the story comes from testimony in one of Lionel's bankruptcy proceedings. When the Albion store went bankrupt, proceedings discovered that $40,000 had been diverted from the clothing business to Lionel's pocket.[400] Proceedings further stated that he had "lost a fortune in gambling on race track tips given him by his brothers, Al and Mert."[401] So even though Lionel does not seem to have invested in gambling houses, he certainly was a compulsive gambler himself.

By the early 1930s, no Wertheimer remained an active gambling impresario in the Detroit area. All four had decamped to Florida to pursue various gambling and real estate opportunities there. From Florida, all went on to pursue other ventures out West in California and Nevada.[402]

Mert Wertheimer's Gray Goose cottage on Burt Lake

Wertheimers Up North

Although by 1915 Mert had moved from Cheboygan to Detroit to pursue business interests, he never forgot his Up North roots. He visited Cheboygan often. He and his wife, Bertha, had a cabin on Burt Lake that they frequently visited; in 1925 they celebrated their anniversary there. The cabin was at the Wabawawa Resort near Cheboygan.[403] However, Mert decided to build a new cottage. He chose a site on the eastern side of Burt Lake at a development called the White Goose Resort. In 1926, Clyde Milliken, the developer of the White Goose Resort,[404] sold property for a cottage to Mert Wertheimer and Ruby Mathis.[405] Mert built the cottage during 1927 "near Clyde Milliken's property." He called it "The Gray Goose," a play on Milliken's "White

Goose Resort."[406] There is a photograph taken from shore that captures the beauty of his spot.[407] In addition to the cottage, Mert had a boathouse on the Cheboygan River where he kept his yacht, the *Wanderlust*; it was still at Cheboygan when Mert died in 1958. At that time, it was captained by Frank DeFond, who during the off season lived and worked in Reno for the Wertheimers.[408]

Ruby Mathis remained a close friend to Mert throughout their lives. Like Mert, a member of Detroit's Chesterfield Syndicate of gambling impresarios, he followed Mert from Detroit to Florida to Nevada as a partner in various gambling operations.[409] The *Detroit Times* reports a humorous story of Mert and Ruby at the Burt Lake place:

> Mert Wertheimer and Ruby Mathis were at Mert's cottage hear Cheboygan getting ready to split one small, tender chicken between them. Along came a car with three visitors from Detroit, all hungry. There was plenty of bread and butter and Ruby started to cut the broiler five ways. 'A leg for me,' said the first guest. 'Me, too,' said the second. 'Oh, give me a leg,' quoth the third, and then little Ruby up and said, 'This is a chicken, gentlemen, not a spider.'[410]

Mert's cottage had another tale to tell. Mert had bought the property from Clyde Milliken, a well-known and respected person in Cheboygan. Milliken, in addition to owning an automobile dealership, was the receiving teller in the savings department of the First National Bank of Cheboygan, an old and very reputable institution. One day Henry F. Quinn, a national bank examiner, came to town to audit the bank. He sealed all records in the savings department, prohibiting Milliken from access. Milliken went to his summer cottage on Burt Lake and shot himself. He knew, as Quinn soon discovered, that over $300,000 was missing (worth perhaps as much as four and a half million dollars in today's purchasing power). How did this happen? Milliken's estate turned out to be worth $120,000, so he was not poor by any means. Local speculation centered on the possibility of large losses in the October 1929 stock market crash. Why had the bank directors not figured out what was going on? A bank employee told Quinn that "he would have been afraid to say or do anything because of Wertheimer and his 'gang'—so friendly to Milliken." Quinn speculated that Milliken's close relationship to the Wertheimers, and through them to the Detroit mob, had intimidated the bank directors and allowed Milliken to get away with his pilfering over a ten-year period. We will never know for sure.[411]

Mert and his wife had a life-long love affair with their place on Burt Lake. Bertha would spend whole summers there. While there, they made frequent trips to Petoskey to shop.[412] This may have also been related to Mert's investment in the Ramona Park Casino gambling operation. At any rate, even after the Wertheimers left Michigan first for Florida and then for Nevada, the lakeside cottage was their summer retreat. Mert would fly back from Florida, California, or Nevada—wherever he was at the time—to spend time at the cottage.[413] After Mert's death in 1958, his wife and close friend Ruby Mathis continued using the cottage into the 1960s.

While Mert was Up North he loved to entertain guests. He had an addition built above the cottage's garage as extra accommodations. The *Cheboygan Democrat* is full of notices of Mert and his friends eating in local restaurants, playing golf on local courses, and seeing fellow gangsters at the Top-In-A-Bee Hotel on Mullet Lake.[414] Mert loved to fish and enjoy his fancy Chris-Craft boat, the *Wanderlust*, on Lake Huron as well as Burt and Mullet Lakes. Mert was also very generous to his Cheboygan friends and neighbors. Gratitude for his contributions to various local causes usually silenced notices about the origin of donated money.

The biggest Up North event in Mert's life began innocently enough. He was at his cottage on Burt Lake when he was kidnapped. I will tell that story in the chapter, "Gangster Pastimes."

While Mert had his place on Burt Lake, his brother Al had a summer home on the "Snow Islands"—that is, the Les Cheneaux Islands across Lake Huron from Cheboygan.[415] These islands are a mere fifteen to twenty miles by water from the islands off Canada that were rife with bootlegging activities. Although pleasant enough locales, the choice of Les Cheneaux cannot have been a coincidence. Al's place was probably on tiny Havens Island off Cube Point of Marquette Island. Just across a narrow strait lies Hessel, "owned" by Joe and Ned Fenlon, well known as bootleggers during Prohibition.[416] There is no direct evidence that Al used his place as a center for arranging for illegal booze from Canada, but it certainly looks like that would have been a motivation for having a place there. Brother Lou does not seem to have had a place Up North though he did have a cabin on Duck Lake, north of Albion, in the south of the state.[417] Lionel Wertheimer does not seem to have owned a cottage.

The Wertheimers are almost unique among gangsters Up North because they were home-grown. But aside from Mert's investment in the Harbor Springs Ramona Park Casino, they did not, as far as we know, operate gambling houses in an area that could have benefitted from them, as could all tourist destinations. Perhaps the lack of a very wealthy clientele around Cheboygan made it unappealing to open such a place. After all, for everyday people, gambling was readily available in the back rooms of many saloons (before 1920) and local speakeasys during Prohibition.

The Grand Hotel on Mackinac Island replicated the gambling available in Petoskey area clubs, and perhaps there was some Wertheimer money there since all gambling was contracted out. In 1907, Al came from the island to visit relatives in Cheboygan. Brother Lou had taken a position in a hotel (unnamed) on the island in 1910.[418] Both men were quite young at the time. It is entirely possible that they just went to the island for summer employment. The history of gambling at the Grand Hotel shows no trace of any Wertheimers' involvement. But, still, the Wertheimer connections Up North and the Grand's need for gambling and booze makes speculation almost irresistible. In addition, Al could very well have been involved in the widespread bootlegging across from Canada in the Cheboygan-Sault Ste. Marie area of northern Lake Huron. But, again, specific evidence is lacking.

The Wertheimers of Cheboygan either kept their illegal activities Up North very well under wraps or they were almost non-existent. The brothers loved the area, especially Mert, but apparently more as a playground than as a venue for their extensive illegal activities.

CHAPTER 11

Gangsters on Vacation
Up North

Gangsters at northeastern Michigan resorts

Throughout the northeastern part of Up North during the 1920s and 1930s, resorters and hunters visited and recreated during the summer and fall each year. Sometimes they patronized permanent camps, cabins, and hotels. Sometimes they bought swaths of land on which to hunt and entertain friends and family. While Chicagoans and others favored more-or-less luxurious housing along the shore of Lake Michigan, Detroiters just as often headed to the lakes and forests of the northeastern part of the state. They could reach these areas by rail or ship, but increasingly the automobile provided access to even very remote places. And remote they were. Roads, when they were not sand and dirt wagon tracks, were most often oiled gravel at best. Passenger railroads existed but missed large areas. In 1920, there were fewer than 70,000 souls in the seven counties of the northeast; one county, Montmorency, had fewer than 5,000 permanent inhabitants and Oscoda fewer still, only about 2,000. Population in the entire area had declined even more by 1930.

Yet this very wilderness, covered with mostly second growth pine and scrub as well as surviving hardwoods, lured city folk north to a rustic experience. Leading industrialists such as Clifford Durant at South Branch Ranch or politicians such as William Comstock of Alpena at

Top-In-A-Bee Resort

his Beaver Lake enclave had extensive holdings where associates were housed and entertained. There were also quite fancy lodges catering to the well-to-do. If gangster leaders came north, they probably would have stayed in one of these.

It seems that Mert Wertheimer was not the only Detroit gangster who enjoyed the Cheboygan area Up North. Mert and Ruby Mathis regularly entertained at their Grey Goose cottage on Burt Lake, but the hotel to stay at was the Top-In-A-Bee on Mullet Lake. Accessible by rail as well as roadway, this luxury hotel attracted a wide clientele. Mark Bicknell, owner of Citizens State Bank in Clare, remembered Joe Bernstein, erstwhile Purple Gangster, staying at the Top-In-A-Bee. Joe had his wife and his long-time chauffeur/bodyguard, Abe Olenik, "a big, heavy fellow," with him. A Cheboygan man named Ed Olney owned the hotel. "Big Ed" once got into an argument with Bernstein. Olney then called Bicknell, who was Joe Bernstein's friend, and told him he was very perturbed because he knew who Joe Bernstein was. In the argument, Joe had said to Ed, "I'll take care of you." Bicknell calmed him down by saying that Joe had a temper, but cooled down fast, too. [419]

A fellow member of the Chesterfield Syndicate of gambling impresarios in Detroit, Lincoln "Fitz" Fitzgerald, also vacationed in the area. He rented

Lincoln Fitzgerald

a cottage on Mullet Lake, or sometimes stayed at the Top-In-A-Bee Hotel. It would be surprising if other members of the Syndicate did not visit as well.

There were several other more or less likely spots for gangsters to go for rest and relaxation in the northeastern part of Up North. These were not fine hotels on the level of the Top-In-A-Bee, but they were substantial and advertised state-wide. Among them were the Greenbush Inn (Harrisville, Alcona County) and the well-known Van Ettan Lake Lodge (Iosco County). I have found no stories about gangsters visiting these places, however.

Some of the more remote areas of northeastern Michigan did not see gangsters. Presque Isle County does not record any sightings, real or imagined. However, Montmorency County, perhaps the most remote of lower peninsula areas, did see some rumors and some actual presence of gangsters. I will mention Hunters Home Dance Hall near Atlanta in the account of rural dance halls; an account of a bank robbery led by a gangster from Detroit features in a later chapter. Rumors of a Mafia-owned retreat, also near Atlanta, fill out what I discovered in that remote area of Michigan.

Alpena was an easy destination by lake steamer. It attracted resorters from early days. William Comstock grew up there. Comstock was a lumber baron, businessman, and devoted Democrat in Michigan politics who served as Michigan's governor from 1932 to 1933. A fairly low-key individual, he did not leave much of a mark in Michigan history, but did appear to have some connections to gangsters. While no overt, explicit evidence exists, he somehow got entangled with Isaiah Leebove and through him with Purple Gangsters. When Leebove came to Michigan from New York City to invest in the Michigan oil boom, he made friends with Comstock. In 1929, Comstock was an early investor in the Clare oil fields where Leebove operated. He was also an original investor in Leebove's Mammoth Petroleum Corporation. Although Leebove cleverly maintained the appearance of honesty in the organization of Mammoth, the tainted money backing him had been arranged by Sam Garfield, an agent of the Purple Gang. For Comstock's failed run for governor in 1929 and his successful bid in 1931, Isaiah

Leebove provided significant funding—in the latter campaign he totally financed Comstock's Detroit and Wayne County operation. Once Comstock entered the governor's office in 1932, he appointed Leebove Inspector of Prisons to assess and reorganize Michigan's penal system. Not coincidentally, it seems, Ray Bernstein, the youngest of the Purple Gang brothers, had recently taken up residence in the Marquette maximum security prison as a result of his conviction for murder in the Collingwood Manor massacre in Detroit in 1931. Leebove visited Bernstein in Marquette, demanding a private audience. He probably worked hard to get Bernstein a new trial and, he hoped, his freedom.[420] Comstock's political enemies cried that he was in cahoots with gangsters. Newspaper accusations flew. But nothing was ever proven.

William Comstock

During this time, Comstock often came to Clare, staying at the Doherty Hotel where Leebove and Purple Gangsters were also staying during their sojourns. He gave Leebove one of his official governor's cars. He continued to invest in Mammoth. He maintained his friendship with Leebove. Overall, it seems very likely that he was a friend of these gangsters, not just a cold, business-only associate.

Comstock also maintained his ties with the Alpena area. However, he leaves virtually no footprint in local history or lore. Certainly, there is not even a rumor in Alpena that he was involved with gangsters, nor that he hosted them at his nearby "camp," a rustic retreat at Bear Lake. A wealthy man's rural refuge often served as a meeting place for friends and business acquaintances—it was an opportunity to network and repay social debts, as well as just to enjoy a quiet life and some good hunting and fishing with friends and relatives. While no report or story places gangsters at Bear Lake, given Comstock's association with Leebove and Purple Gangsters, they probably went there.

Long Lake Lodge also lies in Alpena County. Before it burned to the ground in 1937, it was a favorite resorter destination. An old employee said that the Purple Gang had hideouts all over the Long Lake area. He said they used the Long Lake Hotel on Maple Grove Road and that hidden loot and booze were still to be found around the area.[421]

To the south, in Ogemaw County, several locations claim a gangster presence. Graceland Ballroom attracts the most interest in this regard. I discuss Graceland in the next section, but two other locations also boast extensive rumors.

Kenyon's Resort has, right up to the present, claimed extensive gangster activity in its past. Owners have tried to capitalize on tales to lend

Long Lake Lodge

a sense of history and excitement. Tom Finger's memories of Kenyon from the mid-1940s drew on the accounts of local people who knew the resort during the 1920s and 1930s. Neither he nor anyone else ever saw anyone clearly identified as a gangster, although the customers were all well-heeled. Nor does he report any gangster stories or rumors.[422] Likewise, Sally Kenyon in *The Kenyon Legacy* tells a long story of the place with no mention of gangsters or anything of the sort.[423] Later stories of gangsters at Kenyon's seem to simply be made up, including alleged visits by Al Capone.

Grousehaven was a hunting and fishing retreat near Rose City, also in Ogemaw County. Rumors circulate that Purple Gangsters frequented the place. Henry M. Jewett was an important Detroit automobile manufacturer. In the early 1920s, he purchased over 7,000 acres in an area near Rose City. He was both a sportsman and a conservationist. Not relying on native regeneration, he raised and released game birds and reared fish to stock his property. At the same time, he built a magnificent lodge. In 1925, the work was completed; he opened his retreat to small groups of wealthy sportsmen from America and Europe. These men enjoyed his hospitality as well as the rich hunting and fishing available on the property. Much of this property eventually became state land and is now the Rifle River State Recreation Area.

In the Lupton/Rose City area, tales of gangsters at Grousehaven abound.[424] The remains of the lodge's wine cellar become a bunker for gangsters, as one story has it. But a person involved from the beginning to the end of Grousehaven, Vern Nye, gave an extensive and detailed description of the establishment and management of the retreat. He makes no mention of gangsters, rather the opposite.[425] The rumors prove to be just that, rumors.

Very near Grousehaven another cabin claims Purple Gang residents. The owners advertised that, "this property was previously owned and was used as a 'hide out' by the notorious Purple Gang in the 1920s and 1930s." It is a beautiful, isolated cabin on Eagle Lake that would, indeed, have made an ideal place for a gangster retreat. Unfortunately, upon investigation it turned out that the only evidence was tales told to the current owners when they purchased the place late in the last century.[426]

Purple Gang cottage, Eagle Lake?

Another local person told stories of the activities of the Purple Gang at a lodge on North Dease Lake. One has gangsters rolling a car down a hill and shooting at it until it crashed into the lake, where divers can still find it. This is in line with many other stories of a gangster-related car at the bottom of a Michigan lake.[427] Similar stories are told of nearby Sage Lake and AuSable Lake, both alleged to have Purple Gang cabins on their shore.

On the other side of the state, in Antrim County, another resort may have enticed gangsters. Big Fish Inn is located on Campbell's Lake near Ellsworth. It was built by Lewis Van Skiver in 1924 and passed through two other owners in the 1920s and 1930s. It still exists. During the 1936 FBI investigation of the kidnapping of Edward Bremer by the Barker-Karpis Gang, agents were told to contact Herman Kays in Petoskey as the person who could tell them "more than any other one man in the city." He ran the Kays Patrol and Detective Agency and had been a sergeant in the Michigan State Police. Kays claimed that a "Bob Rosenbloom" had bought Big Fish Inn in 1934. "It was rumored that he did not operate this place as a business venture but merely to keep his following while in that vicinity during the resort season." "His following," Kays implied, were gangsters.[428] Thale Yettaw seemed to validate this. Yettaw, who died in 2003 at the age of ninety-four, was a native of Ellsworth and "was a fishing guide for tourists who stayed at Big Fish Inn, including members of the Purple Gang, movie stars, and CEOs of large corporations."[429]

A history of Ellsworth mentions the Big Fish Inn but, unsurprisingly, does not mention any gangster visits. In addition, the list of owners from the Inn's construction in 1924 until 1966 does not mention "Bob Rosenbloom" as an owner; indeed, the place did not change hands in the year Kays says he bought the place.[430] So, what of "Bob Rosenbloom" and gangsters at Big Fish Inn? Kays stated that Rosenbloom operated a business called "Supplies for Hotels and Restaurants" in Florida. This

Big Fish Inn, Ellsworth

profession was sometimes a cover for gambling operators. In 1932, ten plainclothes Michigan State Police troopers accepted entertainment offers from resorts in Antrim County. While the resorts were providing "much noise and entertainment" for their hosts, the police donned their uniforms and arrested fourteen local residents on liquor charges. Among those arrested were Harold Yettaw (Thale Yettaw's father), who ran a resort near Ellsworth, and Robert Rosenbloom from Ellsworth, who probably was running Big Fish Inn.[431] This detail lines up with Kays' account. While Rosenbloom apparently was not the owner of record of Big Fish Inn, he likely was a lessee. Rosenbloom's permanent residence was Detroit although, of course, that does not mean he was involved with Detroit gangsters.

A visit to Big Fish Inn in 2018 led to a conversation with the current caretaker who repeated stories of gangsters. It is impossible to know whether gangsters stayed at the Big Fish Inn. But as these things go, the evidence is stronger here than at many other places that claim a gangster presence.

Dancing the Nights Away

Alongside the well-outfitted lodges and camps, local entertainment venues also thrived seasonally. These places offered music, dancing, and beverages to all comers. If there were any ordinary gangsters Up North for a bit of fun, they would most likely have found a welcoming spirit. Graceland Ballroom is the most famous of these venues. It was established by a gangster, but was it for gangsters? Truth and myth intertwine once again.

Graceland and the gangsters

The area around Rose City and Lupton in Ogemaw County has very widespread and persistent stories about gangsters coming to the area for rest and relaxation. The central figure in all this is "One-armed Mike" Gelfand. He was definitely something of a gangster.

From a family of Russian Jews who emigrated to New York City in the late nineteenth century, Mike himself was born there on April 12, 1894. He was a rather short man with light brown hair. An accident during his youth left him without his right arm, giving him the nickname "One-armed Mike."[432]

Gelfand's father earned a living making garments. Early in his life, Mike helped him by sewing petticoats.[433] Later, as a young man, he worked, as did so many immigrant Jews, as a travelling peddler.[434] In 1920 he was still in New York City living with his family although he had become a "commercial traveler."[435] By 1925 he, along with his family, left New York and found their way to Detroit, Michigan. In nearby Lucas County, Ohio, he married Grace Drickhame, a Sandusky girl, in 1926.[436] The marriage license still listed his occupation as salesman.[437]

In Detroit, Gelfand seems to have done well. The 1930 Census has him owning a grocery store and living at 3475 Fourth Street in his own house valued at $15,000, which would be about $225,000 in 2019. He also owned a speakeasy in Wayne.[438]

An account has circulated that before leaving Detroit, "One-armed Mike" was part of a Purple Gang faction known as the "Little Jewish Navy." This supposed group is very shadowy even by the standards of gangster stories. One account says these bootleggers—the "navy" that brought booze from the Windsor side of the Detroit River to the American side—were rivals of the Purple Gang, while another says that they were a sub-contractor of that gang.[439] The most likely account is

Collingwood Manor murder scene

that when some gangsters came to Detroit from Chicago, the Purples placed them in their "Third Avenue Gang," a crew charged with the Detroit River liquor trafficking.[440] Then the newcomers got too big for their britches by trying to establish themselves as independent bootleggers. Purple Gangsters murdered them in the Collingwood Manor Apartments in 1931. Newspaper reports then connected these three men to an otherwise unknown and probably invented group, the "Little Jewish Navy."[441] The three victims at Collingwood, Joseph "Nigger Joe" Lebovitz, Isadore "Izzy" Sutker, and Hyman "Hymie" Paul, along with their associate, Sol Levine, are the only names associated with this "navy." There is no mention of Gelfand.[442]

Nevertheless, Paul Kavieff connects Gelfand to the navy. He states in his book, *The Purple Gang*, that Gelfand was "a combination blind pig operator/racketeer" and "one of the leaders of the Little Jewish Navy." He gives an elaborate after-story that combines rumor and fact as he imagines that Gelfand fled Detroit in the aftermath of the Collingwood Manor massacre:

> "One-armed" Mike Gelfand developed a novel idea. In August 1931 Gelfand's sister Lillian had been given eighty acres of land in Michigan. Here, Gelfand planned to build a remote haven to be used by Detroit gangsters on the lam. Gelfand's sister sold him the property for one dollar. He and his wife moved to the area and had plans drawn up for a restaurant and dancing pavilion to cater to local residents while providing a safe house for gangster fugitives. It would become known as the Famous Graceland Ballroom. During its heyday in the mid-thirties, the resort boasted a runway for small aircraft, tourist cabins, and three tunnels, used by fugitives to escape into the nearby woods. The place was visited by many notorious Purple gangsters, as well as underworld characters from all over the Midwest."[443]

This account is widely accepted in Ogemaw County and elsewhere. But who was the real Mike Gelfand? Was Graceland built as a safe place for gangsters? A careful reexamination is needed.

Graceland Ballroom, Lupton

As early as 1928, Mike Gelfand developed an interest in land around Lupton.[444] In April 1929, he bought acreage near the Dease Lakes in Hill Township. Then in 1931 Mike bought from his sister, Lillian, 80 acres of land at the southeastern edge of Rose Township, just outside the village of Lupton.[445] He moved from Detroit with his wife, Grace; they adopted a son, Ronald, in early 1931 or 1932.[446] Gelfand and a person named Jack Smith of Detroit formed the Lupton Recreation Company and proceeded to build a dance hall.[447] Local contractors built the place with wood from local forests. Begun in the summer of 1932, the hall was still not quite completed when it opened on July 4th, 1933.[448] Gelfand and Smith aimed to create "the recreational center of all Northeastern Michigan."[449]

> The architecture and construction of this new building will perhaps surpass any in the state of its kind. It is built of Norway pine logs stripped on the interior with a stained exterior finish. The fixtures are exclusive being carefully designed and manufactured especially for the building's complete harmony with the log structural effect. The artistic interior paintings with the log-effect lighting fixtures make an ideal dancing pavilion with a very spacious floor, measuring 80 by 100 feet...Neither time nor money has been spared in its construction."[450] A dance band from Lansing came up for the opening. "High grade" diamond rings were given away as prizes to entice customers.[451]

Graceland Ballroom interior views

The Lupton Recreation Company operated the ballroom for only five summers, 1933 to 1937. There was always booze available, supplied by local bootleggers, as well as properly bought and sold with a liquor license after Prohibition ended late in 1933.[452] Mike's son, Ronald, recalled that Gelfand was a gambling addict. He would bet on baseball games and boxing and played poker with a vengeance.[453] While stories of Graceland make it clear that dancing and drinking were the entertainment, it is highly likely that gambling also took place in a back room on the premises. A later owner, Floyd Pastula, claimed that gambling devices, meaning slot machines, "were in common use" at Graceland.[454]

"One-armed Mike" had a relatively short run at Graceland. As early as 1935 he was trying to sell it. He listed it with William Dunlop of Clare.[455] A few years later, L. M. Zitomer bought the place and ran it from the summer of 1938 on. At this point, Mike Gelfand left the picture. He moved back to Detroit and the next year his wife, Grace, for whom Graceland was named, divorced him on the grounds of extreme

Graceland Ballroom, Lupton

195

cruelty.[456] Ronald lived with Mike in Detroit after the divorce.[457] That same year, he was in a serious automobile accident near Rochester, New York, along with his brother, Morris, and the wife of his brother, Julius. Ronald was also in the car.[458] The accident in late July was only three months after his divorce from Grace. Gelfand was still in Detroit, living with Ronald and a housekeeper named Mary Knowles, in 1940.[459] He married Mary and the family soon moved to Los Angeles, California.[460] His World War II draft card states that he was self-employed as a lino-leum peddler. However, Ronald Gelfand stated that his father made a living as a jobber dealing in jewelry.[461] Gelfand died in Los Angeles late in December 1944.

Graceland spawned many vivid tales of gangster customers. However, Delores (Dilly) Craft Shore (1921-2019) is the only person I found who could give a first-hand account of involvement with Mike Gelfand and Graceland. Her engagement with the place happened during the time of Mike Gelfand's involvement, from 1932 to 1937. She married in October 1939 and had nothing further to do with Graceland. In 2014 Gayle Miller and Cathy Snider interviewed Dilly. In the interview, she repeated the basic account that is common around the area:

> I worked there! I'll tell you how it all started. Mr. Gelfand, he was One-armed Mike: he was from the Purple Gang in De-troit. They figured Lupton was a good quiet place to hang out, so they built the building and it had the biggest dance floor. After they built the big building, on the end they had to build another small building because they could not have liquor or beer. After about 5 years the state voted and passed a law that said they could have alcohol.[462] So the building on the back was used for the bands when they came up to play the Graceland. They were high classed bands from all over. So, after the new law they went ahead and made the Graceland a dine and dance.

She also related more personal experiences.

> I worked for Mike and Grace taking care of their little boy.[463] They must have figured I was smart enough, so they had me selling dance tickets at the door. There was a big machine gun

in the top of the Graceland even back when I worked there.[464] These guys came up to me at the door and one he said he wanted to buy the last ticket on the roll. I said he could not have the last ticket. The tickets were three for $.25 they had dancing every night and were packed every night.[465] Back to the story, when he came back to the door later and I still told him he could not have the last ticket, he pulled a gun on me, in my face. Petrified, I was on a pedestal and had a buzzer for if I needed help. I rung that buzzer and Mike Gelfand came running up with his gun and fired it one time at the ceiling. Everyone hit the floor. The lights went out. We had no power. The Graceland had a power plant run by several big motors out back and those guys giving me trouble had gone and blown it up. Someone called the police but by the time they got there everyone was gone.[466]

Dilly also worked as a cleaner at the venue. She would clean the floors with a large sack on a broom handle; the sack had wool on the bottom and was filled with rocks to give it weight. It was used to sweep the maple dance floor clean. "The furniture was made of logs. It was heavy to move the tables and when I was cleaning, I would often find money tucked into the logs of the chairs. One time I found a $5 bill, but usually it was just a dollar. That was a lot of money back then and I never told Mike about it."

She also took advantage of the actual entertainment at the Graceland. Her fondest memory was of the music. "The music was fantastic and that is where I learned to dance." The band boys used to say, "Come on Dilly," and she would dance.

Floyd Pastula bought the place in about 1957. He owned the ballroom until its demise in 1981. He had no personal experience with the early days of the Graceland. However, as the centerpiece of his publicity campaign to make Graceland a viable venue he repeated, concocted, and exploited the Purple Gang gangster angle.

His story was that "the famous ballroom was built in the early '30s by the all-time prohibition rumrunners of Detroit that were known as the Purple Gang. It was constructed as a relaxation place and a point of

Floyd Pastula

'hiding out' when things got a little hot, either from police officials or rival gangs in the Detroit area."[467]

Pastula "retained the flavor of the desperate days" he wanted to believe had existed. The myth that the dancehall was built "by and for gangsters" emerges in full flower. Pastula enhanced the image by installing a fake machine gun nest over the entrance and claimed that it had been there in "the old days." He had a safe on display that he claimed had been machine-gunned by the Purple Gang as well as a replica of the gang's supposed concrete coffin.[468] He installed a siren and alarm bell that he could trip from the bar, much as actually existed in speakeasys

Floyd Pastula's fake gangster machine-gunner

CONCRETE
"OVERCOAT -

THIS IS A REPLICA OF THE
PURPLE GANG'S -
CONCRETE-OVERCOAT
OR KIMONO SURE TO MAKE DOUBLE
CROSSERS DISAPPEAR

Floyd Pastula's "concrete overcoat"

to warn customers to skedaddle when the cops arrived. But it was all in good fun, as Pastula himself admitted that the gangster stories were all second- or third-hand. Although locals repeated them, none could be proven. Even he declined to believe that supposed holes in the dance hall's beams had been made by bullets.[469]

The first published description of Graceland's gangster history appears in the *Bay City Times* in 1974. Pat Hunt wrote in breathtaking prose about "the roar of sub-machine guns" no longer echoing through the rafters of the hall. But he knew it was all fake, that "there was no real evidence that the forty-year-old building was ever a gangland battleground."[470]

Graceland burned down in a spectacular blaze the night of Sunday, December 20, 1981.[471] Tom Henry, writing immediately after the incident, demonstrates how Pastula's stories were accepted and passed on. Henry claimed that Al Capone was there, that it served "as a retreat for gangsters," that "she housed Detroit's infamous Purple Gang during the 1930s, sometimes protecting it or other gangs during shoot-outs."[472] Almost none of that is true, but these and similar stories were repeated as truth. An article in 1991 talked of the balcony where Pastula put his fierce mannequin machine-gunner serving "as the guard post for the Purple Gang members. The guards could see anyone coming down the road and give warning if the members would have a need to escape or fight unwanted visitors."[473]

The end of Graceland Ballroom

Ten years later, another article asserted that Gelfand purposely built Graceland as "a safe hideout" for his Purple Gang friends.[474]

Is it possible to fit all the pieces together? The story of Mike Gelfand's life seems fairly normal. He claimed to work in legitimate businesses throughout his life. The only mention of illegal activity comes from his son's recollection of his father running a speakeasy in a small town west of Detroit well before he was born. I have found no documentation to support the statement that Mike was part of the "Little Jewish Navy," nor that he was involved with the Purple Gang. Whatever his life was like in Detroit, he seems to have been quite successful by the mid-1920s. Although rumors claimed that his financing came from the Purple Gang, the Lupton Recreation Company relied on Jack Smith, whoever that might have been, as an investor, along with what money Gelfand himself could raise, most probably by selling his quite substantial home in Detroit.

In principle, founding a dance hall in the late 1920s was not a curious thing to do. Large ballrooms had become fixtures of urban entertainment and they sprang up in rural areas, too. The automobile made it easy to drive to a venue and have a good time dancing and imbibing

GRACELAND BALLROOM, LUPTON

Graceland Ball Room:

Penned and orchestrated
In the bloodiest of times,
The Graceland heard the dance of death
When the gang was in its prime,
Now all that's left is echos
Where in the rafters hang,
Vague shapes and restless spectors,
Of the lawless purple gang.

— SHIRLEY DEE

illegal alcohol if desired. For example, there was a huge dance hall at Walled Lake, just 30 miles from central Detroit.[475] The Wrightington Gardens on the Maple River near Pellston opened in 1926 with big bands from as far away as Illinois. The Avalon ballroom at Barron Lake, near Niles, served that area. Summit Heights ballroom was at Lake Fenton, near Flint. At the Chrystal Palace on Paw Paw Lake and many other similar places, local people pooled their money, bought a dollar's worth of gas, and drove out for a good time. The architecture of these places was exactly like Graceland: a large central structure to cover the dance floor with side halls for eating and drinking areas. There are two oddities about Graceland when compared to these other locales. It was not on a lake, although there are lots of lakes nearby. It was not within striking distance of a large population center, either. But even here, precedents existed such as Johnson's Rustic Dance Palace in Prudenville.

Construction itself need not have been terribly expensive. At Graceland, Gelfand hired local contractors, Lou and Burt Wolfe. Another local, Otto Rosenquist", was one of the builders. Local pine was cut for the structure.[476] The architecture was not complicated. In fact, it was built almost exactly like the Rose City Community Hall that the Wolfe brothers also built.[477] In 1981 when Graceland burned, the owner said it would cost $100,000 to rebuild it. That would be about $18,000 in 1930, about what Gelfand could have sold his home in Detroit for.

The simplest story would be that Gelfand caught a trend—the thriving dance hall business—got a fellow Detroiter to go in with him, found an opportunity to get very cheap land in an area rich in resorters in the summer and hunters in the fall, and decided to try his luck in a new venture. Set beside this benign scenario are all the local stories swirling around Gelfand, gangsters, and Graceland. Could the missing link indeed be Gelfand's involvement in bootlegging in Detroit and subsequent welcoming of his Detroit gangster friends to his new dance hall? It would not be at all surprising to find gangsters Up North enjoying themselves, but hardly hiding out. So perhaps "One-armed Mike" really did have a gangster connection.

Other dance halls

A good example of these rural dance hall bars still exists outside Atlanta, the county seat of Montmorency County. It was called Hunters Home Dance Hall.[478] A later owner reported that his uncle, owner of the place in the late 1940s and early 1950s, had never mentioned anything about gangsters.[479] However, that does not stop stories of gangsters, Purple Gangsters in particular, frequenting the place.

Hunters Home, Atlanta

There are other local stories about gangsters in the area.[480] Supposedly they owned a hunting club on McIntire Road where in later days some dynamite was found. Also, rumors told that the Mafia was said to have owned the Elsman Ranch at the junction of M32 and M33. When the ranch changed hands, the new owners removed lots of 1920s and 1930s furniture, including a large table where supposedly the Mafia capos sat. As in other cases, it is impossible to verify these stories. They were told and retold among friends and family, often with great detail. Without solid evidence they must remain rumors only. But it is important to recall that Mafia capos did own property near Grayling at the South Branch Ranch, only about 40 miles to the southwest.

Johnson's Rustic Dance Palace, Prudenville

Built in 1926, Johnson's Rustic Dance Palace remained a fixture of Houghton Lake resort life for decades.[481] In its heyday, it operated six days a week for the crowds that came to hear well-known bands and dance the night away. Sometimes, up to five hundred cars from a forty-mile radius would be in the parking lot. The building survives today, owned by the Houghton Lake Historical Society, and is used as the Houghton Lake Historical Playhouse. The dance floor still exists; it is possible to get a good sense of what a dance palace like Graceland must have looked and felt like. However, there are no rumors or stories about gangsters at Johnson's. Frank Johnson, the founder, came up from Chicago, but he does not seem to have had any gangster connections there. Sometimes the Mafia types at Higgins Lake and South Branch Ranch would come to Prudenville, but only to see a movie or dance a bit with the other resorters.

CHAPTER 12

Moving Up North

In the course of the accounts of gangsters Up North, we have already come across some who did more than visit, they moved there and resided permanently. From the Purple Gang came Al "Slim" Gerhart, who settled in the Little Traverse Bay area, went into business with the Club Manitou, and stayed in the area except for a time in Jackson prison and, much later, in West Virginia, where he briefly ran an ill-fated gambling establishment. In his later years, he lived on a lake near Alanson in fairly comfortable retirement. "One-armed Mike" Gelfand also came up from Detroit to settle for a time near Lupton, where he operated the Graceland Ballroom for around ten years in the 1930s before moving on to California. From the Cleveland gangsters, Sam "Cheeks" Ginsberg decamped from the shores of Lake Erie and spent the rest of his life on a farm near Tawas City, dividing his time between that area and many visits to Clare. Isaiah Leebove also found Clare congenial as he and his wife, Enid, took up residence in a pleasant home north of town. He lived there until his murder in 1938.[482] Sam Garfield, his good friend and business associate, a consummate minion of a long list of mobsters from the Purple Gang to Meyer Lansky, also lived in Clare from the early 1930s until near his death in the 1970s.[483] A third gangster, Arthur Clark, also wound up in Clare. He had been associated with New York City gangsters such as Arnold Rothstein and Jack "Legs" Diamond, but got cold feet when he was almost assassinated in a Miami, Florida, hit job in 1929.[484] He and his wife, Loretta, moved to Clare. He worked with Leebove in the oil fields, bought a house, sent his son to the local high school, and remained in town most of the rest of his life. He and Loretta were among the very few friends Leebove and his wife had in Clare. Isaiah and Art shared a gangster background and New York connections, while Enid and Loretta, both showgirls when they married, enjoyed each other's company. But there were two other interesting people who moved Up North and had some gangster connections.

Joe Barnes in Clare

Rumors swirled around Clare in the 1960s that a local resident, Joe Barnes, had come to the Clare area from Chicago. Barbara Wentworth, a Clare police dispatcher in the 1960s, assured me that it was true—Joe had been a gangster. She said to me that Barnes had often told her about a gangster life in details that made her believe him. In Chicago, he told her, he had been Al Capone's driver.[485] While my immediate urge was simply to add the "Joe Barnes story" to the long list of mythical connections between Michiganders Up North and Big Al, enough evidence came forward to require that the possibility be treated seriously.

Joe identified himself as Joseph Samuel Barnes, born on January 23, 1878.[486] Sometimes self-presented as having been born in New York, his official documents tell the truth: he was born somewhere in the Russian Empire.[487] Virtually the only late-nineteenth century immigrants from Russia were East European Jews. Barnes was no different. His original name was Baranisky.[488] This surname is preternaturally rare.[489] The obvious Americanization is "Barnes." And so, Joe Baranisky became Joe Barnes.[490] His claim to have been born in New York may indicate that his family entered the country at that port. It may also have been an attempt to claim United States citizenship as no naturalization record exists in his name. The trail of his life only begins for certain in Chicago.

However he got to Chicago, police knew of his illegal activities. By 1917, although he had never been arrested, "for years, without molestation, he had operated roadhouses and resorts and escaped trouble."[491] In that year, he appears as a criminal accused of being a leader in an auto theft ring. He was in cahoots with Lem Nutter, "King of the Auto Thieves," in what police called an "auto thieves trust." Charges against him and an accomplice, Sam "Kinky-haired Jew" Harris, were dropped, however.[492]

His association with Jewish gangsters probably did not begin with this episode, but this is the first documented instance. He and Harris bought a roadhouse called the Burr Oak Inn in Blue Island, Illinois, from Ben F. Hyman.[493] Ameliorated and opened by Barnes and Harris in 1915, the Inn, just over the city limits from south Chicago, was a spectacular example of what a pre-Prohibition nexus of illegal activities could look like. It had the trifecta every gangster hoped for. Physically, it was heavily fortified against police raids (which were quite regular): heavy doors, look-outs posted, armed employees, even, this time for real, an elaborate system of escape hatches and tunnels to allow those caught in a raid to get to the nearby garage and their fast automobiles. Indeed, it was known as "The Castle." The Burr Oak operatives also had total control of the local authorities. The little town of Blue Island, population 3,500, had the usual officials—mayor, police chief, county sheriff, justice of the peace. The gangsters bought them all. In fact, the justice of the peace, Henry Wolske, was the bartender at the Burr Oak![494] The third gangster ideal was a variety of illegal activities. Out back, a madam ran a small whorehouse. An opium den occupied the basement. There was a bar, restaurant, and dance hall. At the time, a local option law governed access to liquor. Many precincts in Chicago and many surrounding communities were "dry." But not Blue Island. In addition, illegal, untaxed booze was a great moneymaker, so the Inn was a center for local bootlegging. As a final entrepreneurial accomplishment, the spot was headquarters for Lem Nutter's auto theft gang. All of this was chugging along just fine when a dispute erupted over the "ownership" of a woman—Barnes and Harris engaged in white slavery as part of the prostitution angle. In October 1916, the dispute led to a gunfight in the Burr Oak bar between employees and a rival gang.[495] In the raid, a hoodlum was shot and killed. Barnes and Harris were arraigned before a grand jury on a charge of murder. But it all just went away: neither was indicted; both went free.[496]

A police operation a few months later, in early January 1917, resulted in Barnes' arrest once again. This time he was charged with conspiracy,

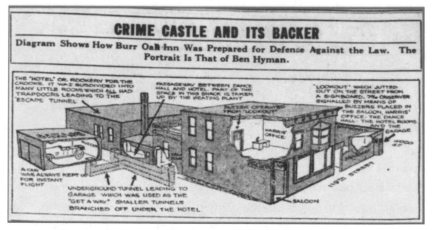

The Burr Oak Inn

bribery, and obstruction of justice.[497] Peace officers under the authority of Illinois' state attorney conducted a well-planned and spectacular raid—local authorities could not be counted on and were kept in the dark.[498] Police arrested Barnes and Harris as well as Lem Nutter, caught while trying to use one of the escape hatches and tunnels from an upstairs bedroom.

What had prompted the raid? Another gangster, Mike "de Pike" Heitler. Mike came from a family of Austrian Jews who had immigrated in the late 1890s. By 1910 he was well known to Chicago police as the owner of cheap whorehouses—customers paid 50¢ a trick (the girl got 25¢ of that).[499] By the early 1920s, Heitler was a major player in Chicago's prostitution scene. He ran the prostitution and graft on Chicago's West and South sides. As a major competitor of Ben Hyman, the man who had sold the Burr Oak to Barnes and Harris, Heitler did not brook competition from small fry. It looks like Barnes got caught in a conflict between these two bigger fish, Heitler and Ben Hyman. Hyman laid the blame for trouble at Heitler's door, stating that, "The whole trouble was caused by Mike "de Pike" Heitler, who wanted to open up out there."[500]

Barnes then seems to have changed camps. He allied himself with Heitler's brother-in-law, Ben Soltnick and got the Burr Oak back. It reopened in June 1918 but was immediately closed by the authorities.[501] With that, we lose track of Joe Barnes, although the Burr Oak did re-open and probably he continued there in some capacity.

When Al Capone came to town in 1921, he started out working for Johnny Torrio as a pimp and bordello manager on Chicago's south side. Prior to bootlegging taking off, prostitution was the most lucrative racket. Big Al quickly became close friends with a man, Jake "Greasy Thumb" Guzik, who controlled a wide range of brothels. Gruzik was Jewish, not Italian, but that did not bother Capone at all. They remained close associates until Gruzik was sent to prison on tax evasion charges in 1932. Guzik ran the prostitution end of Capone's Chicago Outfit.[502] Heitler at first tried to compete, but soon gave up and he, too, aligned with Capone, under Guzik's supervision (which he chaffed at). He continued in his whoremongering ways throughout the 1920s but fell afoul of intra-Chicago Outfit competition and was eliminated in a house inferno in 1931.[503]

The Burr Oak burned to the ground in a mysterious, presumably arson created, fire in 1920. It is highly likely that after the Burr Oak Inn was gone, Joe Barnes continued with Heitler's gang and became involved with running prostitution for the Capone Outfit. There is no specific notice of him during the 1920s, however. The next evidence is his marriage license in 1928 to Edith Hale.

Edith Irene Hale (1897–1986) grew up in Arthur Township, Clare County. She worked in nearby Gladwin and in Sheridan Township, then left home and went to Detroit by 1917.[504] From there she went to

Chicago by 1922.[505] Her cousin, Louis Wasson, also ended up in Chicago. Arlene Milkie, Edith's niece, supplied some details about her life as well as Barnes'.[506]

Recollections of his early years were very scattered, except for the impression that Barnes was not his real name. Joe would talk about his life in Chicago. He claimed to have been a collection manager for Al Capone, a task that would fit with managing bordellos.[507] He told of how he would hop on the running board and speed away when faced with a tense situation.

Another relative recalled that Edith had been a "Gibson Girl" in a speakeasy in Chicago. The term, Gibson Girl, refers originally to the romantic female images drawn by Charles Dana Gibson in the late nineteenth and early twentieth centuries. I have found no reference to Gibson Girl being a synonym for loose woman, rather the opposite. Gibson did con-

1920s Gibson Girls

tinue to draw throughout the 1920s and included flappers in his sketches. But the classic image of the Gibson Girl is the opposite of the flat-chested, short-haired, masculine-looking flapper. However, since Edith was a "Gibson Girl" in a speakeasy, the assumption must be that this is a reference to a loose woman. Women were used in three ways in the speakeasy trade. They were "pushers," that is, they stood outside a place and urged customers to step inside. They were waitresses. They were companions. Prostitution was not far from any of these three roles. It looks like Edith Hale went to Chicago, found employment in a speakeasy, and there met the manager, Joe Barnes.

In December 1928 the two were married in Waukegan, Illinois, north of Chicago. They lived in Chicago for a few years. In the 1930 Census they appear, married, living there with Lewis Wasson, Edith's young cousin from Clare County, as well as with an immigrant from Russia named Barney Siegal.[508] Wasson, age twenty-three, is listed as

Barnes' chauffeur. Joe gives his profession as a scrap iron dealer and his boarder, Barney, lists this as well. Scrap iron collection was frequently a Jewish occupation. But, like Al Capone listing himself as a used furniture dealer or Abe Bernstein of the Purple Gang claiming to be just a shoe salesman, this listing seems to be for window-dressing only.

By 1934 Joe and Edith had left Chicago and took up residence on a farm in Arthur Township, Clare County. Joe claimed that Al Capone had helped him buy the place. People who knew Barnes said that he always dressed well and had a cigar in his mouth. His mien advertised a "don't mess with me" personality. But everyone seemed to like him, and he was great with kids. Chip Shepard, Clare's police chief in the early 1960s, recalls that his nickname was "Spats," but his wife's family never heard him called this. During his time in and around Clare, Barnes worked for Chief Shepard as the Clare dog catcher. At times he also worked for the Clare County sheriff, Jim Darling.[509] And of course he did farm.

Joe was fairly, but not excessively, secretive about his life in Chicago. He would hang out in Clare's bars and at the Doherty Hotel. Shepard said that he did not often speak of his former life. But he did tell his brother-in-law, Glenn Hale, about his Capone connection. He also sat in Bonnie Woodworth's dispatch office at the Clare police department and told her Chicago tales. He told Chip Shepard that Capone had helped buy him the place he owned in Arthur Township.[510]

Chip Shepard also said that Barnes' farm out on Bailey Lake Road was a hideout for Capone's men, that when things got hot, he sent them Up North for some R&R and invisibility. It is hard to know if this could be true.[511] There are no other tales circulating in Clare about Chicago hoodlums coming through—such tales focus exclusively on the Purple Gangsters from Detroit, real and imagined, and to a lesser extent on Cleveland gangster Sam "Cheeks" Ginsberg. However, for what it is worth, the current owners of the farm recall a man who came to their garage sale and while chatting with them said that he was an ex-gangster who had hid out at the farm for a period. This is most probably just a story. But still. Another neighbor told the owners an even more unlikely story—that Capone had slept in the upstairs bedroom of the house!

Suspicion of the stories becomes a bit more difficult, however, after a visit to Barnes' farm. Upper Nestor Lake is a small, natural expanse bordered by only three property owners. It is therefore isolated. The farm extends from Bailey Lake Road back to about a third of the lake's shoreline. Near the road was a house, a barn, a garage, and a chicken coop. The home was and remains a modest farmstead. The current owners of the property bought it in 1967, three years after Joe's death,

Joe Barnes' home (above); his chicken coop converted to housing (below)

directly from Edith Barnes.[512] When they took possession, the chicken coop had been converted into a bunkhouse that would sleep half a dozen or more.[513] There was also an apartment over the garage.[514] In the house, there were two bedrooms besides the one the owner had occupied. There was a baby grand piano in the main parlor.

The barn supposedly had an escape hatch leading from the ground floor to the basement, but close examination turned up nothing but a shoot to dump manure down. By the lake, the ruins of a tar-paper shack still exist. A quite sad affair, perhaps eighteen feet by eight feet, it would have provided minimal protection from serious elements, although it would have kept denizens dry. There are cots and mattresses in it, as well as a broken-down table. A decrepit dock still juts a little into the lake and the ruins of a few rowboats can be seen amidst the trees and ferns.[515]

On the trail leading to the lake, there are a couple of rusted hulks that were once automobiles, but not one dating from the '30s or '40s. It is quite normal for farmers just to drive old vehicles off into an unused place and abandon them.

Joe Barnes' visitors' shack by Nestor Lake

An innocent explanation of all this is that family members did come up from Lansing and occasionally Barnes let visitors camp and fish on his land. Neighbors said that he rented boats, which would agree with the dilapidated craft down by the lake.

In the end, it remains hard to say what is the truth about Joe Barnes and his gangster hangout. The evidence does indicate that he was from Chicago and did have gangster activities in his past. However, that does not mean that he ran a gangster haven in Arthur Township. Neighbors' stories make us think so. But whether those beds and boats were meant for gangsters or just for visiting family and friends from downstate and Chicago, we can never know.

Pat Hayes in Escanaba

Harold C. "Pat" Hayes owned the Hotel Ludington in Escanaba from 1941 until his death in 1969. As his hotel became a favorite place to stay and dine during the wonderful summers by Lake Michigan, he maintained an important place in the community. Passing remarks in newspapers note that he had some association with Al Capone and other Chicago gangsters. He himself downplayed any relationship with Big Al. He told the local newspaper, the *Escanaba Daily Press*, "People say that I was a cook for Al Capone. But they don't say that we inherited the Metropole Hotel in Chicago from the First National Bank and that 30 Days after I took over, he was out."[516]

His account is a bit brief. More is known. A scant five years after arriving in Chicago, reports find him with enough money (or backing, or both) to purchase a major hotel, the Metropole. He claimed to have "made it" by 1923, but just how he did that remains a mystery. He became a significant real estate player in the Windy City owning, besides the Metropole, the Pershing Hotel and various other pieces of property.[517] Out in Dubuque, Iowa he owned the Julian Hotel as well.

He put out the story that he began his hotelier days with the Albert Pick Hotel in Chicago.[518] There is no indication that Hayes ever worked for the Albert Pick. The first notice of him comes only in 1927 as the owner of the Metropole Hotel in Chicago. From 1925, the Metropole was Al Capone's headquarters. Then Hayes bought it. He discovered (or, more likely, already knew) that Capone's gang had taken over part of the hotel—50 rooms in all—on two heavily guarded floors. Access was by elevators the gang controlled. Liquor flowed freely at their own service bars. Visitors gambled openly. Prostitutes came and went at all hours. "On Sunday mornings, especially, the lobby was jammed with criminal lawyers, politicians, and dive keepers, waiting to consult the vice kings." Apparently, Hayes gradually cut away at the privileges the gangsters enjoyed and raised their rates.

Finally, Hayes ejected Capone and his entourage completely. He said he was motivated by "constant peril of wholesale raids by the police, of increased taxes through political influence and, meanwhile, his decent patrons were departing." On July 30, 1927, his "undesirable guests" packed up their belongings and a $100,000 stock of illegal liquor that they had had stored in the hotel's basement. Capone merely moved a short distance away, to the Lexington Hotel. No backstory exists, although one would wonder if Hayes really did have the nerve to eject Big Al had Capone wished to stay. More likely, Capone got better accommodations and a better deal at the Lexington, where he remained.[519]

Hayes' connection with the Capone mob continued. On St. Valentine's Day, 1929, assassins gunned down seven henchmen of the major gangster, Bugs Moran, in a garage in Chicago. One of the alleged torpedoes was a Capone hitman, "Machine Gun" Jack McGurn.[520] Authorities arrested and indicted him on a murder charge. The judge set his bail at $1,300,000 (about twenty million dollars in 2019). Who should come up with bail but Harold Hayes. He put up the Pershing Hotel, valued at the required bail amount, as his bail bond.[521] Evidently, Hayes was being more than big-hearted in doing this. It must have been in his interest to do a favor for Al Capone.[522]

A wealthy man, Hayes did not like to pay income tax. He became closely connected to Frankie Lake and Terry Druggan, very successful Chicago beer barons.[523] They made a lot of money.[524] Their profits of around $2 million a year brought them to the attention of the feds.[525] Together in 1929 they plotted to fix a fake bribery charge on United States District Attorney George E. Q. Johnson, who was spearheading the government's attack on gangsters in Chicago through indictments for tax evasion.[526] Johnson had brought accusation against the pair of cheating the government out of a half million dollars in owed income tax. Capone saw a chance to thwart District Attorney Johnson. He teamed up with Lake and Druggan, offering to intimidate an attorney who then was to implicate Johnson. With some irony, they brought Hayes into the plot, even though the feds later used Hayes as a witness against Capone himself as a tax evader.[527]

But before that, Hayes was the man who whispered the bribery accusation to contacts in Washington. A major investigation of Johnson ensued—but ended abruptly when Hayes could not produce any evidence of the alleged bribery scheme. Hayes protested that, "there's a bigger story behind this if the government would tell the truth," but then refused to explain what he meant.[528]

Hayes was always on the lookout for dodgy ways to increase his net worth. Using his position as major stockholder in the Dubuque (Iowa) Julien Hotel, he diverted $48,000 of company funds to his private use. Minority stockholders blocked him and even filed a counter-suit claiming he had defrauded on his contract.[529] And once at the Metropole he stole $12,000 from a patron's room. It seems the patron had been arrested on a charge of robbery and Hayes did not expect him back.[530]

Through the 1930s, Hayes remained at the Metropole as well as in close connection with Druggan. The two were arrested in 1932 on an unknown charge.[531] Hayes was still owner and manager of the Metropole in 1935 and still skirting the law. He plead guilty to serving alcohol sealed with counterfeit liquor stamps. He sold the Metropole late in 1935 or in January 1936. With that money, he invested in the Cambrinus Company, a Chicago brewery, as secretary-treasurer of the company. His main partner was Druggan. In less than a year, the brewery went bankrupt in March 1937, a costly failure for all concerned. By then, Hayes had already skipped town. By January 1937 he was in Escanaba.[532] His losses in Chicago had been considerable, but he still had some resources. He and Druggan had continued their wily ways, for in 1939 the federal government indicted both Druggan and Hays for concealing Druggan's ownership of the brewery.[533]

An article in the late '40s states that Hayes then bought the Hotel Ludington in Escanaba in 1941.[534] Before that time, in town he was "a salesman for a manufacturer of restaurant equipment."[535] Whether Hayes actually went back to his early 1920s business of selling hotelier equipment, or perhaps just pretended to do this, his purchase of the Hotel Ludington made the hotel his passion for the rest of his life. By the time he died over a quarter century later, he had turned the Ludington into a premier tourist destination with a top-rated restaurant.

Hotel Ludington in Escanaba

Pat Hayes seems to have created a past for himself once he got to Escanaba. He even seems to have invented his nickname, "Pat," or, at least, he is never referred to by this moniker in newspaper stories. His obituary contains many incorrect statements.[536] For example: he married his wife, Maurine, in 1930, not 1924; he never attended the University of Toronto; he did not serve in the Canadian Air Force; he never was employed by Albert Pick in his hotels; "He solved a Cambrious Brewing Company management problem for Pick and was sent to Escanaba to bail out a local brewery" is pure fiction. As I mentioned, there is no indication that he ever worked for Albert Pick. His obituary claims that he served in the Canadian forces as an airplane pilot during the First World War.[537] There is no record in Canadian sources of him having done so. Indeed, he registered for the United States draft in June 1917. There is no record that he ever served, however. In 1920 he was still in his hometown, Boston, selling hotel equipment.[538]

Harold C. "Pat" Hayes definitely knew and worked with Al Capone in Chicago. His hotel business provided him with a headquarters for a time. Hayes must studiously have looked the other way as Capone carried on extensive illegal activities from his hotel rooms. He bailed out a Capone hit man. He later offered the feds incriminating evidence about Capone's activities at his hotel. Hayes also was knee-deep in illegal activities. He probably got out of Chicago because his business dealings there had gone south. Coming to Escanaba gave him a chance to reinvent himself, and he did just that.

Warren Shearer in Crystal Falls

Another supposed refugee and Capone man from Chicago appears to have settled in the Crystal Falls area in the Upper Peninsula. In a Michigan State Police Special Report, troopers Merl Peck and A. J. Haydon followed up a lead in the Lindbergh kidnapping case.[539] As the men interviewed locals, residents pointed fingers at Warren Shearer, a man "reported to be connected with the Capone Gang in Chicago as one of Capone's local agents." He had come to Crystal Falls from Chicago in 1928. Neighbors said that he had made $100,000 in the liquor there (about one and a half million dollars in 2019 purchasing power). About 1930, he married a local girl. He found work at an area golf course. But in fact, "he is reported, from reliable sources, to be connected with a large liquor syndicate in Chicago as a sort of go-between, or agent, with headquarters and a liquor plant located near Spread Eagle, Wisconsin, on what is known as the Charles Mehan farm. Shearer makes a trip to Chicago about once every two weeks, he drives a Buick straight eight sedan, and owns a Chevrolet sedan." The troopers went to the Shearer home on Swan Lake. They did not find him there, but interviews with others indicated that he seemed to be just a normal resident. Unconcerned, apparently, with the accusations and rumors of bootlegging, the troopers went on their way, having investigated yet another dead-end lead in the kidnapping case.

In fact, Shearer was a bootlegger. In Chicago, he had been a federal prohibition agent gone bad. In 1924, he was implicated in the operation of the Mid-City Brewing Company. This had been a legal operation, the Sieben Malt House, before Prohibition, but had continued as Mid-City Brewing after the Volstead Act went into effect in 1920. A Chicago grand jury investigation implicated Shearer as police discovered that he was on the brewery's payroll. Shearer hotly denied doing anything improper.[540] Nonetheless, he seems to have soon left the Windy City for the wilds of Michigan's U.P. and, if rumors are to be believed, continued from his cottage on Swan Lake to engage in Capone's bootlegging operations from Up North Wisconsin.

It seems likely that there were other refugees from Chicago, Detroit, Toledo, and Cleveland gangsterdom who decided that living Up North would be a good idea. Many simply blended in and we may never know their stories.

⤚CHAPTER 13 ⤛

Gangster Pastimes

Bootlegging—Canada is so close by

Prohibition went into effect in the United States on January 17, 1920. In Canada, as in the United States, local and provincial Prohibition had spread widely in the early twentieth century. National Prohibition, a war-time measure, was short lived, 1918-1920. After that, each province determined its liquor laws. Ontario, the only province bordering Michigan, voted to continue dry after the end of national strictures. This measure was strongly opposed by the substantial brewing industry in the province as well as by the working-class population in general. Repeal came in 1927. But even while in force, the Ontario law only prohibited purchase of alcoholic beverages; it never prohibited their manufacture and export. After 1927 there were constraints such as licensing, but all types of liquor could be made, exported, and consumed legally. The Ontario situation meant that throughout America's Prohibition era, beer, wine, and hard liquor was readily available across the

border. Probably 80% of Canadian liquor came into the United States across the Detroit River, but extensive bootlegging also occurred along the St. Clair River and lake, and at the Port Huron/Sarnia crossing. The Michigan Prohibition law of 1918 followed by the

federal law two years later set the stage. Up North, bootleggers did not supply the quantities easily imported downstate, but, still, geography and demand conspired to create an active bootlegging industry.[541]

Lake Superior is a large, often unforgiving, inland sea. Nevertheless, boats loaded with contraband liquor did cross it in order to deliver the goods to Marquette and other destinations. In particular, the western waters proved profitable as booze shipped across from Port Arthur (now Thunder Bay) could easily reach fair-sized cities in Minnesota and could connect by rail to points south.

In volume, however, this never amounted to much. The easiest crossings were from the beginning of the St. Marys River at Whitefish Bay along a winding 75-mile path into Lake Huron. At its narrowest point, the river is well less than a mile wide; one of its Canadian islands, St. Joseph, is a mere 500 feet from the American side at its closest point. Many inlets and islands large, small, and tiny dot its route. Control of cross-border traffic fell to a Sault Ste. Marie Coast Guard post that was grossly understaffed for the task handed to it upon the advent of Prohibition.

Lake Huron posed a greater barrier to bootlegging than the St. Marys River, but less than Lake Superior. Canadian booze came by rail to cities such as Thessalon and Blind River. From there it was loaded onto small craft that set out from the outer islands and headed for Cheboygan or other points across the North Channel.

On all these routes, these small boats were the order of the day. Some craft were larger. But the basic operation was to have a number of independent bootleggers bring the booze to the American side where it was sold to middlemen who in turn shipped the product by ship (the most economical carrier), rail, or, less often and for shorter distances, trucks to downstate Michigan and to the Chicago/Milwaukee area.

Of course, there was some local consumption—the Grand Hotel on Mackinac Island, for example, never lacked for alcoholic beverages. Thomas Pfeiffelmann told me of his grandfather who would take gas bottles up to the Soo with cases of whiskey inside the rows of bottles. For Mackinac, he would meet a supplier on the Canadian side at 3 a.m., load his speedboat, and take it to the Island. Ned Fenlon was another supplier. He would pick up booze at one of the many small Canadian islands opposite Drummond Island and speed it to Mackinac. Probably these two men supplied a good deal of the illegal booze available at the Grand.[542] But in 1930, the entire Upper Peninsula and the northern counties of the Lower Peninsula counted fewer than 350,000 souls out of almost five million in the state. Supplying that population was

Small craft like this could ferry people to and from Mackinac Island—and at night, booze from Canada

very small potatoes compared to supplying the millions in the big cities to the south and, besides, local need was often met by moonshine and home-brewed beer. In the north, the only lucrative market was the resorts whose patrons could and did pay good prices for imported Canadian products. Fenlon was known to supply Al Gerhart at the Club Manitou in Petoskey/Harbor Springs.

There certainly was money to be made. A case of good whiskey brought a premium price, not counting additional profit to be made by cutting the stuff and selling it to unwary customers. Supposedly, agents sent north by the Purple Gang and Capone set up shop on Mackinac Island and arranged for shipments. I have not been able to find any firm evidence for this. After all, Detroit had all the Canadian booze it could drink and shipping excess product across to Chicago from the Detroit/Windsor boundary was much quicker than sailing the booze down from the Soo.

Colorful stories about bootlegging from Canada in the far north abound. There are many tales of how people used their small craft, stowed booze under lumber, took advantage of cruise ships being close to Canada, and so on. But in the end, the quantity did not come anywhere near the booze shipped across at Windsor and across Lake Erie to northern Ohio. Gangsters certainly could have been involved at the Soo and elsewhere, but it would have been a minor aspect of their business, and, in the end, there is no evidence for it. More likely, smugglers and middlemen did the work, got the booze to Detroit or Chicago, and sold it there to the gangster outlets. The popular equating of bootlegging with gangsters then gave rise to local rumors of actual gangsters being involved at the source.

Bank Robbery—The Hillman Heist

Roy Werner, a car dealer in Ferndale, Michigan, wasn't so sure about the two men, Tom Hunt and Alex Graham, who were offering him a $5 bill.[543] They needed a car. Obviously for no good, because they wanted it left by the curb where it could be easily stolen. There was a bank far to the north, in Hillman near Alpena, that was just waiting to be robbed. They would return the car and give him another $45. The men were

Arrow points to the bank in Hillman, Michigan

rough-looking, the one big and burly with a mean smile, the other sort of stooped over, like his back was hurting him. But $50 was not chump change in 1930. Werner agreed to the deal.[544]

Up in Hillman, Beryl Hunt was scratching a living from the sandy pine barrens left behind by ravenous lumbermen, eager to cut green gold and run. The land wasn't good for much besides raising sheep, which is what Hunt did when he wasn't getting into trouble. He had a strong build, big hands, long arms, and a short fuse. Once he had challenged a professional boxer and laid him out cold. That poor fellow wasn't prepared for the rough and tumble slugging a backwoods farmer had to offer. Like many men who lived hard lives just to stay alive, Beryl had a chip on his shoulder and didn't put much stock in getting along with folks. As a later police report said, he "had served a sentence for breaking and entering and he was known to be a hard man." Besides, he was always under pressure to provide for the three others living in the farmhouse—his cousin, Aaron Hunt; his common-law wife, Wilma Margeson; and Wilma's sister, Rebecca.

One day, Beryl saw a Model A Ford coupe come chugging up the drive. Another cousin, Tom Hunt, hopped out with a buddy he introduced as Alex Graham. Over a meal that evening, Tom told him about his time down in Detroit, how hard it was to find work and how he had gotten involved, as had Graham, in bootlegging to make ends meet.[545] The newspapers had been full of stories from around the country about gangsters robbing banks, making off with the loot and eluding police.

The Montmorency County Savings Bank was just down the road in Hillman. What could be easier than knocking it off?

At first Beryl tried, so he later claimed, to talk the pair out of the idea. After all, it was a very small town. Everyone knew everyone else. How could they get away with such a plan? By the light of the kitchen oil lamp, Tom explained how it could be done. With Beryl's help, they could do it. When the cashier, William Niergarth, emerged from his home to go to the bank Monday morning, they would kidnap him, take him to the bank, force him to hand over money, gold, and negotiable bonds, lock him in the safe, and make their getaway.

Alert to stories of bank robberies and the efforts law enforcement went to in pursing fleeing thieves, the men even had an escape plan. Beryl's property included access to the Long Swamp. Well named, it was a ten-mile-long watery wilderness oozing fluid that often reached a man's chest, filled with black snakes and a paradise for mosquitoes. Deep in the swamp, on a spot of higher ground, with Beryl's help the men could prepare a hideout, a makeshift shelter stocked with supplies of food and drinking water. There, the thieves could wait until it all blew over.

Beryl was hesitant, but hesitancy gave way to greed. His farm would be on the edge of a new lake soon to be formed by a dam to flood the Long Swamp. If he had money, he could build a resort at the lake and make a lot more money than farming an unforgiving land. He was in. The men needed a weapon. Beryl offered them one, bought cartridges for it in town and hiked out through the muck to give it to them as they prepared their swamp hideout. Tom drew a map of the operation, including where they would enter the swamp. Everything was ready.

Right on schedule, Wednesday morning, July 30, 1930, Bill Niergarth came out of his house on the way to the bank. According to plan, Tom and Alex confronted him at gunpoint and drove him to the bank. When they got there, two customers were waiting on the sidewalk for the bank to open. They along with Niergarth were hastily forced into the bank. The cashier did as he was told, opened the safe and handed over the contents worth $15,000. The robbers stuffed it all into deerskin bags, shoved the three into the safe, and swung the door shut.[546]

Montmorency County Savings Bank as it looked in 2019

In haste, they tossed the sacks into the Model A and took off. Across the street, Lloyd Taylor watched curiously from his gas station. The five people who entered the bank seemed to him to be acting strangely. As the getaway car drove off, he crossed the street and realized that the bank had been robbed. Not seeing Niergarth and the customers, he realized that they had been locked in the safe. They would die if he didn't act. He shouted for help. Men got a drill from the nearby hardware and tried to force the safe. George Crowley, thinking quickly, drove madly out to the homes of two bank employees, explained the crisis, and brought them back to open the safe. Just in time, as Niergarth had already collapsed in the virtually airless space.

A cry went up in town. Hillman was far from the county sheriff in Alpena and even farther from the nearest State Police post in Manistee over on the other side of the state, so it was up to the local men, who grabbed their guns. An unofficial posse quickly formed and headed out after the robbers and near-murderers. The chase ended only a few miles from town. At the north end of Long Swamp sat the Model A. The robbers had fled, according to plan, into the swamp. One pursuer, William

Savings Bank vault repurposed as a business office, Hillman, Michigan

Banks, tried to track the fleeing men into the swamp, but lost their trail. Things were working out for the gangsters.

Meanwhile, back in Hillman the State Police had arrived and began investigating. Beryl Hunt quickly became the prime suspect. The clue was in the Model A. There, police found material for a disguise and, most importantly, a box of .300 Savage rifle shells with a price mark showing that they came from the local hardware store in Hillman. Beryl Hunt had purchased the shells there the week before.

Michigan State Police Lieutenant Earl Hathaway, charged with the case, went out to the Hunt farm. There he met Beryl as he was walking up to the house. His feet were wet and muddy up to his calves, as though he had been walking in the swamp. At first, Beryl tried to lie his way out of trouble by claiming that he had bought the shells for shooting wild dogs that were ravaging his sheep. That explanation collapsed as Hathaway noted that only two shells were missing from the box. A search of the farmhouse turned up a sawed-off shotgun and several other weapons along with the map showing the bank and the escape route. Police grilled Beryl for three days. He finally broke and told a different story: Tom Hunt and Alex Graham had come to his place on July 22nd. He had bought the shells the next day. Hunt and Graham had taken the shells and the .300 Savage when they left the farm. He continued to deny any part in the bank robbery itself.

Out at the swamp, Hillman resident Nelson G. Farrier led a band of three hundred local men; eventually, eighteen Michigan State Police troopers and several sheriff's deputies and game wardens joined them. Searching the deep and bleak swamp was out of the question. The men set up a siege, assuming that the snakes and mosquitoes would drive the two fugitives out in good time. "Believe me, that's no nice place to be," said one of the troopers. "With water up to your middle in places, scum and dead growth and black snakes by the dozen. They'll get tired of staying in there."

The heist and its exciting aftermath caught the attention of newspapers statewide. *The Detroit Free Press* ran the headline, BANDITS, AT BAY IN SWAMP, ELUDE 225 PURSUERS IN NIGHT MANHUNT. One week into their hiding, the two gangsters emerged at Beryl Hunt's farm, hoping to replenish their supplies. The secret code agreed upon was that the women of Beryl's household would "salt the sheep" as a sign that all was clear. Police, privy to the scheme through their questioning, were on the scene. One trooper took a bead on Alex Graham, pulled the trigger, and...nothing. His rifle had misfired. By the time troopers could pull their pistols and open fire, the hold-up men had run back into the swamp.

At Beryl's farm, police found two knapsacks containing "enough provisions to last two men two weeks"—canned foods, flashlights, face and mosquito lotion, rain gear, blankets, cigarette tobacco, and mosquito netting. Other locals besides Beryl Hunt were helping the miscreants. The area around Hillman swarmed with Tom Hunt's relatives. A cousin, "Bingo Bill" Hunt, also offered aid. Who knew who else might be helping? In addition, the lawmen's perimeter around the swamp leaked like a sieve. It seemed that the fugitives could leave the swamp whenever they wanted. A report from nearby Alpena told of a "ragged, dirty man" with "a roll of bills as big as your fist" coming into a grocery store, making purchases, and then disappearing.

229

Time for a new strategy. Searching the swamp again seemed useless. A band of over two hundred men had tried that following the appearance at the Hunt farm. They had found a rude shelter, clothing, and food to last about two weeks. But no men and no money. Lieutenant Hathaway declared that "it would take 5,000 men to search the swamp and then it is doubtful if the bandits could be found." For the nonce, three sheriffs from Montmorency, Alpena, and Alcona counties, each with a band of vigilantes, maintained the siege on all sides of the swamp. At the two-week mark, Hathaway gave up and returned to the Manistee post, assuming that the robbers had left the area.

But they had not, or, at least, Tom Hunt had not, not yet. Two days later, he had had enough. He walked out of the swamp to George Thompson's farm, about four miles east of Hillman. There, he offered Thompson $500 to hide him and help him escape. Thompson obliged in the first case, hiding Hunt in his barn. But as to the second part, Thompson instead notified the sheriff and State Police. Surrounding the barn, they demanded Hunt's surrender. He meekly complied. Hunt was in bad shape—one eye was swollen shut, he had a terrible cold, and his stomach hurt him a lot. His clothing was in rags, his underwear a grain sack. He told officers he had not had a regular meal in a week but had survived on berries and what he could steal from farm gardens.

But what about the money? What about Graham? Hunt led officers deep into the swamp to the spot where they had stashed their weapons—a small arsenal that included Luger pistols, a .38 automatic pistol, and Beryl Hunt's .300 Savage rifle. "All were loaded with spare clips and a shoe full of extra ammunition." But no money and no Graham. Tom Hunt told the police that Graham had the money, had escaped, and was headed for Lions Head, Canada, where his wife and mother lived. [547] No one believed him. Lieutenant Hathaway stated he "would not be surprised to learn that Tom Hunt killed Alex Graham and left him in the swamp." One week later, Hunt pled guilty to the robbery with a "smirky smile" on his face. He got fifty to sixty years in Jackson Prison, so why was he smirking?

Berkley Police Chief Frank Irons thought he knew. He telephoned Lieutenant Hathaway to tell him that in all probability, Beryl Hunt had planned the robbery and had the money. This, Beryl hotly denied. When he was tried as an accomplice to the robbery, his defense was that he went along with the plot only because he feared that Tom Hunt would kill him if he did not cooperate. Another cousin, Aaron Hunt, even testified that Beryl had tried to talk Tom and Alex Graham out of their plan. It took the jury only nine hours to declare Beryl Hunt not guilty. Willard Klein, a boy of twelve at the time of the heist and an avid student of the affair over the years, later declared, "If they'd a had a good prosecutor, they'd hung Beryl." Instead, Beryl had had a good lawyer and went free.

When it was all over, the town of Hillman tried to forget what had happened. The Hunts were numerous and generally well thought of in the community. Beryl Hunt and his wife went on to lead successful and exemplary lives as upstanding citizens. The swamp became Fletcher Pond, Hunt's property on the lake became a resort. Hunt's Landing was known statewide for its good fishing. He had cabins, a restaurant, campsites, and boats to rent. He prospered.[548]

Alex Graham was never found. Police speculated that Hunt had shot him. His brother assumed that he had died in the swamp. A Hillman local said he was buried under a pile of stones near the artificial lake that had been created to replace the swamp. The money was never found, either. Funny, though—old, larger bills turned up regularly in Hillman over the next decades. Small bills, the size used to this day, were first printed in 1929; in 1930 most circulating paper currency was

Hunt's Landing resort at the lake where the Long Swamp once was

still the noticeably larger pre-1929 issues. Occasionally the police investigators showed up in Hillman, asking questions because the murder case involving Alexander Graham was never closed. Authorities always strongly suspected that Beryl Hunt had masterminded the heist in order to get money for his soon-to-be built resort on the soon-to-be created lake where the soon-to-be flooded swamp existed at the time of the robbery. Talking to old-timers in Hillman, there is more than one reference to a Hunt being able to buy things—a car here, a house there—without obvious wherewithal. One person recalls that Tom Hunt, when he got out of prison in 1949, regularly bought booze for all his friends. Suspicion was that the money from the bank robbery had gotten to the extended Hunt family. But no one ever knew for sure.

Kidnapping—Wertheimer Snatched

Before 1927, it was alleged, kidnapping was not a prevalent crime in Detroit. Or so stated Sergeant Max Waldvogel to a Detroit newspaper correspondent in 1930.[549] Then in the first eight months of 1927, nine kidnappings occurred. These nine targeted prominent gambling operators: Charles T. "Doc" Brady, Meyer "Fish" Bloomfield, "Lefty" Clark, Johnny Ryan, George "St. Louis Dutch" Weinbrenner, Danny Sullivan, Mert Wertheimer, Ruby Mathis,[550] Dick Driscoll, Joe Klein, and Abraham Fein.[551] Reports had it that both Wertheimer and Brady paid $50,000 ransoms.[552] At about this time the extortion and vandalism associated with Detroit's Cleaners and Dyers War had reached its peak. This "war" saw the creation of the Purple Gang out of a bunch of thugs

hired to protect some enterprises and damage or destroy competitors'. One of their tactics was to kidnap leaders of the rival cleaners and dyers organization. But this time, it was out-of-town gangsters who were responsible for the sudden upsurge in kidnappings for ransom, unrelated to the Cleaners and Dyers War.[553]

On September 1, 1927 the Detroit Police Department created the Crime and Bomb Squad within the department to meet this and other underworld threats in the city. Kidnappings continued during 1928, but gambling impresarios seem to have been spared. The focus became on others thought to be wealthy enough to pay a good ransom: Max Ruben, treasurer of the Motion Picture Operators Union (no ransom; purpose was intimidation); Harvey E. Watson, a union official; and Max Mattelson, a malt and hops dealer ($14,000 paid). Some underworld snatches did occur—Eddie McCash, a handbook operator, and Abraham Rosenberg, an alleged partner in a West Side bootlegging syndicate.

In 1929 there were seven successful and one thwarted kidnappings. Fred Begeman, a wealthy Wyandotte bootlegger, paid a $7,000 ransom. Deadly violence entered the picture when in July David Cass, son of Gerson Cass, was taken and in October found near Lapeer, murdered. Shortly after, Matthew Holdrieth Jr., a young student, was kidnapped and held until the ransom was paid.[554]

Law enforcement had little success in catching the perpetrators. They thought that a gang of around ten thugs was involved—a gang that did kidnappings over the entire decade and in several cities besides Detroit. The gang ranged all the way to Miami where it attempted to kidnap the famed boxer, Jack Dempsey, in 1929. In Michigan, they tried to kidnap another boxer, Sammy Mandell, along with his manager as they vacationed at the Top-In-A-Bee Hotel on Mullet Lake.[555]

A *Detroit Free Press* article from 1929 specifically identified the leading kidnappers as Fred "Killer" Burke (originally out of a St. Louis gang) and Purples in Detroit. But no one knew for sure who was doing the snatching. Over all these years and all these snatches, only six kidnappers were convicted and served terms in Michigan prisons and these six were involved in only three of the many kidnappings. The other snatches remained unsolved.

Fred "Killer" Burke was supposedly responsible for the kidnapping of gamblers for ransom, although this contradicts what the Detroit police said in 1930 about another, independent, kidnapping gang. In the Burke scenario, he and a group of four other thugs ranged widely doing hold-ups, kidnappings, and other nefarious deeds. Al-

Fred "Killer" Burke

legedly, this gang was organized about 1919/1920 in Detroit with associates who later became Purple Gang men, such as Abe Axler and "one of the Bernstein boys."[556] This gang was also supposedly responsible for the Miraflores massacre in Detroit in 1927. "Burke's method was to obtain information about the personal habits of the particular gambler or rum baron selected as victim, and at an opportune time seize him and carry him to a hide-out on one of the nearby lake resorts."[557]

Herman Kays, retired Michigan State Police Sergeant and an informant of the FBI, told the FBI in 1936 that Ruby and Mert were kidnapped at Topinabee "in 1929 or 1930" by Fred "Killer" Burke and Raymond "Crane Neck" Nugent, a Burke associate; it was said that they paid $50,000 for their release.[558] Another source stated that Mert was "snatched from a golf course near his Burt Lake cottage and held for ransom by Chicago hoodlums."[559] The most extensive narrative comes from Robert Laxalt, a journalist in Nevada.[560]

Laxalt describes Mert as "a gnome-like little man with a big head, cold eyes, and a rasping voice." As the journalist tells it, Mert asked him if he would like to hear how he was kidnapped. Of course, Laxalt said yes. Mert said that he was on a fishing trip to his place on Burt Lake—he liked to fish and frequently went to his place in Michigan to do it.

He had asked Ruby Mathis to come with him and they took off. Mert continued, "Ruby and I were driving on a mountain road that led to my cabin. We came around a bend, and there was a car blocking the road. I stopped and a couple of guys jumped out of the bushes with guns. One was Turkey Jack, who was a famous kidnapper in Detroit.[561] When I saw him, I knew what was coming off. I had been fingered for a snatch." Mert went on to say that Ruby had been no help at all—had fainted in fact. But Turkey Jack sent

Mert Wertheimer

Mathis back to Detroit with a ransom demand for Mert's brother, Lou. He named a price. Ruby took Mert's car and drove to Detroit. Meanwhile, "Turkey Jack drove me to my cabin, and we all settled down to wait for Ruby and the ransom money." Mert was not tied up or beaten. In fact, the two played cards for two days. The kidnapper was a lousy cook, so Mert did the cooking while they waited. Finally, Ruby showed up. He reported that Lou had refused to pay the ransom.

Supposedly Turkey Jack then said, "I love you like a brother, Mert, even if you cleaned me out in poker. That's not the point. I've got to kill you. For the good of the racket. You understand."

Mert replied, "I understand your position. But let me send Ruby back one last time." Mert then told Ruby to "forget about Lou" and go to Capone in Chicago because "Al owed me a big one and I'm collecting."

Ruby went. Capone got in touch with Turkey Jack and told him to let Mert go. Turkey Jack begrudgingly complied. "So, Turkey Jack left the cabin, and I finished my fishing vacation," Mert concluded.

Laxalt then asked if Mert had learned who had put the finger on him. The reply was, "Oh, sure. It was my brother Lou."

Laxalt: "What did you say to Lou when you got back to Detroit?"

Mert: "Nothing. He's my brother, after all."

This story has all the marks of fiction, of Mert playing with a newspaperman. There are no mountains or anything like it on the way to or near Burt Lake—of course Laxalt, a Nevadan, would not have known this. There is no one named 'Turkey Jack'—perhaps a jest on "Crane Neck" Nugent. A ransom (some say $35,000, some say $50,000) was paid for Mert's release. And surely his brother did not orchestrate the snatch. Also, it seems that Mert continued to elaborate on the story. An entry in his 1958 obituary notes the following: "A Detroit kidnap gang grabbed Mert in the Prohibition mad Twenties. Gamblers were sitting ducks for the mob who freed the victims for a standard fee of $25,000. They took Mert to a hideout in northern Michigan while they negotiated the ransom. He played cards with them and lost. After he was freed, he sent them the money he lost in the card game, although his freedom cost him $25,000. He didn't think this was anything un-usual. 'A man always pays his debts,' he said."[562]

In sum, Mert was kidnapped near Burt Lake in 1927, probably by out-of-town gangsters specializing in this form of extortion.[563] Appar-ently kidnappers had deduced that men on vacation could make easy targets, for there was another gangster snatch at Topinabee at about this time that was unsuccessful. At any rate, Mert paid a ransom. He was freed. His is the only successful gangster kidnapping Up North.

Murder—Isaiah Leebove—the perfect hit?

Among all the stories and events involving gangsters Up North, there is only one murder.[564]

It seemed like a normal Saturday evening. Not much for Isaiah Lee-bove to do after dinner but go down to the Doherty Hotel and have a drink with Pete Geller and his new, pretty wife, Betty. He had his driver, Maxie Levinson, get the car out for the short drive into town. Clare was busy. Saturday night was when the farmers' families came to town. Stores were open a bit later and the feature film at the Ideal Theater—this evening it was *Forbidden Valley* with Noah Beery—was always fun. Leebove was by himself—his wife had not joined him. As a consolation, the oilman sent his nephew out to carry some ice cream back to Wildwood, their home on the Tobacco River. The bar of the

Doherty was busy. Four years after Prohibition ended, you would think it had never happened. Pete and Betty set in a booth on the west side of the crowded room, waiting for him. He sat on the outside. Betty slid over to give a place to his nephew who had just returned from his errand. Pete was Leebove's lawyer; they had a lot to talk about, but this evening was purely social. Chatting away, the party hardly noticed Jack Livingston enter the bar from the door to the hotel lobby.

Livingston was a fixture at the hotel. He had come to Clare at the same time Leebove had, 1929, and had been an early partner with him in exploiting the recent oil boom in the area. Their friendship went back a long way. Both had learned the oil business in Tulsa, Oklahoma, where Jack's father was a successful operator and Leebove as a young man had been the company lawyer. When Isaiah had left for New York, Jack had stayed behind, working as a lease man in the oil fields. The two had drifted apart, but never lost contact.

In Gotham, Leebove had set out on a new career, although he never completely forgot about oil. A smart, personable man, he quickly made friends and married a local girl, the daughter of a prosperous businessman. His gambling habit, first developed while a law student at Cumberland College, drew him to less desirable company. He practiced commercial law, but his combination of intelligence and gambling addiction brought him to the attention of New York's leading underworld figure, Arnold Rothstein. This man had his tentacles in almost all the city's illegal activities ranging from bootlegging to gambling to prostitution to protection rackets. They did not call Rothstein "The Big Bankroll" for nothing. Leebove worked for him as an anti-labor organizer, fixer with a specialty in getting gangsters released on bail, and "mouthpiece," that is, a public relations man. In this new life, he shed his staid wife and married a beautiful showgirl. He made lots of money and was liberal with it, but his gambling habit—he would bet on just about anything— kept his lifestyle, for a successful gangster, quite modest.

His world came crashing down on November 6, 1928. A disgruntled fellow gambler murdered Rothstein. Leebove's main connection and protector suddenly was gone. Once Rothstein was out of the picture, the New York gangland scene became unstable. With Meyer Lansky,

Charles "Lucky" Luciano, and others maneuvering for control, there didn't seem to be a haven for Isaiah Leebove. He tried to establish a new relationship with Jack "Legs" Diamond. No dice. It was time to move on.

Leebove had relatives in Detroit and he had heard about the oil boom in Michigan. He didn't entirely cut his ties with the New York City underworld, but he did pick up and move to the Motor City. Once again, he became enmeshed in the local gambling scene and through that met Sam Garfield, a successful manager of gambling establishments with strong connections to the main underworld operation in Detroit, the Purple Gang. He also met William Comstock, an industrialist and active leader in the state Democrat party. Leebove developed a plan. He would use his oil industry experience to launder ill-gotten gains of gangsters. To do this, he needed an excellent lease man, the person who would get landowners to sign over mineral rights in return for a share of oil revenues, should oil be found. Jack Livingston was active in the nearby oil patch of northwestern Ohio. The four men could work out a successful arrangement. Three of them met in a cabin on Budd Lake in Spring, 1929. Sam Garfield offered to be the link to Purple Gang money for investment in wells; Jack Livingston agreed to be the lease man; Leebove would use his skills to set up a corporation

Isaiah Leebove (l.) and Jack Livingston (r.) in happier days

and his social skills to recruit local investors as a cover for the real, gangster, investors. William Comstock would be an early investor, as well, to provide a link to political connections. Mammoth Petroleum Company was born.

Entwined now with Detroit gangsters just as he had been with New York City mobsters, Leebove soon found his skills sought after. On September 16, 1931, the Purple Gang lured three competing gangsters to the Collingwood Manor Apartments in Detroit and murdered them. The driver of the getaway car was Ray Bernstein, the youngest of the four Bernstein brothers who together ran the Purple Gang. Acting on the information from an informant, police quickly arrested Ray along with two Purple gunmen. Swiftly, a trial ensued. By mid-November the three were on their way to Michigan's maximum-security prison in Marquette, sentenced to life terms. That same month, the State of Michigan voted for a Democrat for president for the first time ever. Fellow Democrat William Comstock was elected governor.

Ray Bernstein's three brothers, and especially the oldest, Abe, had immediately begun efforts to reverse the conviction for murder. They tried to corrupt the witnesses for the prosecution. They argued that due process had been violated. They demanded a new trial. Nothing worked. Now, with Comstock in the governor's mansion, perhaps Isaiah Leebove could do something. They offered him a large retainer. He agreed to free Ray using his connections to the governor. Comstock proceeded to name Leebove Special Inspector of Prisons, supposedly to offer proposals to streamline their operation and save the state money. This looked very much like setting a fox to guard the henhouse, and journalists as well as Republican legislators raised a howl. In the end, nothing came of Leebove's charge and, worse, at the end of Comstock's term in office (he lost his bid for re-election in 1933), Comstock refused Leebove's outright request to help Ray Bernstein get out of prison. Leebove continued his efforts, hoping that the next governor would be susceptible to appeals for at least a new trial. Still nothing worked. In early 1938 Leebove let the Bernstein brothers know that he had done all he could; he offered to return the retainer. But Abe and Joe Bernstein would have none of it.

Meanwhile, relations between Jack Livingston and Isaiah Leebove had soured. From being a central figure in Mammoth Petroleum, Jack gradually drifted away. He had always had a severe drinking problem. Serial treatments for his alcoholism had no lasting effect. When he was sober, he did fine work; when he was not, he wasted Leebove's money and accomplished little. After giving him several chances, Isaiah had had enough. He dumped Jack from all Mammoth operations and then eventually cut off the unofficial salary he kept paying him out of consideration for their long, but increasingly badly frayed, friendship. Jack knew all about Leebove's connections to the Purple Gangsters. Even though the gang itself had disintegrated soon after the Collingwood Manor fiasco, they still had lots of mobster contacts. Jack increasingly felt that Leebove hated him. He became more and more convinced that Leebove wanted to get him out of the way. As his alcoholism became worse and worse, his imagination vividly pictured Leebove as his murderer. He finally broke.

That Saturday evening, Jack came into the bar of the Doherty and looked around. He saw Isaiah Leebove and his friends sitting in a booth by the window. Jack turned, went upstairs to his room, and got his .38 revolver. He came back down, entered the bar, and took a seat with two local girls. Conversing with them, he talked a good deal of nonsense and lapsed into increasingly incomprehensible remarks about life and love. He then moved to the Barrs' table, friends who were Up North at their cabin and in town for dinner and a drink. He was directly across from the booth where Leebove chatted amiably with his friends. Jack slowly got up and stepped over to where Leebove sat. Leebove looked up quizzically from his conversation. Jack stopped and, blinded by his rage, fear, and resolve, he pulled out the .38 revolver, took aim at the man who had once been his close friend, three times pulled the trigger, and muttered, "There, you son-of-a-bitch."

Jack calmly lowered the revolver, turned, and walked back upstairs to his room. Pandemonium ruled the barroom. Someone left to get the police chief. A doctor came, but it was too late to do anything. Summoned by a phone call, Leebove's wife rushed down from her home and seeing her husband dead on the floor, sank down and embraced him,

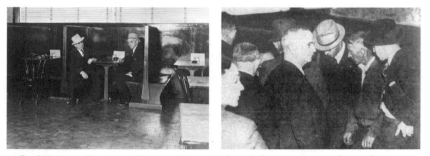

L., William Dunlop, Clare police chief, and George Bates, Clare County sheriff, survey the place where Leebove fell. R., the coroner's jury examines the same spot in the Doherty Hotel bar.

oblivious to his blood staining her evening dress. The chief arrived. He went up to Jack's room and knocked on the door. Jack opened it.

"Did I get him?" Livingston asked.

"You got him, Jack," the chief replied.

Was Jack just carrying out a personal vendetta, killing Leebove because he hated him and feared for his life? Or was there something more? The Bernsteins were fed up with Leebove because he had failed to free their brother. Leebove had recently offered to return the retainer, but that wasn't good enough. They felt they had been misled or even double-crossed by Leebove—their brother still rotted in prison. Local rumor said that the day before, Jack had gotten a call from Joe Bernstein. "Just do it now" was the message. Leebove lay dead, the victim of a crazed alcoholic, the target of a perfect gangland slaying, or both.

Then, Jack beat the rap. Put on trial in Harrison for the murder, he pled insanity and the jury bought it; not guilty, they declared. A month later, state examiners enlisted to determine Jack's mental state declared that he was perfectly sane. He left Harrison a free but troubled man. About ten years later, he committed suicide in New York City.

Afterword

The tales and truths about gangsters Up North offer an aspect of Michigan history never seen before in its entirety. Although individual events and people and myths have from time to time captured the imagination of true-crime buffs and historians, the whole picture remained untold. The extent and fascination of the stories surprises. Piece by piece, a jigsaw of mobsters, mafia, and racketeers assembles into a coherent whole showing how many criminals have found a role Up North. Local boys gone bad—the Wertheimers of Cheboygan, John Hamilton of Sault Ste. Marie—joined Public Enemies, grifters, gamblers, kidnappers, bank robbers, and killers in various deeds throughout the 1920s and 1930s. While unlike the Detroit area, northern Michigan was never a hotbed of gangster activity, there was much more of a presence than has been realized. In addition to the real exploits of so many criminals, the myths linked to them provide additional fascination. Investigating the gangsters produced many unexpected and even at times amusing facts. Future research may hold yet more surprises!

Appendix

Maps

Michigan Counties and County Seats 1930s

Michigan Highways 1920

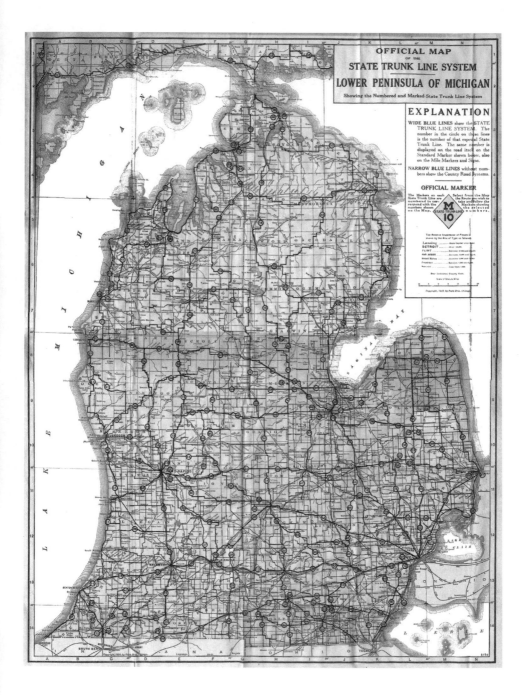

Acknowledgments

So many people have helped me with the project, it is hard to make a full reckoning. But it is a pleasure to try. Since my work went county to county, I would like to express my thanks accordingly.

In Alpena County, Marlo Broad at the Alpena library offered good advice. In Benzie, Jerry Heiman found lots of good information about gangsters in Frankfort. Trevor Dotson and David Miles of the Charlevoix Historical Society provided extensive help with the Colonial Club and other matters. In Cheboygan, Doug Young and Mary Lou Miller made me welcome at the county genealogical society. Susan James (Chippewa County Historical Society) answered questions about gangsters in the Soo area. Researching Harry Bennett's Lost Lake lodge, I benefitted greatly from Bill Gamble's knowledge and owe a special debt for an extensive tour of the lodge and environs; Frank Rowley shared lots of memories and facts from his time as a resident at the lodge. For gangsters in Clare, two interviews with Milan "Chip" Shepard provided many leads that I could follow up. For Prohibition era deeds and criminals, Russell Magnaghi's book proved invaluable, as was his advice about Delta County events and people. Emmett County has a very special local historian in Richard Wiles. He unstintingly shared his knowledge, images, and publications; he also directed me to many other people who subsequently helped my project, people such as Rick Brown, Meryl Hankey, Wendy Morris, Chris Struble, and Tom Fairbairn, all of whom it is a pleasure to thank here. Wiles was particularly helpful about Club Manitou; Barbara Madison added details about Al Gerhart's life; Beth Sylak of the Harbor Springs Area Historical Society helped as well with the Ramona Park Casino nearby. Kim Kelderhouse of the Leelanau Historical Society and Museum opened her files on Al Capone's supposed stay in that county. In Mackinac County, Bob Tagatz, the Grand Hotel's historian, offered good advice while Tom Pfeiffelmann provided good conversation and marvelous stories about bootleggers in the area. In the Upper Peninsula, Samantha Ashby of the Peter White Public Library in Marquette went to great lengths to provide me with an obscure document; Philip Mason also provided good leads. Jennifer Bacon opened up Al Capone's supposed time in Mason County for me. She offered her research, images, and contacts in a most friendly manner. The archives at Historic White Pine Village provided images and newspaper clippings while George Budzinsky went the extra mile in offering advice and contacts, including Annette Hack. Montmorency County might not seem very probable as a gangster location, but Suzanne "Zue" Hudson welcome me to what once was Hunters Home Dance Hall near Atlanta and provided stories and contacts, including Jimmy Richardson. For the Hillman Heist in the county, Rose Creamer of the Hillman Historical Society proved a much appreciated and enthusiastic guide; Jim Stoddard showed me the bank vault; Wes Hills, author of an excellent newspaper story on the heist, shared his knowledge. To the south, in Ogemaw County, many people helped me find gangster information and myths. Cathy Snyder of the Rose City Area Historical Society took me twice around the area looking for gangster hideouts and has always enthusiastically supported the project. In the society, Grace Dooley and George Smith also were very helpful. Sally Rea, Ogemaw County Genealogical Society and Museum, open the archives for me. Finally, Jack Jobst, author of a fine article on the Graceland Ballroom, shared advice on some useful avenues of research. Although Ottawa and Allegan counties are not Up North, I learned a lot from conversation with Randal VanderWater. In Kalamazoo, Catherine Larson provided crucial assistance. Back Up North, Roscommon County proved a surprisingly fruitful area to poke around in. Margaret Karinen shared first-hand experience, as did Pat Maurer and her brother, Jim Richardson; for Higgins Lake, Richard and Mary Roe had stories; Dennis Dusseau of the Houghton Lake Area Historical Society showed me the playhouse/Johnson's Rustic Dance palace.

Beyond the counties themselves, I would express my appreciation to Kenneth Dickson, the reigning authority on gangsters in Toledo, who offered me a good deal of advice and information about Toledo gangsters as they sprang up here and there. He was especially helpful about Toledans at the Ramona Park Casino. Scott Burnstein also deserves special mention. His expertise on Detroit gangsters set me straight on several occasions. In particular, he provided elemental material on Mafia figures in Roscommon County. James Buccellato's advice and book on Detroit Mafia figures proved very useful. The staff at the Clarke Historical Library at Central Michigan University were, as always, extremely helpful.

In the production stage, Thomas Burchfield of Thomas Burchfield Editing and Writing Services once again suggested invaluable technical and organizational improvements to the manuscript. Erin Howarth provided the usual excellent services as editor and production manager.

My wife, Carolyn, was my companion on many trips to check out gangster locations and interview informants. Her presence always added pleasure to any research foray. As a fellow historian, her insightful queries followed by a careful reading and useful suggestions greatly improved the final product. She deserves and receives my warmest thanks.

Bibliography

Alden, Sharyn. "Northwoods Lodges Offer a Nostalgic Getaway." *Milwaukee Journal Sentinel* 2018-05-18.

Arnold, Amy L., Cheryl Chidester, Sandra Sageser Clark, and Louis H. Conger. *Southwest Michigan Roadmap: The West Michigan Pike. Vol. II, Historic Resource Survey.* Lansing, Mich.: State Historic Preservation Office, 2010.

Ash, Agnes. "Contrapposto and Six Dress Suits." *Miami (Fla.) News Miami Magazine,* 1965-10-31: 14-15.

Bair, Deidre. *Al Capone: His Life, Legacy and Legend.* New York: Nan A. Talese/Doubleday, 2016.

Ballard, Charles Edward (Chad), with Janet Kirk Johnson and Anna Marie Borcia. *Charles Edward "Ed" Ballard A Story of Determination, Self-education, and Ultimate Succes.* N.p.: C.E. Ballard Literary Trust, 1984.

Bennett, Harry, with Paul Marcus. *Ford: We Never Called Him Harry.* New York: Faucett, 1951.

Bergreen, Laurence. *Capone The Man and the Era.* New York: Simon & Schuster, 1994.

Bley, Beverly. "Getting to Know Your Neighbor." *Michigan History Magazine* 92.6 (November-December 2008): 28ff.

Blust, Tonya. "Baby Face Nelson Robbed a Grand Haven Bank." Michigan 101 2014-01-24. http://michi101.blogspot.com/2014/01/baby-face-nelson-robbed-grand-haven-bank.html (accessed 2019-01-23).

Buccellato, James A. *Early Organized Crime in Detroit. Vice, Corruption and the Rise of the Mafia.* Charleston S.C., History Press, 2015.

Bueschel, Dick. "I Remember." pp. 55-59 In *A Stony Lake History,* 55-59. Hart Mich: Oceana County Historical and Genealogical Society, 1985.

Burrough, Bryan. *Public Enemies America's Greatest Crime Wave and the Birth of the FBI, 1933-34.* New York: Penguin, 2004.

Carman, Beulah. *Capsules of Time: A Saga of Houghton Lake.* Houghton Lake, Mich.: Bankov Printing, 1987.

BIBLIOGRAPHY

Chilcote, Stephanie. "Harry Bennett: Henry Ford's Man of All Work." Research paper for History 333: History of Michigan, Professor William McDaid, April 2010, 14 pages. Clarke Historical Library, Central Michigan University, Mt. Pleasant, Michigan..

Clock, Bob. "Stork Club of the North." *Harbor Springs (Mich.) Harbor Light,* 1967-12-20: 1.

Cochran, Jennifer M. "Roaring '20s Part of Ice Cream Eatery's History." *Petoskey (Mich.) News-Review,* 1986-07-07.

"Cool Camp: Lost Lake Scout Reservation, Great Lakes Council, Lake, Michigan." *Scouting* (January-February 2012): 52.

Cotsirlos Thomopoulos, Elaine. *St. Joseph and Benton Harbor.* Mt. Pleasant S.C.: Arcadia Press, 2003.

DeMott, Mary. "Ellie's Deli & Pizzeria." *Fairfield (Mich.) Wilderness Chronicle* #41 (December 2003): 13

Dickson, Kenneth R. *Something for Nothing, Gambling in the Glass City 1910-1952.* Point Place, Ohio: ZKDATT, 2008.

Dickson, Kenneth R. *Nothing Personal, Just Business, Prohibition and Murder on Toledo's Mean Streets.* Fremont, Ohio: Lesher Printing, 2003.

Federal Bureau of Investigation (FBI). "Alphonse Capone." Freedom of Information and Privacy Acts. File:62-20034, 62-24153, and 62-27268.

Federal Bureau of Investigation (FBI). "Alvin Karpis and Fred Barker." Freedom of Information and Privacy Acts. File:32-16384, Section 1, Serials 1-3.

Federal Bureau of Investigation (FBI). "Alvin Karpis." Freedom of Information and Privacy Acts. File:62-43010, Section 1.

Federal Bureau of Investigation (FBI). "Purple Gang." Freedom of Information and Privacy Acts. File:62-HQ-29632.

Foreman, Connie England, Gayle Niesen McEnaney, and Arthur D. Smith. *Gun Lake Revisited: A Pictorial History, 1877-1983.* N.p [Mich.]: C. Foreman/G. McEnaney, 1983.

Fraser, Chat. Lake Erie Stories: Struggle and Survival on a Freshwater Ocean. READHOWYOUWANT COM LTD, 2017.

Frazier, Dave. "Scouts Will Camp with a Legend." *Detroit Free Press* 1966-05-01: 13-C.

Friday, Matthew J. Article about Clyde Milliken. *Bank Note Reporter* 2008-02-07. http://www.numismaster.com/ta/numis/Article.jsp?ad =article &ArticleId=3803 (accessed 2018-07-13 but taken down by 2019-04-20).

Friedman, Bill. *30 Illegal Years to the Strip: The Untold Stories of the Gangsters Who Built the Early Las Vegas Strip.* N.p.: Babybook, 2015.

Gilbert, Edith. "High-rolling at Charlevoix's Old Colonial Club. The Ghosts Crap Out to a Bulldozer." In *Summer Resort Life: Tango, Teas and All!,* 73-83. Charlevoix Mich.: Jet'iquette, 1976) = *Detroit Free Press Detroit Magazine* 1974-02-03: 18-21, 23.

Goodboo, Barb. "A Tribute to the Graceland Ballroom." *Momentum Magazine* (Rose City, Mich.), 1991.

Haeffner, C. *Cabins in the Mist.* Philadelphia: Xlibris Corp., 2001.

Hendrickson, Gerth E. *The Angler's Guide to Twelve Classic Trout Streams in Michigan.* Ann Arbor: University of Michigan Press, 1994.

Henry, Tom. "Lupton's 'Grace' dead at 49: May She Rest in Peace." *Bay City Times* 1981-12-23: 3C.

Hills, Wes. "Whatever Happened to the Loot and Alexander Graham following the Great Hillman Bank Robbery of July 29, 1930?" *Atlanta (Mich.) Montmorency County Tribune* 2015-08-25.

Hollatz, Tom. *Gangster Holidays. The Lore and Legends of the Bad Guys.* St. Cloud Minn.: North Star Press, 1989.

Hunt, Pat. "Graceland Ballroom Landmark of Gangster Era." *Bay City Times* 1974-02-20, section C: 1.

Illman, Harry R. *Unholy Toledo.* San Francisco: Polemic Press Publications, 1985.

Jobst, Jack. "Graceland—A Ballroom and Its Builder." *Michigan History Magazine* (May-June 2010): 56-59.

Kavieff, Paul R. *The Purple Gang.* Fort Lee, N.J.: Barricade Books, 2000.

Kelly, Anne. "Let the Dice Roll." *Grand Traverse Scene,* vol. 1 (no. 3, Winter), 2012:16-20.

Kennedy, Robert F. "The Mafia, What It Means." *Saturday Evening Post* August 10-17, 1963.

Knapp Larry. Manuscript account. Clarke Historical Library, Central Michigan University, Mt. Pleasant, Michigan.

Knapp, Larry. "Purple Gang." Clarke Historical Library, Central Michigan University, Mt. Pleasant, Michigan.

Knapp, Robert. *Mystery Man. Gangsters, Oil, and Murder in Michigan.* Clare, Mich.: Cliophile Press, 2014.

——. *Small-Town Citizen Minion of the Mob. Sam Garfield's Two Lives. Purple Gangsters, Meyer Lansky, and Life in Clare Michigan.* Clare, Mich.: Cliophile Press, 2018.

BIBLIOGRAPHY

LaRouche, F. W. "Guardian of Henry Ford." *Little Rock Arkansas Gazette* 1934-05-06: 3, 5.

Laxalt, Robert. *Travels with My Royal. A Memoir of the Writing Life.* Reno: University of Nevada Press, 2001.

Link, Theodore C. "Match Owner is Ex-Convict." *St. Louis Post Dispatch* 1960-02-07: 1.

Lyon, Chriss. *A Killing in Capone's Playground: The True Story of the Hunt for the Most Dangerous Man Alive.* Holland (Mich.): In-Depth Editions, 2014.

Maas, Peter. "The Mafia: The Inside Story?" *Saturday Evening Post* August 10-17, 1963.

Magnaghi, Russell. *Prohibition in the Upper Peninsula and Bootleggers on the Border.* Charleston, S.C.: History Press, 2017.

McQuarrie, Willis John. *Whisky Smugglers of the North Channel.* Gore Bay Ont.: Mid-North Printers and Publishers, 2003.

Meek, Forrest. PurPL99, "Purple Crude." Manuscript in the archive of the Clare County Historical Society, Clare, Michigan.

Meek, Forrest. WBICK2.91, Meek/Willard Bicknell interview 1991. The transcription of the interview is in the archive of the Clare County Historical Society, Clare, Michigan.

Messick, Hank. *The Silent Syndicate.* New York: Macmillan, 1967.

Newton, Michael. *Mr. Mob: Life and Crimes of Moe Dalitz.* Jefferson, N.C.: MacFarland and Company, 2007.

Nye, Vern. "Acquiring Grousehaven." Typescript belonging to Grace Dooley of the Rose City Area Historical Society.

Obituary for William "Al" Gerhart in the *Petoskey (Mich.) News-Review,* 1987-12-17, 1-2;

Rauch, William. "Recalling Harbor Springs in the Cabaret Era of Gambling and Prohibition—A Wide Open Town." *Harbor Springs (Mich.) Harbor Light* Special Centennial Issue July 1, 1981; reprinted in *Harbor Light* 2012-04-04-10: 4B as "A Wide Open Town."

Revolinski, Kevin. "Where Public Enemies Went for a Little Peace and Quiet." *New York Times* 2009-06-25.

Rockaway, Robert A. "The Notorious Purple Gang: Detroit's All-Jewish Prohibition Era Mob." *Shofar* 20 (Special Edition: American Jews) (fall 2001): 118.

Rodgers, Judy. "Resorts." pp. 65-84 In *Harbor Springs. A Collection of Historical Essays,* edited by Jan Morley, 65-84. Harbor Springs Historical Commission. Clarksville Tenn.: Jostens, 1981.

Rodgers, Mary Augusta. "A Serenade to Leelanau." *New York Times* 1985-05-26.

Scroggins, William. *Leaves of a Stunted Shrub: A Genealogy of the Scrogin-Scrog-gin-Scroggins Family*, vol. 4. Cockeysville Md.: Nativa, LLC, 2009.

Spanier, Sandra and Robert W. Trogdon, eds. *The Letters of Ernest Hemingway.* Cambridge: Cambridge University Press, 2011.

Tedsen, Kathleen and Beverlee Rydel. *Haunted Travels of Michigan* vol. 2. Holt, Mich.: Thunder Bay Press, 2010.

Toland, John. *The Dillinger Days*. New York: Random House, 1963 (paper-back, New York: Da Capo, 1965).

Topix. topix.com hosted a forum for contributions to sightings of Capone in Michigan. The site has been taken down and so the thread is no longer accessible.

Trimmer, Elsie. *A History of Ellsworth's First 100 Years, 1866-1966.* Self-pub-lished, 1967.

Turner, Wallace. *Gamblers' Money. The New Force in American Life.* Boston: Houghton Mifflin, 1965.

Wakefield, Larry. "Al Capone Slept Here." In *Ernest Hemingway Fished Here and Other True North Country Tales.* Traverse City Mich.: Horizon Books, 1999.

Wasmer, Rick. *Whenever Rotary Scouts Fall in Line.* N.p.: Lulu Publishing Ser-vices, 2015.

Waugh, Daniel. *Egan's Rats: The Untold Story of the Prohibition-era Gang that Ruled St. Louis.* Nashville: Cumberland House, 2007.

Waugh, Daniel. *Off Color. The Violent History of Detroit's Notorious Purple Gang.* Holland Mich.: In-Dept Editions, 2014.

Wiles, Richard. "Manitou and Ponytail—Hot Spots of Harbor Springs." *Michigan Chronicle*; 39 (no. 4, Winter), 2017: 21-24.

Wiles, Richard. "Cheboygan's Famous (Infamous) Wertheimer Brothers." *Mackinac Journal* (May 2018): 17-21; (June 2018): 20-24, (July 2018): 20-25, (August 2018): 14-17.

Wiles, Richard. "The Infamous Club Manitou." *Mackinac Journal* (December 2013): 12-15.

Image Credits

Chapter 4 More Public Enemies	Dillinger map	*St. Joseph (Mich.) Herald-Press* 1934-04-16
	Dillinger double	*Edinburg (Ind.) Daily Courier* 1934-04-17
	Dillinger in Clare	*Clare (Mich.) Sentinel* 1934-04-27
	Frechette	*Dayton Daily News* 1934-05-23
	Brooks	*Chicago Tribune* 1935-03-23
	Frechette and Dillinger	Wiki Commons
	Karpis	*Sheboygan (Wisc.) Press* 1934-02-09
	Harry Campbell	FBI photo
	Joe Roscoe	*Miami News* 1937-01-27
	Burke	*Wilkes-Barre Evening News* 1931-03-30
	Burke home	*Benton Harbor News-Palladium,* 1931-03-26
	Nelson	*Billings Gazette* 1934-04-17
Chapter 5 Purple Crude	Bernstein brothers	R. Knapp collection
	Purple Gang	government photos
	Garfield	Pamela Schmiedike collection
	Leebove	*Saginaw News* 1938-5-15
	Leebove murder scene	*Detroit Evening Times* 1938-05-16-3
	Lansky	M. Zimmerman, AP photo
Chapter 6 Toledans	Hayes	*Toledo Blade* photo
	Hayes murdered	*Toledo Blade* photo
	Ramona Park Hotel & interior	Harbor Springs Area Historical Society
	Bert Moss	*Detroit Times* 1936-12-30
	Ramona Park Casino 1927 & 1932	Tom Graham Real Estate Harbor Springs & Harbor Springs Area Historical Society
	Boston	*New York Daily News* 1945-02-06
	Jameson	*Stony Lake and Charlie Jameson* p. 4 Oceana County Historical and Genealogical Society
	Pine Lodge Stony Lake	*Stony Lake and Charlie Jameson* p. 3 Oceana County Historical and Genealogical Society
Chapter 7 Cleveland Syndicate	Dalitz	AP photo
Chapter 8 Mafiosi	Zerilli	*Detroit Free Press* 1962-02-22
	LaMare	Wiki Commons
	Corrado	*Detroit Free Press* 1953-12-06
	Zerilli	Wiki Commons
	Profaci	Wiki Commons

Chapter 9	Bennett	AP photo
Harry	Ford and Bennett	*Detroit Free Press* 1951-09-20
Bennett		
	thugs beating UAW leader	AP photo
	Bennett Kefauver	*Detroit Free Press* 1951-02-09
	East Tawas lodge	R. Knapp collection
	Harry and Esther	*Detroit Free Press* 1965-10-24
	Ethel B. Lodge inscription	R. Knapp collection
	Lost Lake lodge	R. Knapp collection
Chapter 10	gambling drawing	*Detroit Free Press* 1925-08-09- Ted
Gambling		Dulyn
	Club Manitou	Wendy Morris photo
	Gerhart	Richard Wiles collection
	Abe Bernstein	*Detroit Free Press* 1928-04-07
	Fatty Bernstein poster	Wiki Commons
	Fatty and Al	Richard Wiles collection
	Al, Jean, and Washburne	Baker photo Richard Wiles collection
	Club Manitou interior	Baker l and r and Wendy Morris photos
	Manitou kitchen	Baker photo Richard Wiles collection
	Manitou customers and Pepper	Baker photo Richard Wiles collection
	Manitou wait staff	Baker photo Richard Wiles collection
	Pepper	Baker photo Richard Wiles collection
	Gerhart park	R. Knapp collection
	John H. Koch	U.S. passport photo
	Colonial Club	R. Knapp collection
	Colonial Club front	Gilbert *Summer Resort Life*_p. 3
	Charlevoix Beach Club	R. Knapp collection
	Grand Hotel	R. Knapp collection
	Chuck-a-luck	AP photo 1931-03-14
	Woodfill	Wiki Commons
	Wertheimer brothers	*Detroit Free Press* 1946-08-02; *Los Angeles Times* 1941-08-17; *Minneapolis Star Tribune* 1941-03-14; *Muncie Star Press* 1924-06-07
	Cheboygan downtown	Doug Dailey image
	Aniwa Club	*Detroit Free Press* 1930-04-20
	Burt Lake view from Gray Goose	R. Knapp collection
	Gray Goose cottage	R. Knapp collection
Chapter 11	Top-In-A-Bee Hotel Resort	R. Knapp collection
Gangster	Lincoln Fitzgerald	*Detroit Free Press* 1946-08-02
Vacations	Hotel Resort advert	*Detroit Free Press* 1934-06-10
	Comstock	Library of Congress

Notes

1   Special Report on case #2499 [the Lindbergh kidnapping], May, 1932, p. 3, Michigan State Police Archive, Lansing, Michigan.

2   Laurence Bergreen, *Capone The Man and the Era* (New York: Simon & Schuster, 1994), 147.

3   http://www.myalcaponemuseum.com/id199.htm (accessed 2018-03-5).

4   Bergreen, *Capone*, 141-145.

5   Bergreen, *Capone*, 162.

6   http://www.myalcaponemuseum.com/id228.htm (accessed 2018-03-5). A *Detroit Free Press*, 1932-04-10, Feature section, 5 article stated, "Al Capone and Sheldon left town [Chicago] hurriedly and went to Hot Springs, Arkansas, to wait for things to cool off in Chicago, where it was 'hot' for them."

7   Bergreen, *Capone*, 172-73.

8   Although others mention this part of Capone's life, Bergreen's research results are the gold standard for discussing it. Deirdre Bair has an account of Al in Lansing and Round Lake in 1926 that closely resembles Bergreen's. Deirdre Bair, *Al Capone: His Life, Legacy and Legend* (New York: Nan A. Talese/Doubleday, 2016), 86-89.

9   Bergreen, *Capone*, 177: Actually, his stays amount to three summers in all, 1926-1928. The summer of 1929 Capone was in a Pennsylvania prison; the summer of 1930 he was on trial for perjury in Miami Beach. Pp. 175-192 provide the core narrative, with some irrelevant asides along the way.

10 Various accounts do circulate. Paul Grescowle, the last owner of Emil's Restaurant in Lansing, was certain the tales of Capone were true. He stated, "When Al Capone would come in, he really loved Coca-Cola and pasta. He was always very polite but had to have the same seat in the back against the wall. If people were seated in his spot, my grandfather would offer to buy their meal in exchange for Al Capone to have his usual spot." "Capone used to come in on his way going back and forth from Canada. He didn't stay long. He loved the food. He'd have a bite to eat, then he was on his way." http://www.secondwavemedia.com/capitalgains/features/emils0903.aspx; http://www.lansingstatejournal.com/story/news/2015/10/30/emils-lansing-institution-closes/74009754/ (accessed 2018-05-13). Vic Spagnuolo offered a second account of interaction with Scarface. "He would come to my dad and uncle and ask for the names of families in Lansing who were having a hard

20 Besides newspaper accounts and local memories, Tom Hollatz treats The Hide Out in *His Gangster Holidays. The Lore and Legends of the Bad Guys* (St. Cloud Minn.: North Star Press, 1989), 67-80, with many images. Unfortunately, Hollatz mostly repeats conventional information about Capone, but he does quote people in the area who claim to have had contact with gangster—claims that in no way, of course, validate Capone's actual presence, since false sightings of Capone are often sworn to by people who claim to be eyewitnesses.

21 "An old man came in here one day and he said Capone was a saint. He said Al Capone took care of him for nine months, feeding his family during the Depression. It was like a mission for the gentleman to come here and look at Al's place." Hollatz, *Gangster Holidays*, 71.

22 *Milwaukee Journal*, 1953-10-16, pt. 8, 8. The place later called The Hide Out is located six miles west of New Post, six miles north of Couderay, and six miles east of Reserve. The current address is 12101 W County Road CC. It is on Pike Lake, not Cranberry Lake. It is ~30 miles west of Barker Lake and ~90 miles west of Mercer. Pike Lake used to be called Cranberry Lake: *Green Bay (Wis.) Press-Gazette* 2000-09-30, B-5.

23 That would be in spring, 1930. *Appleton (Wis.) Post-Crescent*, 1929-05-17, 4. *Wausau (Wis.) Daily Herald*, 1929-05-22, 9 makes it clear that the lodge had not yet been completed and that Capone *planned* to take it up as a summer place.

24 *Milwaukee Journal Sentinel*, 1929-05-21, 1, 4.

25 *Oshkosh (Wis.) Northwestern*, 1929-05-20, 8. In 1953 the property was sold. A descriptive article states that Capone sold it in the early 1930s (*Milwaukee Journal*, 1953-10-16, pt. 8, p. 8). In the 1980s it was run as a resort cashing in on the Capone mythology (Hollatz, *Gangsters*, 70-75). It is now owned by the Lac Courte Oreille Indian tribe. I find no indication that it is being used—the tribal casino is in Hayward, Wisconsin, about 25 miles away.

26 See the intelligent summary compiled by Steve Shukis: https://chicagotruecrime.com/hideout-part-iii-the-big-secret.html (accessed 2019-01-09). He cities good evidence from FBI reports and newspapers.

27 Kevin Revolinski of the *New York Times* ("Where Public Enemies Went for a Little Peace and Quiet," 2009-06-25; https://www.nytimes.com/2009/06/26/travel/escapes/26Gangster.html [accessed 2019-01-16]) wrote: "Today it still has a middle-of-nowhere appeal, and though management for many years flat-out denied there was any evidence that Capone ever stayed or even visited, the stories persist. I nosed around, and a staff member took me upstairs to a renovated event space that believers say was once Capone's room of choice. Another staff member, who — perhaps wisely— insisted on remaining anonymous, said that in the 1920s Four Seasons and three other private

resorts in the area all had armed guards and barbed-wire fences. She repeated management's contention that the gangster pedigree was only hearsay..." The current owners of the resort state the truth: "Rumors often suggested not all customers were the best society could offer, but despite repeated stories that mobster Al Capone was among the Four Seasons' guests Ross and his wife, Marie, were adamant that "Scarface" had never visited the property. 'Don't ever say anything about Al Capone coming here,' Marie Ross said in that same interview. "He never was in our place. Ever, ever, ever." https://www.wisconsin.golf/19th_hole/dennis_mccann/pembine-second-life-for-four-seasons-island-resort-generates-quite/article_d4b4372c-aed9-11e8-b39d-f3399ffc4570.html (accessed 2019-01-16).

28 Revolinski, "Where Public Enemies."

29 Many of the sightings are reported in the web thread called Topix Forum (topix.com), no longer available on the Internet.

30 Basic information (duly questioned) is summarized in Amy L. Arnold, Cheryl Chidester, Sandra Sageser Clark, and Louis H. Conger, *Southwest Michigan Roadmap: The West Michigan Pike. Vol. II, Historic Resource Survey*, (Lansing, Mich.: State Historic Preservation Office, 2010). They give further bibliography about gangsters in that area. My summary is based on this work unless otherwise noted.

31 Noted even in the *Ludington (Mich.) Daily News*, 1931-07-20, 6 (AP).

32 Said to be validated by Berrien County Sheriff's Department records, which I have not seen.

33 Topix entry.

34 For Burke's presence in Michigan, see the excellent book by Chriss Lyon, *A Killing in Capone's Playground: The True Story of the Hunt for the Most Dangerous Man Alive* (United States of America: In Depth Editions, 2014).

35 http://shresort.tripod.com/id12.html (accessed 2019-01-09).

36 Topix.

37 Correspondence with James Schmiechen, local historian in Saugatuck.

38 Diligent search and inquiry fail to turn up any evidence of such trips by boat by Capone. People say that he owned a yacht named either the *Acania* or the *Duchess III*, but no one produces any evidence of this, only the usual hearsay.

39 Connie England Foreman, Gayle Niesen McEnaney, and Arthur D. Smith, *Gun Lake Revisited: A Pictorial History, 1877-1983* (n.p [Mich.]: C. Foreman/G. McEnaney, 1983). I have not seen this book; it appears in no library collection, nor through any internet merchant.

40 Charlotte Weick of Advanced Newspapers posted this at https://www.mlive.com/penaseeglobe/index.ssf/2009/02/on_the_trail_of_al_capone_in_a.html (accessed 2019-01-09).

41 Topix.

42 This scout camp started in 1911 so apparently folks thought that Al hid out with the boys.

43 https://www.michigan-sportsman.com/forum/threads/what-is-your-home-town-famous-for.243620/ (accessed 2019-01-13).

44 *Indianapolis Star,* 1930-07-15, 3. The full story is told in the chapter "More Public Enemies Up North."

45 Topix.

46 See chapter, "Toledans at the Beach." The noted accounts were found on Topix.

47 Jennifer Bacon in correspondence. I have not seen the photo, nor can it now be located. Of course, a man, even Capone, standing by a car in a rural area could have been taken in any number of places.

48 Drew McVicker, in correspondence. Another local person, almost ninety in 2017, stated with certainty that Capone never stayed in the Opitz Hotel. A third source told me that Opitz did not allow liquor in her hotel. That certainly would have discouraged a visit by Capone unless he was attracted by Opitz' famous fried chicken dinners! McVicker points out that there was a second hotel on the lake, perhaps named the Round Lake Hotel, that was tawdrier than the Opitz; Bacon confirms that this hotel continued to operate well after Capone's time. However, not even rumors indicate that Al Capone stayed at that one.

49 http://www.bigstarlakehistory.com/Hotel.htm (accessed 2019-01-10).

50 Topix.

51 As usual, no one actually says s/he has been in one of these supposed tunnels. The best that is witnessed is (alleged) bricked up openings in various structures. The person who once owned the Hotel Frankfort stated that he did a lot of remodeling in the basement, including digging out several walls by hand, and found no evidence of tunnels. Jerry Heiman in correspondence.

52 Topix.

53 https://www.annlake.org/?page_id=389 (accessed 2019-01-13).

54 http://lakeanncottage.com/the-cottage/ (accessed 2019-01-13).

55 https://business.facebook.com/lakeanncorner/posts/606031986449829 (accessed 2019-01-13).

56 The article is republished as the chapter "Al Capone Slept Here" in Larry Wakefield, *Ernest Hemingway Fished Here and Other True North Country Tales* (Traverse City Mich.: Horizon Books, 1999), 41-45.

57 Theodore C. Link, "Match Owner is Ex-Convict," *St. Louis Post Dispatch*, 1960-02-07, 1.

58 *House of Representatives Congressional Record 1950*, p. 8434.

59 Mary Augusta Rodgers, "A Serenade to Leelanau," *New York Times* 1985-05-26. Also picked up by William Scroggins, *Leaves of a Stunted Shrub : a Genealogy of the Scrogin-Scroggin-Scroggins Family*, vol. 4, (Cockeysville Md.: Nativa, LLC, 2009), 158-159.

60 http://static.record-eagle.com/2000/dec/02sale.htm.

61 Sharyn Alden, "Northwoods Lodges Offer a Nostalgic Getaway," *Milwaukee Journal Sentinel*, 2018-05-18. This Spider Lake Lodge was built in 1923. The lodge is near Hayward, Wisconsin, in an area that saw actual gangsters vacationing.

62 Supposedly he had a residence in Harbor Springs; also, supposedly he "lined up a family and tommy gunned them;" one of his bars is now a township hall "somewhere." One person claims his father did landscaping for Big Al "in the early 80s"! Topix. Beth Sylak of the Harbor Springs Area Historical Society in correspondence categorically rejects these claims.

63 Although there is no proof, Daniel Waugh, the author of the best book on the Purple Gang (*Off Color. The Violent History of Detroit's Notorious Purple Gang*, Holland Mich.: In-Dept Editions, 2014) accepts mythical encounters in Detroit itself with both the Purple Gang and Detroit's Mafia, pp. 135, 143. Capone himself never set foot in Detroit, although the stories go back to the 1920s themselves. Of course, it is entirely possible that Capone's men did visit the Motor City on his behalf.

64 Around $30,000 in purchasing power today.

65 Mafalda is referred to as "Mae," the name of her sister-in-law, Al's wife, in newspapers as early as 1959. This is not just a confusion with the name of her sister-in-law, who is also mentioned as "Mae" in the same reports. John Maritote always called Mafalda "Mae". Beverley Bley, "Getting to Know Your Neighbor," *Michigan History Magazine* 92.6 (November-December) 2008, 28ff.

66 Possibly Mafalda liked the rural—very rural—life in Oscoda from her time spent in Mercer, Wisconsin. One newspaper report asserts that she owned her brother, Ralph's, retreat in that town and she may have been there often. *Baton Rouge Advocate*, 1961-06-20, p. 8. After Mafalda's death, John Maritote moved to California to be with his daughter.

67 The article cited above by Beverly Bley describes her condition at this time. This article gives a very good description of the Maritotes' stay in Oscoda.

68 Posted by "LoriLyn" at http://chicagocrimescenes.blogspot.com/2008/10/mafalda-capone-maritote.html (accessed 2019-03-27).

69 But Russell Magnaghi in correspondence tells of a person in Sault Ste. Marie who recalled his grandmother cooking spaghetti for Big Al.

70 1930 road map of Wisconsin at http://content.wisconsinhistory.org/cdm/singleitem/collection/maps/id/16052/rec/10 (accessed 2019-01-16).

71 http://www.myalcaponemuseum.com/id196.htm (accessed 2019-01-16).

72 This was a real place. It specialized in Chevrolets.

73 Topix. See the material on William Shearer of Swan Lake, below. His bootlegging may be the origin of this Capone myth.

74 http://heritagenews.com/archive/article.asp?ID=413861 (accessed 2018-06-01).

75 Saari died in 2015. I could not locate this book or its author. Inquiries at the University of Michigan where Lampinen supposedly wrote the book as his dissertation revealed that he was never a student there. Philip Mason, a retired history professor at Wayne State University and an expert on bootlegging, etc., does not recall this person or this book. Russell Magnaghi (Northern Michigan University) could not find it, either. Lampinen's sources must, therefore, remain a mystery.

76 Unfortunately, glaring mistakes in Saari's account (referring to "Frankie Yalie" instead of Frankie Yale and to "Johnny Tario" instead of Johnny Torrio, along with serious errors in a description of Al's brother's life) throw doubt on his investigative standards. It is regrettable, too, that the "local historian" is not named.

77 Topix.

78 Russell Magnaghi, *Prohibition in the Upper Peninsula and Bootleggers on the Border* (Charleston, S.C.: History Press, 2017).

79 Topix. Another Topix contributor states that the tunnel went from the Ludington to Capone's house. That would be about a two-mile tunnel.

80 Indeed, some rumrunning did take place across Lake Superior as well as across the St. Marys River at Sault Ste. Marie. See Magnaghi, *Prohibition*.

81 *Marquette (Mich.) Mining Journal*, 1931-03-25, 4. Samantha Ashby of the Peter White Public Library in Marquette kindly found a copy of this article and aided in deciphering the poor microfilm version of the newspaper.

82 Larry Chabot, "Prohibition Gangsters Weren't Strangers to the U.P.," *Marquette Monthly*, June 2012, offers a sensible assessment of this piece of evidence and other reports of Capone in the area.

83 John Binder, *Al Capone's Beer Wars* (Amherst N. Y.: Prometheus Books, 2017), communicates in correspondence that only the *Acania* is documented as Capone's boat. I have not been able to find any reference of any kind to a boat in Great Lakes waters called the *Norco*.

84 Marriage date and place attested on divorce decree, Michigan divorce records. John and Sarah came to Nottawa Township, Isabella County. In March 1882, John opened a blacksmith shop in Calkinsville (Rosebush), Michigan. Their first child, William, was born the next year, also in Nottawa Township, Isabella County.

85 John B. Hamilton Jr.'s death certificate (1852-1923) from the State of Illinois states that he was born in "Ontario." On the 1910 U.S. Census his birth is listed as "Canada." All the other children were born in Michigan. The eldest, William, in 1883, Elmer, in 1885, Claude, in 1887, and Joseph Sylvester in 1893 were all born in Isabella County. The sibling immediately before John, Anna, was born in 1895 in Sault Ste. Marie; the one after him, Valentine "Tiny" came in 1901, also born in the Soo. Finally, Joseph Foy(e) was born in 1909. All but John are undoubtedly Michiganders. John Jr., born in 1898, does not appear in the admittedly incomplete Ontario birth records. The *Detroit Free Press* article 1934-11-29 states that Hamilton was born in the Soo. Another *Free Press* article (1935-08-29, 2) states he was born in Two Rivers, Ontario: "As a youngster he had been brought from tiny Two Rivers, Ontario." On John's marriage certificate to Mary Stephenson he asserts that he was born in Byng Inlet, Parry Sound District, Ontario.

86 Valentine was interviewed directly after Hamilton's body was discovered in 1935: Mabel Norris, "Normal Youth to Desperado!" *Akron (Ohio) Beacon Journal*, 1935-08-29, 1. One of the Hamilton children perhaps died young, for there were eight, not seven children in all. Examinations of Hamilton's life appear in the *Detroit Free Press* articles cited in the last note. Bryan Burrough, *Public Enemies. American's Greatest Crime Wave and the Birth of the FBI, 1933-1934* (New York: Penguin Books, 2004) provides many of the details of Hamilton's life as a criminal.

87 Details of the accident: *Sault Ste. Marie (Mich.) Evening News* 1909-06-16, 1. The event was changed in the telling so that later the story circulated that Hamilton lost his fingers on a dare when he thrust his hand between the wheels of a fast train and didn't pull it back in time to avoid being run over: *Detroit Free Press* 1935-08-29, 2.

88 *Sault Ste. Marie (Mich.) Evening News* 1910-11-21, 1.

89 *Sault Ste. Marie (Mich.) Evening News* 1914-09-18, 1.

90 The next year, 1915, Sarah lists herself in the Soo city directory as widowed,

which is strange since on the family gravestone John's death is given as 1923. Newspaper account seem to indicate that he was dead by 1914 or 1915, shortly after he had gone a bit crazy and threatened his family. That cannot be true, for why would a wrong date be carved into a gravestone that mentioned both John and Sarah? Apparently, Sarah, ashamed of the divorce, called herself a "widow" in 1915 and again in the 1921 Sault Ste. Marie city directory. Then when John Sr. died in 1923, he was buried in the family plot, again to hide or minimize the fact of his desertion and their divorce. Sarah died in 1933.

91 These and later details are a composite based mostly on three newspaper articles: *Detroit Free Press* 1934-11-29, 3; *Detroit Free Press* 1935-08-29, 2; and *Akron (Ohio) Beacon Journal*, 1935-08-29, 1 (the interview with his sister, Valentine).

92 *Sault Ste. Marie (Mich.) Evening News* 1919-12-27, 3.

93 The robbery, arrests, and interrogation are described in great detail in the *South Bend (Ind.) Tribune*, 1927-03-16, 1-2.

94 The men were pleased that they had not been extradited to Michigan where they would have faced a life sentence for bank robbery. However, they were chagrined at the long Indiana sentence. With discretion of between 10- and 25- year sentencing, the judge had opted for the longest possible sentence because, he said, he was also considering the Michigan robberies.

95 Divorce decree, Sault Ste Marie, 1928-10-19.

96 Burrough, *Public Enemies*, 296.

97 Details of this trip rely on Burrough, *Public Enemies*, 296-298 and newspaper accounts as cited. Given the detail Burrough offers, it is probable that much information came from Patricia Cherrington who gave a statement to the FBI after she was later arrested and, subsequently, also gave some interviews.

98 Her maiden name remains unclear. Her marriage license to Arthur Cherrington in 1932 gives her name as Patricia Young. Her sister is mentioned in newspaper accounts as Opal Long; that does not appear to be a married name, so Patricia may have been born a Long.

99 *Chicago Tribune* 1933-09-03, 3. Welton Spark, Billie Frechette's husband, and Roy Little were also arrested and sent to prison. Cherrington was transferred to the new prison on Alcatraz Island in 1934.

100 Burrough, *Public Enemies*, 297-298. He also adds details that seem to come from newspaper reports.

101 *Green Bay Press-Gazette* 1934-07-14, 1.

102 Oddly, both the time sentenced and the place the time was served differ in various accounts. Either she was sentenced to three or four months or six

months of detention; she served her time in Milan, or in the jail in Traverse City, or in the jail in Sault St. Marie.

103   Part of the government argument was that Mrs. Steve had helped Dillinger and Hamilton on their journey that eventually ended up at the Little Bohemia Lodge in Northern Wisconsin. This is the origin of the incorrect statements in newspapers and books that the gangsters went directly from Sault St. Marie to Little Bohemia and the deadly events there, travelling west across the Upper Peninsula through Newberry and Iron Mountain. Extensive and clear evidence, especially Patricia Cherrington's, decisively refutes a trip across the U.P. and validates the account followed here.

104   Also very near Mercer, where Ralph Capone had his cottage.

105   Burrough, *Public Enemies*, 407-409.

106   Federal authorities suspected that the tip had come from Anna Steve, but it is hard to imagine how she would have learned where Hamilton had been buried. *Detroit Times*, 1935-09-01.

107   International News Service story in the *(Hammond, Ind.) Times*, 1935-08-30; Associated Press story in the *Reno (Nev.) Gazette-Journal*, 1935-08-31, 2.

108   *Edinburg (Ind.) Daily Courier*, 1934-04-17, 1.

109   A. C. Haeffner, *Cabins in the Mist* (Philadelphia, Pa.?: Xlibris Corp., 2001).

110   *Detroit Evening Times*, 1932-05-18, 2.

111   Knapp manuscript in the Clarke Historical Library, Central Michigan University, Mt. Pleasant, Michigan. Larry Knapp is not related to the author.

112   *Clare (Mich.) Sentinel*, 1934-04-27, 1.

113   Before any careless thinking takes place regarding the possibility of Dillinger, Hamilton, and the woman coming south from the Soo, the dates would not match up. By April 21st, the date of this sighting, Dillinger and his group were already in Little Bohemia in northern Wisconsin.

114   The 1930 Census says nothing about her mother and gives her father as "mixed blood." I do not know where the "French" ancestry information comes from—perhaps just a deduction from her last name. The 1900 Census lists her as Mary Labell, living on the reservation, and as ½ Indian. The 1920 Census only lists her mother and gives her as "Indian." The 1920 Census says her mother was a janitress—U.S. Government Indian Office. On one of the Indian Census tallies, Evelyn is listed as "½", that is, half-Indian. In the Indian censuses from 1903 until 1924, the mother only is listed as head of household. She continues to have children through the teens, but never an official husband.

115   The 1920 Census says she went to school. 1930 Census says she had no schooling. Another source says she was sent to South Dakota for schooling.

116   Per William Frechette's birth certificate.

117   State of Illinois birth certificate. The father is listed as unknown. Michigan Attorney General Harry S. Toy in his desire to raise his visibility for a possible run for governor, claimed that John Dillinger was the father. However, as newspapers quickly pointed out, the birth date of the child was well before Frechette met Dillinger. *Evening San Diego (Calif.) Tribune*, 1935-01-24, 1.

118   Michigan Certificate of Death. The father is listed as unknown. The presence of syphilis is indication, but not proof, that Frechette had worked as a prostitute.

119   *Fort Worth Star-Telegram*, 1935-01-24, 2.

120   She appears regularly in the June Indian Census for most of the years of her life. Since we know she lived elsewhere some of the time, she must have just kept a registration in the Census whether she was actually present in any given year.

121   Either she was never actually married to Albert or had divorced him. Sparks was in Leavenworth on a 25-year sentence in 1932 (*Cincinnati Enquirer*, 1934-03-10, 2). She had a divorce case pending as of January 1934 (*Milwaukee Journal*, 1934-05-18, 2). Newspapers have her as the divorced wife of Welton Sparks, "Leavenworth convict," in 1934 (*Minneapolis Star Tribune*, 1934-03-11, 6). Newspapers also got the names mixed up, writing that she was the wife of "Sparks" Frechette, serving a fifteen-year sentence for bank robbery at Leavenworth. *Indianapolis Star*, 1934-01-28, 2.

122   Toland, *Dillinger*, 120, 127, states they met sometime just before late September 1933.

123   Federal Bureau of Investigation case originating at Cincinnati, Ohio. Report made at Detroit, Michigan, 1936-04-16 by W.H. Hoffman. File 7-25.

124   Their Ohio Marriage license lists him as "Clarence C. Miller," a fictitious name. The 1936 Karpis-Barker FBI report gives the name "Bob Miller."

125   FBI 1936 report on Barker-Karpis Gang.

126   FBI 1936 p. 2. His Italian name was Rascio per correspondence from Kenneth Dickson.

127   A full story of Middle Island and Joe Roscoe is in Chat Fraser, *Lake Erie Stories: Struggle and Survival on a Freshwater Ocean* (READHOWYOU-WANT COM LTD, 2017), 191-194.

128   *Toledo Blade*, 1937-01-28.

129 Accounts state that Burke committed land fraud in Michigan, but that crime was earlier, in Kansas. We do not know exactly what kind of fraud landed him in Michigan's prison system. Chriss Lyon in correspondence.

130 Federal Bureau of Investigation case searching for Barker-Karpis Gang originating at Cincinnati, Ohio. 1936. *Detroit Free Press*, 1929-12-18, 2: "Burke's method was to obtain information about the personal habits of the particular gambler or rum baron selected as victim, and at an opportune time seize him and carry him to a hide-out on one of the nearby lake resorts. In this manner Mert Wertheimer was seized at Burt Lake and held for $35,000 ransom, which was paid." It must be noted that a *Detroit Free Press* article 1932-12-31, 2 states that both Al and Mert were kidnapped and taken to a house in Oakland (a Detroit suburb) and were not snatched Up North. That is not Mert's own story: See chapter "Gangsters Pastimes."

131 For Burke in Michigan see Lyon, *A Killing*.

132 Lyon, *A Killing*, 2002-207 for the hideout and sightings.

133 Ibid., 249-255.

134 A good account of this episode is Tonya Blust, "Baby Face Nelson Robbed a Grand Haven Bank," Michigan 101 (2014-01-24) http://michi101. blogspot.com/2014/01/baby-face-nelson-robbed-grand-haven-bank.html (accessed 2019-01-23).

135 What follows is fully documented in Robert Knapp, *Mystery Man. Gangsters, Oil, and Murder in Michigan* (Clare Mich.: Cliophile Press, 2014) and *Small-Town Citizen Minion of the Mob. Sam Garfield's Two Lives. Purple Gangsters, Meyer Lansky, and Life in Clare Michigan* (Clare Mich.: Cliophile Press, 2018).

136 What follows is based upon Kenneth R. Dickson's well-researched books, *Something for Nothing, Gambling in the Glass City 1910-1952* (Point Place, Ohio: ZKDATT, 2008), and *Nothing Personal, Just Business, Prohibition and Murder on Toledo's Mean Streets* (Fremont, Ohio: Lesher Printing, 2003). I also learned much from correspondence with Dickson. There is a summary article dealing with this chapter's subject by Anne Kelly, "Let the Dice Roll," *Grand Traverse Scene* Vol. 1 (no. 3, Winter) 2012, 16-20.

137 *Toledo News Bee and Blade*, 1926-09-10.

138 Not to be confused with their cousin, Peter Licavoli, who was in Michigan's maximum-security prison in Marquette.

139 On St. Louis gangsters of this time, see Daniel Waugh, *Egan's Rats: The Untold Story of the Prohibition-era Gang that Ruled St. Louis* (Nashville Tenn.: Cumberland House, 2007).

140   Assistant Prosecutor Harry Friberg for the first time in a capital case used the Ohio statues on aiding and abetting a conspiracy to gain a conviction.

141   Located at 631 St. Clair Street, Toledo.

142   Dickson, *Nothing Personal*, 179-180.

143   Quoted by Dickson, *Something*.

144   Dickson, *Nothing Personal*, 175. Ed Warnke had been with Hayes since the earliest days when they both had been hack drivers on Toledo's streets in the 'teens.

145   Harry R. Illman, *Unholy Toledo* (San Francisco Calif.: Polemic Press Publications, 1985), mentions Jimmy Hayes on pp. 89 and 152, but does not mention the Ramona.

146   The Ramona Park Casino must not be confused with the Ramona Park Hotel. The hotel, built in 1909 and opened in 1910, became a prime destination for wealthy resorters from Chicago, Detroit, Cleveland, Cincinnati, St. Louis, and many places in-between. There was gambling there—it was raided as late as 1947—but its primary purpose was as a summer resort. There was a beach, a health spa, and much else. A very luxurious operation. Demolition crews took it down in November 1994. There is no sign of gangster involvement except, perhaps, as guests. The gangster connection seems limited to the casino, perhaps not by chance as the hotel encouraged the casino to be constructed (see below).

147   Dickson, *Nothing Personal*, 102, 183.

148   Judy Rodgers, "Resorts," pp. 65-84 in Jan Morley, ed. *Harbor Springs. A Collection of Essays* (Harbor Springs: Harbor Springs Historical Commission, 1981), 83-84. It is not clear which Studebakers are referred to here, but the family of automobile millionaires was based in South Bend, Indiana.

149   *Detroit Free Press*, 1934-10-05, 7.

150   *Detroit Free Press*, 1909-05-10, 1.

151   *Detroit Free Press*, 1912-10-13, 15. Bernstein became the leader of Detroit's Purple Gang around 1924-1925.

152   *Detroit Free Press*, 1916-11-08, 8.

153   *Detroit Times*, 1919-03-03.

154   *Detroit Free Press*, 1922-02-23, 2. It was the fifty-second police raid on the place.

155   *Marshall (Mich.) Evening Chronicle*, 1931-10-17, 1 (U.P.).

156   Cremer was an industrialist from Milwaukee. The Ramona Park Hotel seems to have either changed hands or re-branded itself, for in 1928

it advertised itself as the Traverse Shores Country Club with the Ramona Park Hotel part of the complex. *Detroit Free Press*, 1928-06-17, pt 6, 23.

157 This description comes from the *Petoskey (Mich.) Evening News*, 1926, courtesy of Richard Wiles.

158 I have not been able to find out anything about this Edward Young.

159 The Addison Hotel was run by one of the investors, Bert Moss, a major gambling impresario in Detroit at that time. See below.

160 Herman Kays, a local Petoskey private detective and cottage security person. The FBI interviewed him in 1936 as part of their investigation of the infamous Barker-Karpis Gang. "Mr. Kays spent considerable time with Agent gratis and it is believed he would be of considerable assistance at Petoskey and vicinity if there is ever any activity by the Bureau there. He accompanied Agent to Harbor Springs and personally pointed out the clubs..." The FBI report contains many interesting details about criminal life in the Harbor Springs/Petoskey area. https://vault.fbi.gov/barker-karpis-gang/bremer-kidnapping/bremer-kidnapping-part-219-of%20459-/view No. 219 (accessed 2018-06-15).

161 Kays, FBI.

162 *Detroit Free Press*, 1940-08-11, 1-2.

163 *Miami Herald*, 1930-02-11, 11. He appears as an owner only in 1930, but that may be just because the club's playbills stopped listing the owners of the club.

164 Dickson, *Nothing Personal*, 89.

165 These names and this piece of information come from Kays, FBI. One does wonder, however, if all of the named Detroit gamblers actually had a piece of the action. The list of investors reads rather like a list of well-known Detroit gambling overlords.

166 *Detroit Times*, 1931-09-17, 16; 1936-04-15, 17.

167 The details of ownership come from Herman Kays' interview with the FBI.

168 Kays, FBI.

169 *Marshall (Mich.) Evening Chronicle*, 1931-10-17, 1 (U.P.).

170 *Petoskey (Mich.) Evening News*, 1932-06-25 [no page given].

171 Dickson, *Nothing Personal*. Hayes seems to have bought this place, built about 1923-1924, as a first-class dinner club. Newspapers first mention him and his fellow Toledan, Louis Kaufman, as owners in early 1930. When he purchased it is unknown. However, it may have been that very year as Hayes

also expanded his gambling empire Up North in 1930. Was this simply expansion, or was Jimmy hedging his bets as the Licavolis moved in on his gambling turf in Toledo itself beginning in 1930?

172 Tripp specifically stated that the Petoskey Bay View Country Club, run by the Methodist church, "undoubtedly did not cater to gambling rackets." He also stated that the Walloon Lake Country Club, a stock company operated by one Chalmers Curtis, President of the First National Bank, "and other substantial people of the community," did not have anything to do with hoodlum or racketeering elements.

173 FBI report.

174 *Detroit Free Press,* 1934-10-05, 7.

175 Kays, FBI.

176 His presence was unknown to R.D. Tripp, Petoskey postmaster and long-time resident per the FBI report. Kays in his interview asserted he saw him there in the summer of 1935.

177 The Michigan State Police raided it in August 1938: *Marshall (Mich.) Evening Chronical,* 1938-08-18, 1.

178 I tell his story in the chapter "Gamblers and Gambling."

179 Gerhart used some salvaged materials to refurbish his recently acquired Booth's Bar, renamed Al's Pier Bar, in Harbor Springs. Richard Wiles, "The Infamous Club Manitou," *Mackinac Journal* December 2013, 12-15, p. 15.

180 At the demise of the Ramona Park Casino, a casino was opened in the Ramona Park Hotel itself, probably in the early 1950s and certainly, to judge from newspaper advertisements, by 1953.

181 Per Richard Wiles and Kenneth Dickson.

182 "In general, casual betting or gaming by individuals—as distinguished from betting or gambling as a business or profession—is not a crime in this state [of New York]." *Sacramento Bee* 1947-02-28 p. 14 (INS). Details on Boston's life in mid-town Manhattan: http://daytoninmanhattan.blogspot.com/2018/06/urban-living-enhanced-240-central-park.html (accessed 2019-02-05)

183 *Milwaukee Sentinel,* 1946-12-21 p. 17 (INS).

184 *Detroit Free Press,* 1947-09-27.

185 Jameson died in 1961.

186 Basic information from Dick Bueschel, "I Remember," pp. 55-59 in *A Stony Lake History* (Hart Mich.: Oceana County Historical and Genealogical Society, 1985).

187 Guarda L. Spellman, 1884-1935. She is buried in Shelby. Her father was a blacksmith in Shelby.

188 Bueschel, *Remember*, 56.

189 Information supplied by Kenneth Dickson.

190 Bueschel, *Remember*, 55. Subsequent quotations are also from Bueschel's account.

191 Quoted by Bueschel, *Remember*, 55. Jameson also told Reames, "Kid, when I was your age, I was stealing with both hands." And, "If I thought I had an honest dollar I'd throw it away."

192 "Perhaps the most colorful character in Stony Lake history was Charlie Jameson, a Toledo grifter, rumrunner, bootlegger and racketeer who had ties to the notorious Purple Gang." "A Brief History of Stony Lake, Michigan," based upon Bueschel's article. The author adds, "Many stories are told about Charlie's business sense, his fishing obsession, and his generosity to area residents." http://www.stonylakepropertyowners.com/docs/A%20Brief%20 History%20of%20Stony%20Lake.pdf (accessed 2018-11-07).

193 Bueschel, *Remember*, 57.

194 Ibid., 59 says she was buried in Toledo, but her gravestone is in the Mount Hope Cemetery, Shelby, nestled among the graves of her Spellman relatives. Her husband, Charlie, is also buried in that cemetery.

195 Hank Messick, *The Silent Syndicate* (New York: Macmillan, 1967) has full details on the Cleveland mobsters. See p. 42 for these four central figures.

196 Ibid., 50.

197 Ibid., 135.

198 Wallace Turner, *Gamblers' Money. The New Force in American Life* (Boston: Houghton Mifflin, 1965), 73 calls him a "lifelong friend."

199 He also involved his brother, George, in Leebove's oil operations. George and his wife and daughter even lived in the Doherty Hotel in Clare for a time. Then they rented Willard Bicknell's mother's duplex. Willard told Meek, "They lived over there, but they couldn't keep him sober." Purples and Cleveland gang brought into oil investment: Meek/Willard Bicknell interview 1991 p. 9-11.

200 *Detroit Times*, 1938-05-19, 4.

201 The FBI file on Moe Dalitz has a memo about Strong dated 1939-06-01. Michael Newton, *Mr. Mob: Life and Crimes of Moe Dalitz* (Jefferson N.C.: MacFarland and Company, 2007), 77, 88.

202　World War I draft card.

203　*Cleveland Plain Dealer,* 1900-07-18, 6.

204　An article in the *Cleveland Plain Dealer,* 1931-10-06. 1 has Assistant City Law Director Henry S. Brainard stating that Ginsberg was "a Cleveland gambler of 25 years' standing."

205　1912 is the first notice I have found of Ginsberg being called "Cheeks." The origin of this epithet remains unknown.

206　*Pittsfield (Mass.) Berkshire County Eagle,* 1920-05-12, 21.

207　*Baltimore Sun,* 1928-11-12, 2.

208　*Montreal (Canada) Gazette,*1920-06-05, 14.

209　*New York Daily News,* 1920-05-15, 2.

210　*(Cleveland Plain Dealer,* 1920-05-30, 8.

211　*Dayton Daily News,* 1920-10-31, 19.

212　*Pittsfield (Mass.) Berkshire County Eagle,* 1924-05-13, 1.

213　*New Castle (Penn.) News,* 1924-05-13, 18. *Investigation of Hon. Harry M. Daugherty, formerly attorney general of the United States. Hearings before the Select Committee on Investigation of the Attorney General, United States Senate, Sixty-Eighth Congress, first session, pursuant to S. Res. 157, directing a committee to investigate the failure of the attorney general to prosecute or defend certain criminal and civil actions, wherein the government is interested.* Government Printing Office, 1924, 2253-2254.

214　His daughter, Maude, married in 1917. She was born in Tawas according to her marriage record.

215　*Detroit Free Press,* 1900-07-03, 10.

216　*Saginaw (Mich.) Herald,* 1905-05-25, 4.

217　Miss Kitty Kaiser and her mother visited in 1923: *Tawas (Mich.) Herald,* 1928-08-17, 1. Mother living in Bay City with daughter Maude and son Clarence: 1920 U. S. Census. Daughter Ella Kaiser Budd married in Tawas in 1924: marriage record.

218　Occupation: farmer; location: Tawas Township. Kitty's mother was living with them: U. S. Census 1930.

219　Newton, *Mr. Mob,* 29-38.

220　Apparently, he had lived high while in Cleveland. Willard Bicknell in Clare recalled that Ginsberg came to him in the forties and ask him for a loan, leaving Kitty's diamonds as collateral. Then Ginsberg came to him again and said, "Give me so much and keep it [the diamonds])!". Forrest

Meek, Bicknell Willard interview (WBICK2.91), 14-15. The transcription of the interview is in the archive of the Clare County Historical Society, Clare, Michigan.

221 *Akron Beacon Journal,* 1931-10-06, 28; *Cleveland Plain Dealer,* 1931-06-06, 8.

222 Details in Robert Knapp, *Small-Town Citizen.*

223 County deed records of Ogemaw County. They were all in Town 22N Range 4E. The oil boom in Ogemaw began when the first producer struck oil in July 1933, although exploration had begun some years before.

224 Forrest Meek, "Bicknell Willard interview (WBICK2.91), 30-31; "Doherty Hotel Chat 1990-12-20," 15. The interviewees also recalled that Ed Strong, Ginsberg's associate, showed up from time to time at the Doherty. Forrest Meek, "Purple Crude-PurPL99," 56 incorrectly states that Ginsberg had an outstanding New York State warrant for his arrest on a murder charge. I have found no evidence of this, although his earlier bond schemes might have gotten him into trouble with New York law. Transcriptions of the interviews are in the archive of the Clare County (Mich.) Historical Society.

225 *Clare (Mich.) Sentinel,* 1954-07-30, 1.

226 For an excellent survey, see James A. Buccellato, *Early Organized Crime in Detroit. Vice, Corruption and the Rise of the Mafia* (Charleston S.C., History Press, 2015).

227 When the *Saturday Evening Post,* August 10-17, 1963, ran articles about the FBI investigations into *La Cosa Nostra*: Robert F. Kennedy, "The Mafia, What It Means," and Peter Maas, "The Mafia: The Inside Story?" A reporter asked Zerilli about the allegation that he was a big man in the Mafia. He replied, "If my name is in there (the *Post*), it must be a mistake. I don't know anything about (*La Cosa Nostra*). I've never heard of the organization or any of these man in the *Post*. I've been in the bakery business for 36 years." *Detroit Free Press,* 1963-08-06, 1.

228 Per city directories on Ancestry.com, a Peter Corrado place is located at 225 Pine Bluffs Road, .2 miles south of the Zerilli place at 225 Hawthorn Trail. These may be the two of the properties in question. This property was all on the east side of Higgins Lake. There are stories that "gangsters" or "the Purple Gang" owned a cabin on the west side of the lake in Lyons Township, but I have found no evidence of this. The purchases noted are recorded in the Grantor and Grantee deeds, Roscommon County Courthouse.

229 Grantor and Grantee deeds, Roscommon County Courthouse. The Corrados also apparently bought lots north of their original property on Higgins and built what is now called "Corrado Condos." In 2010 there was

a case in 34th Circuit Court, Roscommon, featuring Gerrish Township vs Peter Corrado and Jeannette Corrado. "Plaintiff's motion for entry of default was granted." *Houghton Lake Resorter* Court News, 2010-09-09, 2. Peter and Jeannette are children of Anthony J. Corrado. Allegedly there are abandoned cabins off a two-track road west of Houghton Lake. The area is fenced by the DNR to keep vandals out, but the rumors have it that they were safe houses. Robinson Lake Road goes east and west; Higgins Lake is on the west end; Robinson Lake on the east. http://www.topix.com/forum/state/mi/TLF7CKUF3UNVFVHOA/p3 (no longer accessible).

230 Pete Corrado also had a 100-acre farm in Price, Ontario, Canada, where he spent time and invited Mafia associates to visit.

231 Unless otherwise noted, the information comes from Scott Burnstein.

232 FBI "JFK Assassination Records" record 124-10336-10389 (1964).

233 *Grayling (Mich.) Crawford County Avalanche* 1953-11-19, 6; Pete Corrado also donated $250. Salvatore Zerilli, 22, was found guilty, along with Joseph John Ventimiglia, 48, of hunting deer with artificial light in 1981: *Avalanche*, 1981-02-05, 7.

234 I have been told that another mafioso, Mike Rubino, also had land Up North, but I have been unable to verify this.

235 Greg Stejskal wrote for the *Ann Arbor News*: In the early 1970s, the FBI set up a special squad tasked with surveillance of mobsters in Detroit. Greg Stejskal was assigned to the group surveilling the Detroit Partnership (Mafia). This information was added as a comment by 'oldrustynail' to Stejskal's story about mob surveillance. http://www.annarbor.com/news/retired-ann-arbor-fbi-agent-recalls-taking-infamous-photo-of-a-mafia-meeting-in-the-dexter-area/ (accessed 2018-02-22).

236 There are extensive articles about the early days of the Dance Palace in the *Battle Creek Enquirer*, 1926-08-28, 11 and in the *Lansing State Journal*, 1927-06-29, 10.

237 Beulah Carman, *Capsules of Time: A Saga of Houghton Lake* (Houghton Lake Mich.: Bankov Printing, 1987), makes no mention of gangsters.

238 *Detroit Free Press*, 1910-03-22, 3; *Bay City Times*, 1910-03-26l 8l.

239 *Detroit Free Press*, 1906-02-19, 2, 5.

240 *Lansing State Journal*, 1915-11-03, 1.

241 *St. Petersburg Tampa Bay Times*, 1932-04-1, 12. Given that Durant's land was marketed in 1932 as the South Branch Ranch, it may be that he bought not only the 1,800 acres along the river, but the inland ranch as well. His divorce from his third wife, Lea Gapsky, in 1932 might also have contributed

to the decision to sell the land. Dan Fishel, *Roscommon (Mich.) Roscommon County Voice*, 2012-01-07, 1.

242   Gerth E. Hendrickson, *The Angler's Guide to Twelve Classic Trout Streams in Michigan* (Ann Arbor: University of Michigan Press, 1994), 53 cited a Mrs. Margaret Jenson (1982). The widow was Charlotte Philipps Durant (originally from Los Angeles); they had married in 1935.

243   That property is now the Forest Dunes Golf Club.

244   *Grayling (Mich.) Crawford County Avalanche*, 1940-06-13, 3.

245   Basic information from the Forest Dunes Golf Club website. The skepticism about tunnels and hidden rooms is my own. https://www.forestdunesgolf.com/index.php/history (accessed 2019-03-11).

246   *Detroit Free Press*, 1952-11-26, 3.

247   *Grayling (Mich.) Crawford County Avalanche*, 1964-09-03, 1 with other notices in following years.

248   *Grayling (Mich.) Crawford County Avalanche*, 1969-08-28, 1.

249   *Detroit Free Press*, 1997-08-19, 3C.

250   In 1940, there were twenty-one buildings on the property. *Grayling (Mich.) Crawford County Avalanche*, 1940-06-13, 3.

251   *Grayling (Mich.) Crawford County Avalanche*, 1969-08-28, 1.

252   It is not quite clear how many actual sea-going seamen and navy types would have been hanging around Detroit during the 1910s. Detroit did have a naval reserve, founded in 1893, a sort of millionaires' navy as it was satirically dubbed. But men from this reserve (naval state militia) unit served in both the Spanish-American and First World Wars. Perhaps it is these men who sat around Cass Park and swapped tales to the eager ears of young men like Harry.

253   At this point in American history, enlistment in the Navy was highly competitive; only about one in four was accepted. Lieutenant Carlos Bean oversaw recruitment in Cincinnati. Later, Bean knew Bennett—it is possible that they served together on a ship since Bean seems to have had more than a passing experience with Bennett, but it is also possible they first met in the interviewing for enlistment. This could have happened if Bennett had gone to Cincinnati, not Cleveland, to enlist, or if Bean had been in charge of both places.

254   Bennett's World War I draft card states that he served 4 years in the Navy as a fireman; enlistments in those years was for two years at a hitch. It also states that he supported his mother and wife at the time of the draft, 1917.

255   It is fair to say that every account of Harry Bennett's life is full of contradictory and even erroneous details, including his own, Harry Bennett with

Paul Marcus, *Ford: We Never Called Him Harry* (New York: Faucett, 1951). For example, his Navy life: He says in his memoirs that he enlisted for eight years and left the Navy in New York, in 1916, having last served on the USS *Nashville*, a battleship then serving in the Caribbean. He then met Ford as per the story above. There is no mention of any adventures in French West Africa. His tattoo noticing enlistment in 1909 would mean leaving the Navy in 1917, not 1916. In addition, his draft card, dated mid-summer, 1917, says he served for 4 years, not 8. Finally, the *Nashville* was not in New York in 1916—it was in New Orleans for a short time that year, but never in New York. http://navalwarfare.blogspot.com/2009/07/uss-nashville-pg-7.html (accessed 2018-06-07).

256   The plant complex closed in 2004; the last car produced was a red Mustang. The site is now a huge parking lot. *Sic transit gloria mundi.*

257   Bennett has slightly different details but essentially the same story in his memoir, *Ford.*

258   *Detroit Free Press,* 1937-06-30, 3. He put the total number at 340 while others offered a figure three times that.

259   A popular adage among Ford workers was that they were paid $5 a day and all they could steal.

260   A *Detroit Times,* 1932-03-08, 28 editorial heroized Bennett in this confrontation: "He was at one-time a lightweight fighter, and always has been reputed to be fearless. He had nothing to do with starting the riot, and when it spread to property that he was charged with protecting, he demonstrated a type of courage for which it is difficult to find a parallel in these times when peace officers have learned to resort immediately to their guns when in danger. Although Bennett has always avoided public notice, he has loyal friends on every level of society, and their best wishes go out to him for a speedy recover from his wounds."

261   *Detroit Times,* 1937-05-26, 1.

262   Buccellato, *Early Organized Crime,* 141-142. *Detroit Times,* 1947-10-03, 6.

263   F.W. LaRouche, "Guardian of Henry Ford," *Little Rock Arkansas Gazette* [printed elsewhere as well], 1934-05-06, 3, 5.

264   Buccellato, *Early Organized Crime,* 141.

265   Ibid., 143.

266   *Detroit Free Press,* 1951-02-09, 12.

267   Bennett, *Ford,* 119. LaMare was a major Mafia figure in Detroit who was murdered in a gangland slaying in 1931.

268   Buccellato, *Early Organized Crime,* 138-146.

269   He said, "I'd treat them all right if they [came to my house]." *Detroit Free Press,* 1951-02-09, 12.

270   Bennett also owned a ranch near Palm Springs, California by summer, 1943. He regularly spent winters there until 1953, when he took up permanent residence until he moved to Las Vegas in 1974. Bennett, *Ford,* 295.

271   It is at the corner of Pontiac Avenue and Huron Hills Drive; its lot extends from the lake across Huron Hills Drive to Baldwin Resort Road. Dale Harwood recounts on Facebook: "This was on Baldwin Resort Road and right next door to our summer cottage. We used to sit around a campfire after dark, tell ghost stories and then dare someone to run over and touch the house." https://www.facebook.com/groups/270539595338/permalink/10153981514190339/ (accessed 2018-06-09). *Detroit Times,* 1935-02-05, 1 says it is near Oscoda. Oscoda township is just to the north of where the cabin was.

272   Fred Jennett: "My Grandfather worked for Ford and Bennett. Ford built the cabin for Bennett. There was a beautiful piano room on the lake side of the house. Grandpa came up from Detroit to play for Harry. My Grandfather also was the orchestra conductor at the Fisher Theater [in Detroit]. Been in the house many times."

273   Deed filed in the Iosco County Courthouse.

274   A slight variant: "Harry Bennett's house is next door at end of Huron Hills. The sidewalk has Esther Bennett 1934 in the cement." Skip Kubiac (Facebook) In 1934 Harry was still married to his second wife, Margaret; they divorced in June 1935 (*Detroit Times,* 1935-06-09, 1). He married Esther Beattie in November 1936. Esther was from a wealthy Pontiac family. She also was a trained nurse. One might wonder about a labelled trysting spot for Harry and Esther while Margaret was still on the scene. In fact, the date, 1937, is on the slab in question—Margaret was out of the picture—and there is no heart.

275   This was just a covered-over sluice-way, like the one at the Castle, that made it easy to get from the house down to the boat. No tunnel. The same "exits out of every room" is part of the mythology of Bennett's place at Lost Lake, as well (see below).

276   Although Bennett did keep a couple of tame circus cats at his Castle in Ypsilanti, he never had cats prowling about or, indeed, any large cats at all except for these tame lions. Certainly, there was never a leopard at the East Tawas cottage. Close examination of all existing cement yields no paw prints.

277   There were, indeed, stables. But what would mounted guards do on such a small property?

278   The choice of the name "Ethel B. Lodge" remains a mystery. There is no Ethel Bennett or Ethel Beattie (Esther's maiden name). Esther's middle name was Arabella. The name in the cement is no accident; the same name is repeated in the cement step outside the lakeside entrance to the cottage. Did a worker make a mistake when putting the writing into the cement, Ethel B. for Esther B.?

279   The deed transfer dated June 1939 shows Bennett deeded the Lake Huron property to Ford for $1—not the actual price necessarily, as "$1" is often given on deeds to hide the true sale cost. It looks like Ford, in turn, deeded the Pagoda to Bennett for an actual $1, if the story is true.

280   *Detroit Free Press,* 1974-01-20, 15.

281   *Detroit Free Press,* 1986-11-03, 1, 10.

282   *Detroit Times,* 1957-01-10, 11. Recall that Bennett also probably named the Lake Huron retreat after Esther. The name on the pavers there is "Ethel B. Lodge." Most likely this is a mistake for "Esther B. Lodge." See the note just above.

283   Bennett, *Ford,* 310. In an article by James Sweinhart he mentioned three homes: the castle on the Hudson River in Ypsilanti; the ranch 30 miles outside Palm Springs, California; and a large farm near Ann Arbor. Curiously, there is no mention of Lost Lake. *Detroit News,* 1945-10-03, 4.

284   *Detroit Times,* 1953-07-05, 8.

285   Ibid.

286   *Detroit Times,* 1957-01-10, 11.

287   *Detroit Free Press Detroit Magazine,* 1974-01-20, 15. A *Detroit Free Press* story says it was sold "shortly after" Bennett was fired by Henry Ford II in 1945. "Shortly after he sold his Clare County property to a Detroit junk dealer who tried unsuccessfully to develop it as a resort." But this is not true. *Detroit Free Press,* 1986-11-03, 1, 10; *Detroit Free Press,* 1966-05-01, 13-C says that it was sold "to a Detroit area company" "about six years ago" (i.e., ~1960). "The company had plans to develop the property for its employees, but never followed through."

288   "Long time Clare county residents tell of armed guards patrolling the estate, of secret passageways, high-stakes gambling and moonshine whisky." *Detroit Free Press,* 1966-05-01, 13-C. Local moonshine is always a possibility, but Prohibition was long gone when Bennett set up at Lost Lake.

289   Rick Wasmer, *Whenever Rotary Scouts Fall in Line* (n.p.: Lulu Publishing Services, 2015), p. 77

290   Ibid.

291 *Detroit Free Press,* 1986-11-03, 1, 10. Rowley died in 2008.

292 Posted January 14, 2013 at 9:59 am | Permalink: http://markmaynard. com/2012/02/walking-the-secret-passageways-of-harry-bennets-heavily-fortified-ypsilanti-castle/ (accessed 2019-03-14).

293 Unless otherwise noted, the material about the Club Manitou is based upon the following sources: Judy Rodgers, "Resorts," pp. 65-84 in Jan Morley, ed., *Harbor Springs. A Collection of Historical Essays.* Harbor Springs Historical Commission (Clarksville TN: Jostens, 1981); William Rauch, "Recalling Harbor Springs in the Cabaret Era of Gambling and Prohibition—A Wide Open Town," *Harbor Springs (Mich.) Harbor Light* Special Centennial Issue, July 1, 1981; reprinted *Harbor Light,* 2012-04-04-10, 4B as "A Wide Open Town;" obituary for William "Al" Gerhard in the *Petoskey (Mich.) News-Review,* 1987-12-17, 1-2; Richard Wiles, "The Infamous Club Manitou," *Mackinac Journal,* Dec. 2013, 12-15; Richard Wiles, "Manitou and Pony-tail—Hot Spots of Harbor Springs," *Michigan Chronicle* 39 no. 4, Winter, 2017, 21-24. I cite below only exact quotations from these sources.

294 *Grand Rapids Herald,* 1899-09-15, 2.

295 *Grand Rapids Press,* 1915-09-28, 4.

296 *Muskegon (Mich.) Chronicle,* 1917-07-16, 4.

297 *Cheboygan (Mich.) Democrat,* 1924-01-03, 1.

298 Ibid.

299 Ibid.

300 Gerhart's father, Max Schwendner, died in Reading Pennsylvania in 1924. At that point, the obituary referred to Gerhart as "Allah Schwendner" and noted that he, his brothers Irvin and Frederick, and sister Eveline (married to a King) all lived in Detroit.

301 *Port Huron (Mich.) Times-Herald,* 1925-05-08, 12.

302 *Port Huron (Mich.) Times-Herald,* 1925-06-23, 5.

303 *Port Huron (Mich.) Times-Herald,* 1925-08-28, 7.

304 *Detroit Free Press,* 1929-05-25, 2.

305 *Detroit Free Press,* 1929-05-24, 1, 2. Note that in this episode, Gerhart is not called "Al," but rather "William." In later newspaper accounts, sometimes Al, sometimes William appears. I found no indication that Gerhart and Wood were arrested, much less charged, in this incident.

306 *Detroit Free Press,* 1927-11-13 (robbery); 1928-03-13 (robbery); 1928-05-26 (robbery); 1929-07-28 (murder); 1929-07-30 (running a saloon); 1929-08-08 (running a blind pig); 1931-01-15 and 01-17 (attempted

kidnapping); 1931-02-27 (witness to murder); *Detroit Times* 1931-03-27 (assault); *St. Joseph (Mich.) Herald-Press*, 1936-06-03 (burglary); *Detroit Free Press*, 1942-09-14 (gambling).

307   *Petoskey (Mich.) News-Review*, 1987-12-18, 1.

308   *Petoskey (Mich.) Evening News*, 1935-01-15.

309   *Lansing State Journal*, 1935-09-19, 2; *Lansing State Journal*, 1935-11-16.

310   *Charlevoix (Mich.) Courier*, 1935-12-6, 1.

311   *Lansing State Journal*, 1935-01-15, 1.

312   *Detroit Free Press*, 1935-02-01, 1.

313   *Lansing State Journal*, 1935-01-15, 1.

314   *Fremont (Ohio) News-Messenger*, 1935-01-18, 10 (AP).

315   *Windsor (Ont.) Star*, 1927-09-29, 17.

316   Federal Bureau of Investigation File Number 7-576 Section 185 1935-1936, April 1936.

317   *Harbor Springs (Mich.) Emmet County Graphic*, 1947-01-16.

318   *Lansing State Journal*, 1947-08-20. The police had obtained a warrant to raid the near-by Ramona Park Hotel's Sea Gull Cottage gambling spot. It seems a bit suspicious that they failed to get one for the Manitou.

319   *Detroit Free Press*, 1947-09-27.

320   *Washington Post*, 1964-09-09, C9.

321   The information in this and the next paragraph come from Al Gerhart's obituary in the *Petoskey (Mich.) News-Review*, 1987-12-17, pp. 1-2.

322   Quoted by Rodgers, "Resorts," 83.

323   Rauch, "Recalling Harbor Springs," gives this description. It is hard to imagine this many doors; the description does not agree with the firsthand account of Larry Knapp, quoted below.

324   Bruce Snoap, Kingtones keyboard player http://www.westmichmusichysstericalsociety.com/club-ponytail/ (accessed 2019-04-03).

325   Ibid.

326   Pepper (1890-1958) is an interesting person in his own right. Born in Poland, he came to the States as a teen in 1907. In Detroit, he worked as a waiter but was expelled from the Hotel and Restaurant Workers Union for selling booze. Apparently, this recommended him to Al Gerhart. He worked not only at the Manitou, he also ran his own blind pigs. In 1932 he was arrested along with some Detroit men for running an extensive joint out of a garage

basement in Petoskey. There was an 85-foot bar; the State Police seized 6 barrels of beer and over 100 bottles of Canadian whiskey. It must have been either a big basement or a very crowded one, for the police found 200 patrons imbibing. Only four men, Pepper among them, were held, however.

327 Quoted in Rodgers "Resorts," 82. These are all near-by resort areas.

328 *Petoskey (Mich.) News-Review*, 1987-12-18, 1.

329 Larry Knapp, "Purple Gang," manuscript in the Clarke Historical Library, Mt. Pleasant, Michigan.

330 Knapp's description of the entrance door differs markedly from the heavy steel doors I described above. Could that description be a myth, not fact?

331 *Escanaba (Mich.) Daily*, 1938-08-24, 1.

332 Quoted by Rauch, "Recalling Harbor Springs."

333 Quoted by Wiles, "Infamous Club Manitou," 14 and "Manitou and Pony-tail," 23.

334 *Battle Creek Enquirer*, 1948-01-25, 16.

335 Bob Clock, "Stork Club of the North," *Harbor Springs (Mich.) Harbor Light*, 1967-12-20, 1.

336 Agnes Ash, "Contrapposto and Six Dress Suits, *Miami (Fla.) News*, 1965-10-31 *Miami Magazine*, 14-15.

337 *Cheboygan (Mich.) Democrat*, 1914-03-06, 4. The article has a definite "tisk-tisk" tone: "We cannot believe that Petoskey and Mackiac [sic; i.e., the Grand Hotel] are tarred with the same gambling stick. We acknowledge a little freeze out, some drawing and a trifle of stud poker, but nothing more [in Cheboygan itself]." Actually, Koch maintained his gambling activities in Toledo even while starting up the club Up North. In 1920, thieves broke into his gambling establishment there, broke locks on two doors, pried the door of his safe, and made off with $10,000 in Liberty Bonds and $2,588 in cash *Sandusky (Ohio) Star-Journal*, 1920-01-12, 8. Koch's obituary in the *Charlevoix (Mich.) Courier* states that he came to that city in 1916.

338 *Charlevoix (Mich.) Courier*, 1920-06-16, 5.

339 1923 fire: *Charlevoix (Mich.) Sentinel*, 1923-09-06, 1. The disaster was also reported on the front page of the *Detroit Free Press*, 1923-09-02, where the club was described as "widely known as one of the big summer resort homes of Michigan; the building was one of the most palatial on the western coast of Michigan." The *Cheboygan (Mich.) Democrat*, 1923-09-06, 2 notes that "a new fireproof structure immediately will take the place of the old one, Mr. Koch announced." The first notice of the new building comes in 1927, but it may well have been opened sooner.

340   Like the Club Manitou and other seasonal establishments, there were rooms on the second floor of the Colonial Club to house the summer help that came up from Florida for the season—the dealers, croupiers, and chefs.

341   Edith Gilbert, "High-rolling at Charlevoix's Old Colonial Club. The Ghosts Crap Out to a Bulldozer," *Summer Resort Life: Tango, Teas and All!* (Charlevoix Mich.: Jet'iquette, 1976), 73-83. Also in *Detroit Free Press,* 1974-02-03, *Detroit Magazine,* 18-21, 23.

342   Quoted by Gilbert, "High-rollering," 76 from Constance Cappel Montgomery's book, *Hemingway in Michigan,* (New York: Fleet Publishing, 1966). The letter read: "Came home yesterday and all went in to the Voix [Charlevoix] and played at Cook's [Koch's]. I had only six seeds to my name and was thinking I'd have to write to the Bank at home for more or work in the cement plant and then I played roulette until 2 a.m. this morning and won fifty-nine. Was going strong playing the rouge and noir, the way I learned in Algeciras—but the men made me quit as they wanted to go home. Hemmingstein luck." Sandra Spanier and Robert W. Trogdon, eds., *The Letters of Ernest Hemingway* (Cambridge: Cambridge University Press, 2011), vol. 1, 237-238.

343   Orestes Gatti got his start as a manager in famous New York City hotels. He managed the Palm Island Club, later renamed the Latin Club, in Miami Beach from 1921-1924. Koch persuaded Gatti to manage the Palm Island Club restaurant in Miami Beach during the winter (in 1924 Gatti opened his own restaurant there; it survived for decades as a high-class place) and the Colonial Club in the summer. Koch eventually sold the Palm Island Club. Gatti continued with the Colonial Club. Agnes Ash, "Contrapposto and Six Dress Suits," 14-15. Al Capone was an investor in the Palm Island Club, but only after Koch had sold it.

344   Gilbert "High rolling."

345   Federal Bureau of Investigation case originating at Cincinnati, Ohio. Report made at Detroit, Michigan, 1936-04-16 by W.H. Hoffman. File 7-25. Main informant: Herman Kays.

346   David Miles of the Charlevoix Historical Society in correspondence, "Von Dolke was the son-in-law of the owner, Martha Elston Baker, who had developed the Beach into a nationally known hotel with a sterling reputation. Upon her death in Miami in 1922, it reverted to her giddy daughter who had not a whit of her mother's operational or business savvy, and she and hotshot husband [Von Dolke] proceeded to fritter away the inherited fortune (for its time) and run the establishment into the ground until it went into receivership in the 1930s." Rumors abounded that Von Dolke "had shady connections."

347 Jennifer M. Cochran, "Roaring '20s Part of Ice Cream Eatery's History," *Petoskey (Mich.) News-Review*, 1986-07-07.

348 This and many of the following details come from the excellent history of the hotel, John McCabe, *Grand Hotel Mackinac Island* (Lake Superior State College, Sault Ste. Marie, Mich.: Unicorn Press, 1987).

349 William Randolph Hearst published a scathing account of gambling at French Lick in the *Chicago American*. This is reported and quoted at great length in the *Indianapolis Morning Sun*, 1906-06-11, 1, 3. It claimed Ed Ballard and Thomas Taggart (Democratic National Committeeman) ran wide-open gambling at French Lick. Hearst was angry at Taggart for not supporting his favorite political causes.

350 June 1917.

351 *Ironwood (Mich.) Times*, 1919-09-06 reports: "The raid followed a series of articles in the *Soo News* discussing the character of the play at the Grand and open defiance of the laws there." The *News'* articles can hardly be called an expose—the gambling at the Grand had been too notorious to make an expose unnecessary. Supposedly, the *News* forwarded copy of its articles to the down state newspapers, so that they could publish simultaneously with their publication in the Soo, thus assuring the early attention of state officials. The intent was to throw the hotel's gambling into bold relief and force the state officials' hand. But, I find nothing in the *Sault Ste. Marie Evening News* around that date. There is no exposé published in any Michigan newspaper I have access to, although reports of the raid were subsequently widely published.

352 An attorney for the Grand submitted, then withdrew a replevin suit (that is, a suit to return goods seized).

353 *Fort Wayne Journal-Gazette*, 1910-03-06, 5.

354 A particularly lyrical account is in the *Chicago Daily National Hotel Reporter*, 1919-09-03. The same account also appears elsewhere, e.g., the *Muskegon (Mich.) Chronicle*, 1919-08-28, 2.

355 *Ironwood (Mich.) Times*, 1919-09-06.

356 *Saint Joseph (Mich.) Herald-Press*, 1920-10-04. The same article appears in the *Mt. Pleasant (Mich.) Isabella County Enterprise* on October 1st. This raid seems to have taken place in early October, but may have been earlier, as the Grand Hotel normally shut down for the season in early September each year.

357 A detailed account of the raid is in the *Lansing State Journal*, 1921-09-21, 8.

358 Edward Ballard's gambling empire in French Lick and West Baden steadfastly maintained the position that no gangster elements were involved.

Charles Edward (Chad) Ballard with Janet Kirk Johnson and Anna Marie Borcia, *Charles Edward "Ed" Ballard A Story of Determination, Self-education, and Ultimate Success* (n.p.: C.E. Ballard Literary Trust, 1984) states that Ed Ballard never brought gangsters into French Lick: "He was adamant in keeping away the offensive element so often associated with gambling" (p. 34), even when that would have saved the casino in 1932 (p. 60). However, a list of Ballard's investments in gambling (p. 63) is a list of gangster-influenced if not gangster-owned establishments. In 1934 he still owned an interest in the Palm Island Club; another investor was Al Capone (p. 64). Investments in other gambling-related establishments in Saratoga Springs, New York, and Hot Springs, Arkansas, were hotbeds of gangster activity and ownership.

359   Magnaghi, *Prohibition*, 101-105.

360   John Koch's forbidding of beverages in his gambling room at the Colonial Club in Charlevoix is an exception.

361   Willis John McQuarrie, *Whisky Smugglers of the North Channel* (Gore Bay Ont.: Mid-North Printers and Publishers, 2003).

362   *Port Huron (Mich.) Times Herald,* 1928-05-21, 1. This was to date the largest shipment seized on the Great Lakes.

363   McCabe, *Grand Hotel,* 107.

364   Newspaper accounts trace Nowak's suit as it advanced to the Michigan Supreme Court. However, I could find no account of the result after Nowak got hold of the accounts. He may have published something in his *Michigan State Digest.* W.W. Liggett's Prohibition era magazine, *Plain Talk,* has an article about this according to Magnaghi, *Prohibition,* 104-105, who seems to quote from it.

365   *Benton Harbor (Mich.) News-Palladium,* 1937-08-26, 1; 1937-08-31, 1; 1934-09-16, 14.

366   *Detroit Free Press,* 1938-02-21, 12.

367   *Port Huron (Mich.) Times Herald,* 1937-07-30, 1: "Our force with its limited personnel has done the best it could to check gambling in the state. We have co-operated at all times with local law enforcement agencies, but our force is so small it's all we can do to cope with the traffic situation."

368   McCabe, *Grand Hotel,* 137.

369   Thomas Pfeiffelmann, a local expert on Mackinac Island and vicinity, as well as Robert Tagatz, the official historian of the Grand, strongly hold the position that no outsiders were involved either in the bootlegging or the gambling on the island.

370 Rick Wiles, "Cheboygan's Famous (Infamous) Wertheimer Brothers," provides an extensive look at the Wertheimer clan: *Mackinac Journal*, May 2018 pp. 17-21, June 2018 pp. 20-24, July 2018 pp. 20-25, August 2018 pp. 14-17.

371 U.S. 1870 Census.

372 *Cheboygan (Mich.) Democrat*, 1882-01-29, 3.

373 *Detroit Free Press*, 1889-12-17.

374 *Cheboygan (Mich.) Democrat*, 1888-01-29, 4 and 1885-02-05, 1.

375 1907 Dunn and Bradstreet Directory for Cheboygan. Note that the Model Pool Room was not one of them. It began sometime between 1907 and 1911.

376 On April 27, 1917 Al drove a car that struck and killed a bicyclist in Detroit. He was charged with vehicular manslaughter but a year later, October 8, 1918, the charge was dismissed. *Detroit Free Press*, 1918-08-10, 5.

377 *Detroit Free Press*, 1958-07-21, 3.

378 *Cheboygan (Mich.) Democrat*, 1924-01-31, 7.

379 Ibid.

380 *Cheboygan (Mich.) Democrat*, 1924-08-7, 1.

381 *Detroit Free Press*, 1929-03-29, 3.

382 *Cheboygan (Mich.) Democrat*, 1920-03-26, 2.

383 *Detroit Free Press*, 1927-05-01, 1 has the story.

384 *Detroit Free Press*, 1923-05-27, 23.

385 *Detroit Free Press*, 1925-12-29, 7.

386 *Detroit Free Press*, 1922-04-04, 3.

387 A colorful account of the place appears in *Detroit Free Press*, 1927-05-01, 1. In 1923, Mert was arrested and tried for running this gambling establishment. However, a recorder's court jury did not convict. *Detroit Free Press*, 1924-06-20, 1, 8.

388 *Detroit Free Press*, 1925-05-01, 1; 1927-07-13, 1.

389 *Cheboygan (Mich.) Democrat*, 1924-05-22, 3.

390 *Detroit Free Press*, 1923-05-27.

391 Ibid.

392 This was on Grand Avenue.

393 The wagon master claimed that he didn't make much profit, but he admitted that he paid $1 a case for the beer and sold it to Wertheimer for $5.50 each. *Detroit Free Press*, 1923-01-19, 1.

394　Full story first appeared in the *Detroit Times*; it was reprinted in the *Cheboygan (Mich.) Democrat*, 1924-01-31, 7.

395　*Detroit Free Press*, 1929-03-13, 1.

396　*Detroit Free Press*, 1929-03-14, 3 consistently names Al, not Mert, Wertheimer in this episode. The corresponding *Lansing State Journal* story got the name wrong, calling the protagonist Wertheimer Mert, not Al.

397　*Lansing State Journal*, 1929-03-13, 1. Two other men, Charles Adler and Oscar Herman, were charged with Mert.

398　*Detroit Free Press*, 1929-03-14, 3.

399　*Detroit Free Press*, 1929-03-14, 1.

400　*Jackson (Mich.) News*, 1924-07-08, 6.

401　Original story in the *Detroit Free Press* reprinted in the *Cheboygan (Mich.) Democrat*, 1924-12-18, 9.

402　Details in Wiles, "Wertheimers of Cheboygan," July 2018 pp. 20-25 and August 2018 pp. 14-17.

403　I have been unable to locate this resort.

404　*Cheboygan (Mich.) Observer*, 1930-06-12, 1.

405　Warranty deed on file in the Cheboygan County Courthouse.

406　*Cheboygan (Mich.) Democrat*, 1927-01-27. The architect/contractor was Lee Fish: *Cheboygan Democrat*, 1927-02-03. In fact, the cottage was part of the White Goose Resort and even today lies on a private road lined with expensive cottages along the lake shore. Besides the cottage, Mert may have had a club on the shore of that same lake: "During the summer months Wertheimer has a club on the shore of Burt Lake near Cheboygan." *Detroit Times*, 1929-03-13 p. 10. But nothing more is known of this and it may be a confusion with his cottage itself or perhaps with his investment in the Ramona Park Casino in Harbor Springs (see below).

407　*Cheboygan (Mich.) Democrat*, 1927-11-03. The image appears in the *Detroit Free Press*, 1927-10-30, 117.

408　*Cheboygan (Mich.) Daily Tribune*, 1958-07-27. In 1955 he is listed as an employee in the Riverside Casino, Reno. Reno 1955 City Directory. His boathouse is now a restaurant.

409　*Detroit Times*, 1936-07-23, 2

410　*Detroit Times*, 1927-02-11, 17.

411　Matthew J. Friday, article in the *Bank Note Reporter* 2008-02-07 http://

www.numismaster.com/ta/numis/Article.jsp?ad=article&ArticleId=3803
(accessed 2018-07-13 but taken down by 2019-04-20).

412   As stated in Mert's obituary in the *Petoskey (Mich.) News*, 07-21-1958.

413   *Cheboygan (Mich.) Daily Tribune*, 1958-07-21.

414   Wiles, "Wertheimer Brothers," June 2018, 23.

415   *Detroit Times*, 1926-10-25, 13

416   *Detroit Times*, "Michigan Page," 1929-08-31, 6. Fenlon's name is mispelled as "Ed."

417   *Jackson (Mich.) News*, 1920-07-03, 8.

418   *Cheboygan (Mich.) Democrat* 1910-04-22.

419   Forrest Meek interview with William Bicknell, 1990, manuscript in the archive of the Clare County Historical Society, p. 7.

420   Details in Knapp, *Mystery Man*, 67-88. Allegedly, the other Bernstein brothers paid Leebove to achieve this. In the end the authorities thwarted all attempts to retry the Collingwood case. Ray remained in prison until 1964, shortly before his death.

421   http://www.treasurenet.com/forums/treasure-legends-michigan/46866-purple-gang-2.html (accessed 2018-04-18).

422   Typescript owned by Grace Dooley of the Rose City Area Historical Society.

423   Copy in the archive of the Rose City Area Historical Society.

424   For example, http://lostinmichigan.net/notorious-purple-gang-connec-tions-mid-michigan/ (accessed 2018-12-07).

425   Vern Nye, "Acquiring Grousehaven," typescript belonging to Grace Dooley of the Rose City Area Historical Society. Information is summarized in a document by Marvin Wilber, 2008-08-16, held by the Rose City Area Historical Society. For the bunker, see http://lostinmichigan.net/remains-grousehaven-lodge/ (accessed 2019-04-21).

426   Interview with the current owner.

427   Account found at topix.com thread which has since been taken down from the internet. "One-Armed Mike" Gerhart's first property purchase was at Dease Lake (Ogemaw County grantor/grantee deeds). This may have given rise to rumors about gangsters since Gerhart's Graceland Ballroom was a magnet for such stories.

428   FBI Bremer Kidnapping Part 219 of 459- p. 12.

429   Obituary, *Petoskey (Mich.) News* 2003-10-03 (on line).

430   Elsie Trimmer, *A History of Ellsworth's First 100 Years, 1866-1966* (Self-published, 1967). Available on line at http://bankstownship.net/gleanings.html (accessed 2018-05-13).

431   *Marshall (Mich.) Evening Chronicle,* 1932-06-18, 1 (U.P.).

432   World War I draft card, 1917. So, he had lost his right arm before he was 23.

433   Jack Jobst, "Graceland—A Ballroom and Its Builder," *Michigan History Magazine,* May-June 2010, 56-59. This is a well-researched summary of what we know about Gelfand. Jobst was able to interview his adopted son, Ronald. Many details otherwise unattested are recorded here on good authority.

434   World War I draft card.

435   U.S. Census 1920.

436   The divorce decree from 1939 states her birthdate as 1925-05-23. The marriage certificate states 1926-06-12.

437   Marriage certificate.

438   There are no Gelfands or related Feldmans (Mike's mother was a Feldman) in Wayne, Michigan, Census records report. But as this information probably comes from Mike's son, Ronald, it may well be accurate. Jobst, "Graceland," 58.

439   Rival: Kavieff, *Purple Gang,* 110-112. Unfortunately, Kavieff does not provide any documentation. Sub-contractor: Robert A. Rockaway, "The Notorious Purple Gang: Detroit's All-Jewish Prohibition Era Mob," *Shofar* 20 (Special Edition: American Jews), Fall 2001, 118. They probably began as a sub-contractor but branched out and tried to establish themselves as an independent gang.

440   Waugh, *Off Color,* 179, calls them the "Third Street Gang." Kavieff, *Purple Gang,* 111 refers to them as the "Third Avenue Terrors." Third Avenue ran down to the Detroit River. A U.S. Navy recruiting station was located there. Ironically, or perhaps intentionally, this gang thus became known as a "navy."

441   Paul R. Kavieff, *The Purple Gang* (Fort Lee N.J.: Barricade Books, 2000), 10. All reports of the Little Jewish Navy that I have found have their origin in a single United Press distributed newspaper account of the Collingwood Manor murders dated September 17, 1931. Neither the *Detroit Free Press* nor the *Detroit Times* ran this story. In fact, these papers' coverage of the murders do not mention the "navy" at all. Both refer to the victims as members of a "Third Avenue Gang." These account also stress that the dispute with the Purples was not about bootlegging, but rather about a dispute over money owed to the Purples.

442   Newspaper accounts never mention the navy until the reporting regarding the Collingwood Manor murders in 1931.

443   Kavieff, *Purple Gang,* 10, 119-120; however the author provides no documentation. Kavieff told LuAnn Zettle that old-time Detroit gangsters had mentioned the tunnels to him; Kavieff admitted that these gangsters probably never set foot in Graceland and had only heard about the tunnels. It is worth noting that when Short Excavating of Lupton removed the debris after Graceland burned, they did not find any evidence of tunnels. The details Kavieff offers about "One-armed Mike" Gelfand, his purchase of the property, and his relationship to the Purple Gang and the Little Jewish Navy probably also come from his conversations with the old-timers since none of this is mentioned in Detroit newspapers. Some of those details are correct, so perhaps there was some recollection, real or imagined, of Mike Gelfand, his dance hall, and Purple Gang involvement among Kavieff's sources in Detroit.

444   Grantor/grantee deeds in Ogemaw County show Michael Gelfand purchasing land in Rose Township in September 1929.

445   Country records show that Lillian had acquired this by a will, presumably from a relative. She sold it to Mike for an undisclosed sum—the deed states "$1", but this is a common action to avoid putting the actual sale price of a property on the deed transfer. In accounts of Graceland, Gelfand's name is often misspelled as Gilfan or Gilfand.

446   His obituary gives 1931; a public record gives 1932. Jobst, "Graceland," 59 states that Ronald was adopted. This information presumably comes from Ronald himself; there is no indication of an adoption in records that are publicly accessible.

447   *West Branch (Mich.) Ogemaw Herald,* 1933-05-25, 1. Jack Smith is a very common name. There are a number of residents in Detroit who are bootleggers, burglars, and the like. None is immediately identifiable as Gefland's partner in the Lupton Recreation Company. But it would not be odd if Gelfand and another bootlegger teamed up to invest in Graceland. Tom Henry claims that the plans to build date to 1928. There is no evidence of this: "Lupton's 'Grace' Dead at 49: May She Rest in Peace," *Bay City Times,* 1981-12-23, 3C.

448   The featured band was Nate Frye's dance band—a 10-piece outfit composed of students from Michigan State College. *Adrian (Mich.) Daily Telegram,* 1932-09-23, 2. So, some events began in the hall in the summer of 1932 with the grand opening only in June 1933: *West Branch (Mich.) Ogemaw Herald,* 1933-05-25, 1.

449   The owners specifically identified nearby towns as the target audience: West Branch, Mio, Tawas, Standish, Gladwin, Roscommon, Graying, and Rose City. None of these is more than 50 miles from Lupton. However, during the summer months—the only months Graceland was open—the area's population increased substantially because of tourism.

450   *West Branch (Mich.) Ogemaw Herald,* 1933-05-21, 1.

451   Later in life, Mike Gelfand was a jewelry merchant. Rings were, indeed, actually given away. On this occasion Oka Millard of Tawas City and Josephine Lally of West Branch were the lucky winners. The week before, rings were awarded as well. *West Branch (Mich.) Ogemaw Herald,* 1933-06-01, 5; 1933-06-08, 5.

452   George Smith told me that when Hank Nelson was the sheriff, he did not stop the booze business at Graceland. It all come from local farmers—the sheriff did raid the local stills quite regularly. At Graceland there was a trap door leading to where the bootlegged booze was hidden. One time his wife descended on Graceland and smashed all the bottles.

453   Jobst, "Graceland," 59.

454   *Graceland News-Gazette.* Pastula printed this broadsheet to hype and advertise Graceland. This edition is "volume 15 no. 216"; it dates to sometime after 1959. Copies of other editions are at the Rose City Area Historical Society in Rose City, Michigan.

455   The for-sale advertisement read: "Graceland ballroom 80x100 ft. including restaurant 26x52, 9 room cottage and 40 acres land, complete electric power. Wonderful summer business, good opportunity for some one. Lupton, Mich., 18 miles from West Branch. Inquire Wm. E. Dunlop, Clare." *Clare (Mich.) Sentinel,* 1935-04-12, 8. William Dunlop leaves no trace as a real estate agent in Clare; he did become city police chief in 1938. Why list the Graceland for sale with a Clare person not otherwise engaged in real estate?

456   Divorce record from Wayne County, Michigan, granted April 28, 1939.

457   U.S. Census 1940.

458   So, too, two children of his brother, Julius. *Rochester (N.Y.) Democrat and Chronicle,* 1939-07-20, 16.

459   U.S. Census 1940. His son apparently remembered things differently. His recollection was that Mike headed west in a new 1939 Plymouth "packed with suitcases" to southern California, where Gelfand had relatives.

460   Jack Jobst in conversation for Ronald was told that he was adopted. Dilly Craft, who babysat for Ronald when he was an infant, did not mention his being adopted by Mike and Grace Gelfand. At Ronald's death, an obituary

gave Mary Wood as his mother. Wood cannot be his natural mother as she does not enter the picture until 1940, after Grace's divorce from Gelfand. She may have adopted him after Gelfand died in 1944.

461 There is no indication of this profession in earlier documents. However, at Graceland one of the come-ons was to award a "diamond" ring to two patrons on the dance floor. Several women attest that they won the rings. It may be doubted that the diamonds were real. Locals also recalled jewelry sales at the ballroom. Jobst, "Graceland," 59.

462 Prohibition ended late in 1933. So, liquor was legal at Graceland from the 1934 season on.

463 Ronald was born in January 1932, the year Graceland opened. Dilly was 11 at the time.

464 This seems to be a recollection based on Floyd Pastula's later creation of a machine gun totting mannequin at the place.

465 Since Dilly states that dances became 10¢ or three for 25¢ after Prohibition ended, this event must take place in the 1934 season or later.

466 This "lights out" event seems to be the same one referred to in another, slightly different, account: "The Graceland had its own power plant and an area native and hardware store owner, now dead, told Pastula not long after the ballroom opened someone was flicking the main power switch, causing the lights to go on and off. The hardware man was outside when he felt a gun in his ribs and he hastily explained to a tough gangster-type he was not the man who was tripping the power switch." *Bay City Times,* 1974-02-20, section C, 1.

467 *Graceland News-Gazette.* Note the similarities to Kavieff's narrative.

468 Note that the machine gun held is an incorrect version of the Thompson submachine gun; that weapon had a disk to hold the bullets, not a rectangular magazine. It remains unclear why one would machine gun a safe. Another local story reported by Mel Conway has it that the gang would bring safes up from Detroit to Graceland, open them there, and distribute the goods. Conway said that his father recalled the Purples driving a large vehicle with a set of pull-out tracks, so they could unload the safes. Emails archived at the Rose City Area Historical Society.

469 Pat Hunt, "Graceland Ballroom Landmark of Gangster Era," *Bay City Times,* 1974-02-20, section C, 1. Pastula's fictions had become fact by the time of Mary DeMott, "Ellie's Deli & Pizzeria," *Fairfield (Mich.) Wilderness Chronicle* #41, December 2003, 13. The Hunt article is reprinted in the *West Branch (Mich.) Ogemaw Herald,* summer 1976, section 2, 14.

470 Hunt, "Graceland," 2.

471   *West Branch (Mich.) Ogemaw Herald,* 1981-12-24, 1, with images of the burned ruins. The same account appears in the *Bay City Times.*

472   Tom Henry, "Lupton's 'Grace' dead at 49: May She Rest in Peace," *Bay City Times,* 1981-12-23, 3C. The Capone myth is also repeated by DeMott, "Ellie's Deli."

473   Barb Goodboo, "A Tribute to the Graceland Ballroom," *Momentum Magazine* (Rose City, Mich.), 1991. Written in 1985.

474   DeMott, "Ellie's Deli."

475   There is evidence that Purple Gangsters went up to Walled Lake for some rest and relaxation.

476   One local rumor has it that Gelfand never paid the contractors!

477   LuAnn Zettle email in the archives at the Rose City Area Historical Society. This building was torn down in the seventies for development. The Wolfe brothers as contractors: Conway, email in the Rose City Area Historical Area Society archive, also confirms that the two structures were almost identical.

478   The image is of the back of the hall. The current owner, Zue Hudson, provided the identification.

479   Jimmie Richardson interview.

480   Paul Williams interview.

481   There is a long 1927 story describing the dance palace in the *Lansing State Journal,* 1927-06-29, 10. The *Battle Creek Enquirer,* 1926-08-28, 11 indicates that it first operated the year before.

482   Knapp, *Mystery Man.*

483   Knapp, *Small-Town Citizen.*

484   Knapp, *Mystery Man,* pp. 124-125 and notes.

485   Wentworth declined to elaborate the stories, telling me that she had promised Joe never to repeat what he told her.

486   World War II draft card.

487   World War II draft card.

488   Source uncertain; perhaps his marriage certificate?

489   Ancestry.com has fewer than a hundred Baranisky/Baraniski, and only six with the first name, Joseph. None is this Joseph Samuel Baranisky.

490   There is no World War I draft card under either Baranisky/i or Barnes. Nor is there any naturalization record.

491   *Chicago Tribune* 1917-06-03 p. 1.

492   *Chicago Tribune* 1917-02-14 p. 13.

493   Hyman was one of the Big Four gambling powers in Chicago at the time. His claim to fame was the ship City of Traverse that was a literally floating craps, bookmaking, pool playing, gambling craft anchored in State of Indiana waters to avoid Illinois police.

494   The sheriff, perhaps disingenuously, remarked when asked why did didn't do more to close down the place, "Deputies tell me Justice of the Peace Henry Wolske of Burr Oak tends bar and so what could a fellow do?" *Chicago Tribune* 1916-10-14 p. 15; 10-15 p. 2.

495   Barnes and Harris had gone to the local constabulary asking for protection against the anticipated attack. The advice of the police: the owners should arm the bartender and waiters and take care of the affair themselves.

496   *Chicago Tribune* 1916-10-02 p. 1; 10-14 p. 15;

497   *Chicago Tribune* 1917-06-05.

498   *Chicago Tribune* 1917-01-26 p. 12.

499   *Chicago Tribune* 1917-06-06 p. 1. Supposedly, his sobriquet came from being called a 'piker' in the prostitution business because of the cheap price for a trick at his whorehouses.

500   *Chicago Tribune* 1917-06-21 p. 12.

501   *Chicago Tribune* 1918-06-09 p. 13.

502   Bergreen, *Capone* pp. 90-91.

503   Information at http://undereverytombstone.blogspot.com/2015/04/head-of-vice-trust-in-chicago-michael.html (accessed 2019-02-28)

504   *CS* 1912-07-19 p. 2 (1912, Gladwin); *CS* 1915-01-15 p. 8 (Sheridan); *CS* 1917-08-23 p. 5 (Detroit).

505   *Clare Courier* 1922-07-07 p. 1.

506   I interviewed both Arlene Farmer Milkie and her daughter, Annette Marsh Carper.

507   The Slanecs, current owners of the Barnes property near Clare, say they were told by neighbors that Joe had claimed to be Capone's bookkeeper. Since one of Jake Guzik's jobs was keeping track of payoff and such, and Barnes seems to have worked with Guzik, this just might be true. Recall that Barnes told Barbara Wentworth that he had been Capone's chauffeur.

508   In North Chicago at 4448 Sunnyside Avenue, a nice, if modest, family home today.

509   According the Chief Shepard, Darling knew about Barnes' farm on Bailey Lake Road.

510 Pat Zinser, a neighbor down the road, told a different story—that Joe had "escaped Capone" by leaving Chicago. This makes a bit more sense, considering that Barnes was probably allied with Mike "the Pike" Heitler, a man who was rubbed out by Capone's men in 1931, about the time Barnes left the Windy City.

511 Chief Shepard also told me that Capone's men vacationed at what is now the Boy Scout Camp Rotary north of Clare. This seems impossible, as the camp dates from 1925 and so the land there would not have been available for a gangster hideout.

512 Mel and Joanne Slanec graciously spoke to me about their recollections and allowed me to roam the estate. They said that when they bought the house, neighbors regularly came by to tell them stories of gangsters.

513 Arlene Milkie confirmed that this coop was used as a house when Joe lived there.

514 When the Slanecs took possession, there were cots and bunks in the coop and cots in the apartment above the garage.

515 Arlene Milkie said that this array was a boy scout camp, but that is highly unlikely.

516 *Lansing State Journal,* 1999-03-14, "Vacation Escapes," 5.

517 He paid a million dollars for the Persian, with a $680,000 mortgage. It was somewhat distressed, having been closed for twelve months by the feds for violating the Volstead Act in its Club Bagdad. *Chicago Tribune,* 1928-11-08, 27.

518 *Escanaba Daily Press,* 1969-01-28, 1.

519 Account in the *Sioux City (Ia.) Journal* ("Special Dispatch to *The Journal*"), 1927-09-02, 1.

520 Despite this name, McGurn was through and through and Italian. Born in Sicily, he came at a young age to Brooklyn. Trying his hand as a prizefighter, he changed his name to "Battling Jack" McGurn because an Irish name would help him in his boxing career. Early on he moved to Chicago and became a notoriously vicious killer in Capone's Outfit.

521 *Chicago Tribune* 1929-05-03 p.4, *San Francisco Chronicle* 1929-05-03 p. 6. Hayes' money was safe. Numerous delays by the prosecution eventually led to the dismissal of the charge against McGurn in December 1929.

522 In almost every mention of Hayes in Chicago newspapers, it is pointed out that Hayes' Metropole Hotel was the former headquarters of Al Capone.

523 John J. Binder, *Al Capone's Beer Wars. A Complete History of Organized Crime in Chicago during Prohibition,* Amherst N.Y.: Prometheus Books, 2017.

524 The profits from illegal beer were tremendous. Lake and Druggan sold their brew at $50 a barrel to speakeasies and $30 a barrel at wholesale to other gangsters. The barons paid about $2 a barrel in actual production costs and around $7.50 in graft per barrel. Even with some other overhead, the pair made between $20 and $40 a barrel.

525 Binder, *Al Capone's Beer Wars* p. 107.

526 Johnson eventually got convictions for Ralph "Bottles" Capone, Al's brother, for Capone henchmen Frank Nitti and Sam Guzik, and finally for Big Al himself in 1931.

527 Ultimately prosecutors did not use Hayes' testimony against Capone because they did not consider him a reliable witness. He had detailed in a long statement how Capone and Dennis "The Duke" Cooney had run illegal enterprises from the Metropole. Cooney, he said, had rented several rooms for his prostitutes and paid Hayes weekly. Hayes also averred that Capone had paid off a Chicago police captain from his hotel room. *Chicago Tribune*, 1931-10-05, 2.

528 Details in a United Press story, *The Taylor (Tex.) Daily Press*, 1931-09-27, 1.

529 *Daily Times (Davenport Iowa)* special, 1929-04-24, 25; *Sioux City (Ia.) Journal* (AP), 1929-04-30, 1.

530 *Chicago Tribune*, 1931-12-23, 6.

531 *Chicago Tribune*, 1932-10-18, 7.

532 *Escanaba Daily Press*, 1937-01-31, 21.

533 The *Escanaba Daily Press* has a lengthy story about this, 1939-08-11 p. 5. By 1939 Hayes had established himself in town but had not yet gained the good reputation that would later quash any mention in the *Daily Press* of his shady past. Federal prosecutors dropped his case in 1943.

534 By the late 1940s this hotel was known as the House of Ludington.

535 *Escanaba Daily Press*, 1949-11-08, 5.

536 *Escanaba Daily Press*, 1969-01-28.

537 Interestingly, there is a Harold Clement Hayes, born in England in 1894, who did serve in the Great War as a private in the Lincolnshire Regiment. He also died in 1969, the year our Harold Clement Hayes died. However, this Hayes is buried in England.

538 1920 U.S. Census.

539 Special Report on case #2499 [the Lindbergh kidnapping], Michigan State Police Archive, Lansing, Michigan.

540 *Chicago Tribune*, 1924-05-23, 3.

541 In this analysis I follow the fine account of Magnaghi, *Prohibition*.

542   Tom Pfeiffelmann interview. Edward "Ned" Fenlon (1903-2010), born and raised in Hessel, he went on to be elected to the Michigan House of Representatives (1933-1938) and later served as a circuit court judge (1951-1974). He seems also to have been active in bootlegging across the St. Marys River at the Soo (Meryl Hankey interview).

543   This account is based upon the excellent summary of events by Wes Hills, "Whatever Happened to the Loot and Alexander Graham following the Great Hillman Bank Robbery of July 29, 1930?" *Atlanta (Mich.) Montmorency County Tribune,* 2015-08-25. Also, the Montmorency County Historical Society holds a transcription of the story. The issues of the *Tribune* from mid-July to late August 1930 have disappeared. Extensive accounts of events survive in the *Alpena (Mich.) News. Detroit Free Press* stories about the robbery over the period July 30-October 11, 1930 provide information with some details missing from the Hills account.

544   Werner later denied that he had made any such deal when questioned by police after the robbery. George Alexander Graham grew up in Lions Head, Ontario, Canada. In 1928 he married in Royal Oak, Michigan, just two miles from Ferndale; both towns are just north of Detroit. His marriage license gives his occupation as "sewer contractor."

545   *Detroit Free Press,* 1930-07-30, 1, 3 calls these two men gangsters. The story also adds a third man, Carl Reed, also of the Hillman area, as an additional gangster. "Reed is a native of this vicinity [i.e., Hillman] but resided for many years in Ecorse where, officers say, he as a police record as a gangster and bootlegger." But Reed does not subsequently appear in any accounts because police early on cleared him of involvement in the robbery. Hunt, who lived in Wyandotte, and Graham are also called "Detroit gunmen," 1930-08-08.

546   The safe, fully large enough for three people, was subsequently removed from the bank and survives as the office of a businessman in Hillman.

547   George Alexander Graham was raised in Lion Head. In 1928 he married in Royal Oak, Michigan. George Alexander Graham's wife, Sadie Murray, remarried in April 1932, barely 8 months after the heist and presumed death of Alex. Michigan marriage certificates.

548   Later, locals' recollections morphed this into a Purple Gang heist. Sue "Zue" Hudson reports this.

549   *Kingsport (Tenn.) Times,* 1930-02-10, 3 (AP). Curiously, this AP story appears in neither the *Detroit Times* nor the *Detroit Free Press.* The narrative that follows is based upon the AP reporting.

550   The AP report wrongly gives his name as "Meter" Wertheimer. Mathis' name is wrongly given as "Mathas." The *Detroit Times* account (1930-02-08,

2) mauls the list even more: Ruby Mathis becomes "Matthews;" Mert Wertheimer becomes Al Wertheimer. The account in the *Marshall (Mich.) Evening Chronicle* 1930-06-19, 1, also has Al Wertheimer as the kidnapee.

551   Klein's name is added to this list from the *Detroit Times* article, 1930-02-08, 2. Fein's name comes from *Detroit Free Press*, 1929-12-18, 2.

552   *Marshall (Mich.) Evening Chronicle*, 1930-06-19, 1. *Detroit Free Press*, 1929 12-18, 2 gives the following ransoms: Brady ($40,000), Bloomfield ($40,000k), Ryan ($50,000), Matthews [Mathis] $(25,000), Driscoll ($20,000), Klein ($10,000), Abraham Fein ($14,000). Other reports put Wertheimer's ransom at $35,000.

553   *Detroit Times*, 1930-02-08, 2 (a different article than the AP wire service one).

554   Per the *Detroit Free Press*, 1928-09-27, 2 "more than a score" of kidnappings had happened during the current frenzy.

555   *Marshall (Mich.) Evening Chronicle*, 1930-06-16, 1.

556   *Detroit Free Press*, 1929-12-18, 2: "The [Purple] gang was originally organized in Detroit something less than ten years ago, Garvin said. At that time Abe Axler and one of the Bernstein boys, who later were to organize the Purple gang among Detroit thugs, were associates of Burke."

557   *Detroit Free Press*, 1929-12-18, 2.

558   FBI file 7-25, Cincinnati Office, April 1936: "Mr. Kays recalled that Fred "Killer" Burke and "Crane Neck" Nugent, deceased, kidnapped Mert Worthhiem [sic] and Ruby Mathews [sic] at Topinabee, Michigan, near Petoskey in 1929 or 1930 and these men were reputed to have paid $50,000 for their release."

559   Mark Beltaire at Wiles, "Wertheimer Brothers," June 2018, 23-24.

560   Robert Laxalt, *Travels with My Royal. A Memoir of the Writing Life*, Reno: University of Nevada Press, 2001, pp. 82-86. Laxalt wrongly makes Mert "a member of the Purple Gang." It must be noted that a *Detroit Free Press* article 1932-12-31, 2 states both Al and Mert were kidnapped and taken to a house in Oakland (a Detroit suburb) and were not snatched Up North. The article also states the ransom as $35,000, not $50,000. That is not Mert's own story.

561   I find no reference to any hoodlum by this name.

562   *Detroit Times*, 1958-07-21, 3.

563   *Detroit Free Press*, 1929-12-18, 2. Burke is given as the kidnapper.

564   The following is based upon Robert Knapp, *Mystery Man*.

Index